OPA!

OPA!
THE
HEALTHY
GREEK
COOKBOOK

*Modern Mediterranean Recipes
for Living the Good Life*

Theo Stephan and Christina Xenos

ROCKRIDGE
PRESS

For general information on our other products
and services or to obtain technical support, please
contact our Customer Care Department within
the U.S. at (866) 744-2665, or outside the U.S. at
(510) 253-0500.

Rockridge Press publishes its books in a variety of
electronic and print formats. Some content that
appears in print may not be available in electronic
books, and vice versa.

Photography © Hélène Dujardin/Food styling by
Lisa Rovick: cover, ii, 20, 40, 54, 67, 73, 76, 88, 97, 102,
114, 122, 135, 144, 154, 159, 181, 188, 195, 204, 211, 214,
216 & back cover; Ivan Solis/Food styling by Jessica
Boone: v, xii, 10, 25, 28, 33, 45, 68, 82, 87, 109, 149, 168,
184 & 201; @yanos/Twenty20.com, pp. vi-vii; Aaron
Thomas/Stocksy, p. viii; @talbegalxo/Twenty20.com,
p. xi; Verpeya/Shutterstock.com, p. 5; Helen Sotiriadis/
Stocksy, p. 6.

All illustrations: © 2017 Tom Bingham

Authors' photo credits: Anita Williams, p. 248;
Courtesy of Christina Xenos, p. 249.

ISBN: Print 978-1-939754-12-7
eBook 978-1-939754-97-4

Theo:

For my sisters Renee and Kathy, with love and hopes for a lot more "OPAs!" in our lives together

Christina:

For my *yiayias* Helen, Chrysanthe, and Polly, who nurtured my love for Greek cooking and culture

Contents

Introduction ix

CHAPTER ONE
UNDERSTANDING GREEK CUISINE 1

CHAPTER TWO
IN THE GREEK KITCHEN 11

CHAPTER THREE
MEZZETHES 21

CHAPTER FOUR
SALADS & SOUPS 41

CHAPTER FIVE
BEANS, RICE & PASTA 69

CHAPTER SIX
VEGETABLE MAINS 89

CHAPTER SEVEN
SEAFOOD MAINS 123

CHAPTER EIGHT
MEAT MAINS 155

CHAPTER NINE
DESSERTS 189

Holiday Menus 217

Glossary 221

APPENDIX A
The Dirty Dozen & the Clean Fifteen 224

APPENDIX B
Conversion Tables 225

Recipe Index 226

Index 229

Introduction

Christina Like in many Greek families, my love of food and cooking was passed to me by my *yiayia*. Grandmothers are a fixture of Greek clans, and we always had one living with us. They had the luxury of time and would spend all afternoon meticulously picking through cups of rice, beans, and lentils for quality control before finessing them into some delicious creation over the stove. My earliest memory of cooking was my *Yiayia* Chrysanthe sending me out to her backyard to pick grape leaves off her chain-link fence so we could make *dolmathes*. The grapes grew next to her bountiful garden stacked with rows of rhubarb, tomatoes, and zucchini. Foraging and cultivating was the way of life back in Crete, our family home; those traditions traveled with her to the United States, and she passed them on to me. We would sit at her table and roll the meaty mixture into the grape leaves and then stack them in her pot to steam.

I was also "adopted" by many other *yiayias* every summer when my mom took me to our local Greek church to cook for our annual festival. While my friends spent their days poolside at the local country club, I sat in the company of experts, brushing phyllo leaves with butter and rolling countless spanakopita and *tiropita* triangles. The baking weeks were my favorites, though, using my nimble fingers to roll out spiral *koulouria*, layer spiced nuts onto paper-thin phyllo leaves to make baklava, and braid the traditional sweet *tsoureki* bread.

Dining together is the cornerstone of Greek culture. We would come together nightly over hearty stews, grilled fish with *pilaffi*, and, no matter what, a dish of boiled *horta* field greens floating in tangy lemon juice and olive oil. These greens—spinach, chicory, dandelion, and green amaranth—are the backbone of a healthy Greek diet, one rich in olive oil, vegetables, legumes, and fish, with meat on special occasions. These recipes and way of living define the way I cook for my family, friends, and clients—preparing healthy food for longevity.

Theo OPA! Growing up Greek, to me, meant either having a party at our house every weekend or going to Greek friends' homes, bursting with warm aromas of freshly baked breads, pitas, and desserts. Greek music blared as families and friends ate, drank, and danced with a lively attitude, sharing "opas" with friendly slaps on the back, lots of cheek pinching, and kissing.

An actual excitement arose in my heart—and stomach—weekly for these cultural gatherings, filled with laughing *yiayias* in colorful aprons, juxtaposed with the pungency of brined feta, olives, and countless dishes from *mezze* to meats anointing my every sense. Endless ribbons of dishes covered all flat surfaces in the kitchen—even the top of the fridge! Colors and textures flowing across my eager palate gave way to a satiated sense of love and respect . . . love for these wild and wonderful people who shared such fascinating conversation and respect for the deliciousness and health, which I then took for granted.

My friends tease me that I live for my next meal. I am not embarrassed; it's true! Planting Santa Barbara County's first olive grove specifically for extra-virgin olive oil in the mid-1990s came directly from my childhood love of my family's weekly culinary forays. Every harvest and olive pressing reminds me of my Aunt Lou, who introduced me to olive oil on a Wonder Bread bun, and my mom's insistence on the importance of oregano (*Greek* oregano, not Italian!) while friend Grace declared nutmeg as the secret ingredient to all Greek meat dishes. Now, with constant experimentation in my own kitchen, converting favorite family recipes into my own, I still recall the taste of steam from my *yiayia's glyko* (candied oranges) and will never forget the gargantuan size of my mom's hand-rolled phyllo dough. We spoke only Greek in our house because my *yiayia* didn't know English; and I think it made everything taste better somehow. The dynamics of the language have been interpreted into flavor creations my "American" friends look for, too, whenever their taste buds cross my threshold.

I am 57, and Christina is 37. We both grew up with delicious Greek foods playing a central role in our daily lives, no matter the day of the week, holiday or snack time. What we didn't realize as children is that we were also eating healthy. We both grew up in Dayton, Ohio, but because of our age differences, we didn't know each other there. Christina and I met through our mothers 10 years ago, after they discovered their daughters both moved to California. We immediately compared notes on family traditions, careers, and our own

interpretations of growing up in a Greek kitchen. Creating this book together is a fun, natural way for us to share our heritage, history, and love for the classic Greek diet. To us, it is not a diet at all but a compilation of the best in Greek food! In the following pages, we hope you will appreciate the savory qualities of our stories and recipes. We have modernized, made easier, and added our own tasty touches to delectable favorites we know you will enjoy cooking.

Here's to livening up your own kitchen with new recipes that will inspire you to relish a healthier, more flavorful lifestyle. OPA!

CHAPTER ONE

Understanding Greek Cuisine

Despite it being the food of the gods, you don't need the help of an oracle to discover the secrets of Greek cooking. Read on to discover how Greece's traditions, from ancient times to the modern day, have shaped its cuisine and culture. Travel through the many regions of Greece and learn how geography inspires key recipes. Get a feel for how Greeks embrace feasting with family and friends and how this plays into their eating habits, which make them some of the healthiest, longest-living people in the world. Learn how to stock your own Greek pantry at home, so you have the tools to make your own Greek-inspired dishes.

Ancient Food History

The essential ingredients of Greek cuisine are the same today as they were for the Bronze Age Minoans thriving on the Island of Crete. Wheat, grain, legumes, and fruit have always been ubiquitous—as is the veritable pillar of the Hellenic kitchen, fresh-pressed olive oil.

The ancients celebrated the cycles of planting and harvest religiously, offering sacrifices and libations to the gods who protected their bounty. Demeter was the goddess of agricultural fertility; her daughter, Persephone, the goddess of spring growth; and Dionysus, the infamous god of wine, indulgence, and transcendence. Dishonor them at your own risk . . .

Traditionally, Greek food was prepared in simple ways. Cheese and olives greeted guests as they sat at the table, and wines cut with water flowed freely, pairing perfectly with roasted lamb, meat stews, and lentil or bean soups. The

A valued servant brought in bread and set it down before them,

and added many tasty delicacies as well,

taking freely from the food she had in store.

A carver lifted platters with all sorts of meat

and served them, then set down in front of the two men goblets made of gold. Fair-haired Menelaus welcomed both of them and said:

"Help yourselves. Enjoy our food. And once you've had your meal,

we'll inquire you who you are . . . "

Menelaus spoke. Then with his own hands he picked up

the roasted meat and set it down in front of them,

the fat back cut of beef they'd placed in front of him, a mark of honour. So the two men helped themselves, eating the fine meal prepared and set before them.

—Book IV, Homer's *Odyssey*

ancients raised goats, sheep, pigs, and cattle, and were highly skilled fisher-men. Cooks simmered octopus in wine, while preserving other fish in salt. As sugarcane had yet to reach the diaspora, honey was used as a sweetener, often served with yogurt and walnuts, a simple yet mouthwatering delicacy still enjoyed today.

Above all, the Greeks took pride in providing the highest level of hospitality to their guests. Food and wine were at the center of every pan-Hellenic festi-val, from the Olympics to the Theater Festival of Dionysus and the Eleusinian Mysteries. Stories of elaborate feasts are found throughout Homer's *Iliad* and *Odyssey*; in Platonic dialogues, such as *The Symposium*; and in the plays of Aeschylus, Sophocles, Euripides, and Aristophanes.

These feasts, however, were more than a culinary ritual. They were a custom and a code of ethics. The term *philoxenia* is Greek for "the love of strangers." By classical standards, an excellent host welcomed guests with open arms, treating them with the highest respect and restoring them to their best selves before even inquiring who they were.

Rich Food Culture

At the heart of Greek culture and *philoxenia* is food. When a guest is welcomed into a home, she is immediately given whatever is on hand, typically cheese, olives, and even a square of spanakopita. Meals are the social center of life and bring families and communities together. Greeks use meals as their social outlet, dining with friends and family in their homes or out at restaurants. In more relaxed parts of the country, it's typical for neighbors to drop by in the early evening with a snack or bottle of grappalike *tsipouro*, or *tsikoudia* if you're in Crete, to catch up on the day's events. As lively conversation thrives—as it always does when you get a group of Greeks together—those gatherings often turn into ones with even more food and drinks that linger into the evening.

Greek holidays are nothing without a spread of dips, cheeses, olives, pies, and roasted meats. These feasts are the reward for fasting—eating only approved foods during a specific time of year. Although there are numerous fasting periods throughout the year, Great Lent is the longest, and Easter is the most indulgent holiday on the Greek calendar. After 40 days of fasting, Greeks announce that Christ has risen at midnight of Holy Saturday and punctuate that with a bowl of *magiritsa* and the cracking of eggs dyed red to represent

THE FOOD REGIONS OF GREECE

Greece's location as a peninsular archipelago in southern Europe makes it a culinary crossroads for the rest of the continent, Africa, and Asia. Its landscape travels from mountainous regions to vast plains, which allows its people to graze animals and cultivate grains, vegetables, and fruits, and Greece's 8,498 miles of coastline boasts bountiful seafood offerings, from sea bass to octopus. With such a varied geography, the country has developed a diverse array of dishes with strong regional origins.

1. Northern Greece

Greece's mountainous region in the north is bordered by Albania, FYROM (the Former Yugoslav Republic of Macedonia), Bulgaria, and Turkey. The northern Greek regions of Thrace, Macedonia, and Epirus have a distinct food culture. Olives don't thrive in the north, so this is the part of the country where buttery pies and rich local goat's and sheep's milk cheeses shine. Corn is farmed here, too, and is common in dishes from Epirus. Farther toward the east, Pontian cuisine from the Greeks who settled around the Black Sea features grain dishes. Macedonia is known for its irresistible sweets, many having Turkish influence. The regions of Macedonia and Thrace have expansive coastlines, and with those come delectable seafood dishes.

2. Central Greece

The heart of Greece is also its breadbasket. Central Greece extends from the thriving metropolis of Athens to the mountainous monasteries of Meteora in the great plains of Thessaly. This region produces everything from organic vegetables to meats and cheeses cultivated from animals grazing on the plains.

3. Peloponnese

Olives and citrus take center stage in this peninsula that makes up southern mainland Greece. Kalamata is the second largest city of the region, and it is from here that the region's prized namesake olive is cultivated. In everything from sweet to savory dishes you'll find hints of citrus, such as orange blossom and juice, flavoring thick honey syrup in sweets, and even used to flavor sausages.

4. Islands

Half of Greece's population lives within its island groups, made up of the Saronic Islands, Ionian Islands, Cycladic Islands, Dodecanese Islands, Aegean Islands, and Sporades Islands. All have distinct characteristics, such as the iconic, whitewashed buildings of the Cycladic Islands or the sought-after beaches of the Ionian Islands. The latter group was occupied by the Venetians for 400 years and incorporates that influence into its pasta-laden stews and thick tomato sauces. The islands are also where you'll find some of the best seafood in the country, from whole octopus hanging on a clothesline to fresh sea urchin, whole sea bass, and grilled red mullet. You'll also find some of Greece's prized wine on Santorini, a mineral-y Assyrtiko or sweet Vinsanto.

5. Crete

Greece's largest island boasts a food history that spans millennia—one influenced by many cultures. It existed as a part of the Roman Empire and Byzantine Empire before the Venetians occupied it for more than 400 years and, subsequently, the Ottomans for 200 years. As a major participant of the Greek War of Independence, Crete help push the Ottomans out of its territory in 1898, giving way to an independent Cretan state, which existed until 1913, when Crete became a part of Greece. Crete is also one of the healthiest regions in all of Greece. The foundation of its cuisine is built on the back of wild greens, legumes, olive oil, fresh fish, and cheese.

6. Cyprus

Greek and Turkish cultures collide on this independent island country in the eastern Mediterranean. *Halloumi* cheese reigns supreme in its gastronomical offerings; the semihard cheese with an elastic texture is either grilled or served fresh and can be eaten along with or incorporated into salads and other dishes. Cyprus also produces a variety of fresh vegetables and legumes used in its cuisine. The island is also known for its confections: *Flaounes* are savory cheese-filled pastries that traditionally include raisins and ground *mahlepi* (a distinctive Greek spice with a fruity, cherry taste). If you have a sweet tooth, you can indulge in many traditional Cypriot desserts, such as *loukoumades* (fried dough balls in honey syrup) and *loukoum* (Turkish delight).

MAKING A MODERN LIFESTYLE
FROM THE OLD WORLD

The island of Crete offers a contemporary, adaptable approach to our daily food intake that can truly make us feel better. Theo was recently in Crete, where she asked 10 elderly people about aspects of life on Greece's largest island, where countless people thrive in an engaging existence well beyond the norm.

The quick answer: eating one main meal a day, usually a plate of greens or beans smothered with olive oil and a chunk of cheese or yogurt (always with Cretan honey made from bees that feed on mountain thyme and other herbs carrying therapeutic qualities), with fruit after the meal. Simple mezze (small dishes), such as sliced tomatoes, feta, and olives, are typical in the late afternoon; *raki* (alcohol made from grape peelings after wine production), before bed. Larger family-style meals shared on weekends feature platters of meats and red wine. Desserts happen mostly on special occasions or in the early afternoon, with a coffee.

There are three eating "habits" unique to Crete:

1. Rusk—a hard, crunchy bread made from barley flour—is high in protein. Historically, Cretans relied on agriculture and breeding stock, with rusk a cheap, tasty, long-lasting staple.
2. Olive oil from Crete has a high density and extremely low acidity, with higher polyphenolic (antioxidant) qualities compared with any other oils in the world.
3. Dittany, a healing herb, can be found growing wild only on the island of Crete. It is made into tea with just a few leaves, warding off most illnesses, or combined with rue, parsley, and peppers as a sauce, dating back to Cretan antiquity.

the blood of Jesus Christ. An epic feast follows on Easter Sunday, with roasted lamb and lemon potatoes, spanakopita, tzatziki, cheese, olives, and many other traditional dishes from the cook's repertoire. Christmas and New Year's incorporate generous feasts, with the traditional *vasilopita* sweet bread being served on New Year's Day. A coin is hidden within the bread and the person who receives that piece is said to gain luck for the year.

Greeks also connect food with the passing of a loved one. Traditionally, following a funeral service, those in attendance are invited by the family to a *makaria*, where the menu offers fish to symbolize Christ's Resurrection, because Greek Orthodox Christians believe that at His Resurrection, Christ shared a meal of fish with his disciples. Memorial services follow at 40 days, three months, six months, nine months, and annually, where the family often offers *koliva*—a sweet mix of boiled wheat, raisins, powdered sugar, almonds, and other additions—to the church congregation in memory of those departed.

Essential Flavors

The first time Theo tasted "raw" olive oil was when her Aunt Lou pulled a pack of Wonder Bread hamburger buns off the fridge and poured that liquid gold into a cup for her to dip. Her action was prompted by Theo's question: "Why does your cooking taste so good?" She was quick to compare Theo's mom's cooking using Crisco to hers with Greek olive oil, admonishing her playfully for "going American." It was 1968, after all! That moment opened Theo's palate to her own culinary curiosities and appreciation for the fresh flavor of olive oil. The first time she went to Greece, she visited family north of Thessaloniki, where her *Thea* Hariklia (Aunt Harriet) served an endless array of platters featuring lemon, olive oil, dill, garlic, yogurt, honeyed fresh fruit intertwined with phyllo, and homemade cherry sauce. It all made her taste buds dance just as they did getting ready for those annual Greek festivals when she was a little girl.

Personal experience as an olive oil producer has further taught her the savory versus spicy qualities of Greek cooking. Californian and Italian olive oils tend toward an herbaceous or peppery finish. Greek extra-virgin olive oil tickles the back of your throat with a sensuous, resonant layering, lingering lightly on eggs, vegetables, main dishes, and even desserts. The balance of acid (lemon, wine vinegar) to the delicate richness of goat's-milk yogurts and cheeses weaves itself into recipes shared here in a natural, flavorful, simple, yet elegant manner.

Naturally Healthy

The Greek "diet" is naturally healthy, but it's so flavorful, you never actually *feel* like you're giving anything up. Sugar is never a featured ingredient or flavor, even in desserts that are rich and savory. Greeks are, indeed, omnivores who love their meat, but it is not the cornerstone of Greek cooking. Meat dishes are typically reserved for Sundays and holidays. Fava beans, green beans, *horta* (which most commonly refers to young dandelion greens), and tomatoes are the most commonly used vegetables. Seldom will you see a meat-and-beans combination or a beans-and-rice (or other grain) dish common in other ethnic cuisines. Goat's-milk–based yogurts and cheeses, more Greek food staples, are naturally lower in fat than cow's-milk products. Healthy fats, such as in olive oil and nuts, play a significant role, too.

A true Greek diet proves that all fats are not created equal. Several olives, a small chunk of feta, a peach, a plum, and a handful of grapes or cherries are all essential breakfast staples. Key foods comprising the largest meal of the day—lunch—are vegetables or grains, most frequently prepared with olive oil and fresh herbs. Eating leg of lamb (try *Gemisto Podi Arniou* / Stuffed Leg of Lamb, page 158, or *Arni Psito* / Roasted Leg of Lamb, page 161) or pork shoulder (*Hirino me Damaskina kai Syka* / Braised Pork Shoulder with Plums and Figs, page 170) doesn't mean gorging on a half-pound plate of meat at lunchtime! Portions stay in the 4-ounce range, with healthy heaps of flavor-rich vegetarian accompaniments.

As a slew of "modern" diet books feature, you absolutely *must* eat healthy fats to maintain optimal weight, let alone frame of mind. Omega-3s (from nuts, seafood, or spinach) are considered as good for your brain as they are for keeping inflammation in check. You sure see a lot of *yiayias* trolling the promenades of Greek villages late into the night. They're living proof the Greek way works!

GREEK CUISINE AND THE MEDITERRANEAN DIET

The Greek diet is essentially what's called in broader terms the Mediterranean diet. You will find that it's not an actual diet for which you carefully measure ingredients and count calories on a daily basis. It's truly a lifestyle supplanted with fresh vegetables, local foraging, whole grains, and nuts. And while meat is included, it's not eaten on a daily basis. Sure, there's a fast-food culture in the big cities, like Athens and Thessaloniki; however, even the small village *tavernas* serve real food, such as that day's fresh catch, that morning's harvest, and that cousin's red wine.

The less-meat, plant-based, healthy-fat principles of the Mediterranean diet make this way of eating one of the healthiest diets overall. Living the Greek lifestyle is all about eating your way—deliciously and responsibly—through life, joining friends and family for enlivening conversation and an exchange of food (and sometimes wine!) in the process.

The top characteristics of a Mediterranean diet's healthy profile, as noted by the Mayo Clinic, include the following:

- Eating primarily plant-based whole foods, such as fruits and vegetables, whole grains, legumes, and nuts

- Replacing less healthy butter with healthy fats, such as olive oil

- Using fresh herbs and spices instead of salt to flavor foods

- Limiting red meat to no more than a few times a month

- Eating fish and poultry at least twice a week

- Enjoying meals with family and friends, which provides social support

- Drinking red wine in moderation (optional)

- Getting plenty of exercise

CHAPTER TWO

In the Greek Kitchen

Welcome to the modern-day Greek kitchen. In this sacred spot you will discover the fundamentals of traditional flavors in the Greek pantry, useful cooking techniques, and the tools you'll need to get started. Pay particular attention to common flavor combinations. While Greek food has its own traditional flavor patterns, you can have fun improvising your own interpretation of Greek cuisine once you master the basics.

The Greek Pantry

Healthy Greek cooking starts with certain simple key ingredients. The best way to master the art of Greek cooking is to have them at the ready in your pantry and refrigerator. Stocking up on these ingredients and learning their distinct characteristics will give you the tools you need to complete any Greek recipe and make improvisations of your own.

OLIVE OIL: Greece is one of the world's top producers of olive oil, and the revered ingredient is the very foundation of Greek cooking. Greeks use olive oil in everything from salad dressings to desserts and do not shy away from frying or baking with it.

LEMON: This fruit is another building block of Greek recipes. It takes center stage in *avgolemono* soup (the Greek version of the ever-healing chicken soup); *avgolemono* sauce, which dresses everything from vegetables to meat; and *ladolemono*, an emulsion of lemon and olive oil that is a perfect simple sauce for fish or a dressing for salad and vegetables.

VINEGAR: Small bottles of red wine vinegar (and olive oil) dress the tables in most casual restaurants in Greece. People commonly use it in salads, soups, dips, and fish dishes. However, the original *horiatiki* (village) salad does not use vinegar at all, only a savory Koroneiki or Kalamata Greek varietal extra-virgin olive oil.

GREEK OREGANO: Greek oregano, *rigani*, is one of the most common herbs used in Greek cooking. Use dried oregano to spice fish and meats—a pork souvlaki would be one-dimensional without it—and sprinkle it over feta cheese in the classic Greek village salad. Oregano is also used in many sauces and dips. Italian or Mexican oregano will not impart the same flavors; use the Greek varietal for the most genuine flavor.

BASIL: Not only do most Greek households have pots of basil growing around their homes to deter bugs and bring luck, but they also use the herb, which has historical associations with royalty, in their cooking. Greek "globe" varietal basil is a natural accompaniment to tomatoes in sauces and salads. Like Greek oregano, the authentic globe varietal (you can easily get seeds and grow it in any window box) gives you authentic flavor in your foods; use it fresh. If only

COMMON FLAVOR COMBINATIONS

The successful Greek home cook knows the most authentic flavors result from using fresh, organic ingredients. In Greece, GMO (genetically modified organism) crops don't exist, and chemicals in the garden are taboo. The best Greek flavors arrive using simple flavor combinations, creating a balance of acidity and savory flavors to create the quintessential Greek dish. Our favorites:

Garlic, lemon, and extra-virgin olive oil: Use a 1:2 ratio of freshly minced garlic to both freshly squeezed lemon juice and Greek extra-virgin olive oil as a marinade formula for chicken, seafood, oven-roasted vegetables, and even peaches on the grill.

Greek oregano and feta cheese: One teaspoon dried Greek oregano to 1 ounce feta cheese makes just about anything taste Greek.

Nutmeg and freshly ground black pepper: Use a ratio of ¼ part nutmeg (which is intense) to 1 part freshly ground black pepper. The goal with this secret addition is bringing out flavors, especially in spanakopita, sauces, and meat dishes. Keep the ratio light relative to the other spices in the dish.

Dill, Mediterranean sea salt, and tomato: A fist-size tomato benefits greatly from a sprinkling of real Mediterranean sea salt crystals (easy to find anywhere, and it contains less sodium than table salt) and dried dill. Dried herbs are more flavorful than fresh herbs and will rehydrate when heated. Don't use old dried herbs, however; keep them fresh or dry them from your own garden if possible. Herbs more than a few months old lose their flavor qualities.

Mediterranean sea salt, dill, and garlic: An instant Greek meat or seafood flavor rub can be made by combining a ratio of 1 part salt to 1 part dill to 2 parts garlic. You can use a mortar and pestle or combine larger amounts in a small food processor. If you make a big batch, freeze leftovers in ice cube trays for convenient use later.

Greek basil, lemon, and extra-virgin olive oil: Combined in equal measurements, Greek basil, lemon, and extra-virgin olive oil create a natural, Mediterranean, savory flavor to be used as a marinade or salad dressing, or even blended together for a pesto consistency. This combination can easily be frozen in ice cube trays for convenient use any time.

Honey, cinnamon, and lemon: Not just for dessert. Combine 1 part honey to ½ part lemon to ¼ part cinnamon. Dress a fruit salad, marinate seafood or chicken, or drizzle on Greek yogurt to turn the ordinary into extraordinary Greek-inspired dishes.

common basil is available, chiffonade (pile the leaves, roll into a cigarlike shape, and thinly slice crosswise into ribbons) the delicate leaves to keep them from becoming bitter from being overworked.

MINT: This fresh herb is easy to grow (best in pots to contain it) and flavors signature Greek dishes, such as *keftedes* (Greek meatballs), stuffed peppers, and zucchini balls. Greeks also believe mint plays a part in aiding digestive problems and other mild ailments.

PARSLEY: Fresh flat-leaf parsley enhances everything from fish dishes to sauces. Greeks use it as a key herb in their various phyllo pies and in stuffings for peppers, tomatoes, and zucchini.

DILL: The unique earthy quality of dill makes it essential in Greek dips (such as tzatziki), phyllo pies, and stuffed grape leaves. Dill's qualities are stronger when it's fresh, but you can use dried dill for most applications.

CINNAMON: This warming spice catches people off guard when Greeks use it to take their meat sauces to the next level. Cinnamon is also commonly used to spice fillings and syrups for sweet confections.

TOMATOES: You haven't really tasted a tomato until you've eaten one in Greece. Fresh tomatoes are the star of the ever-simple Greek village salad. They are also grated and used for fresh sauces. If you can't find tomatoes in season, use a can of good-quality whole or chopped tomatoes for stews and sauces.

Equipment

Greeks have been creating beautiful, delicious dishes since ancient times, so modern cooking conveniences aren't necessarily needed, but they are time-savers. Here are some key pieces of equipment to consider stocking your kitchen with before embarking on creating the recipes in this book.

FOOD PROCESSOR: From chopping vegetables to whipping up dips, a food processor is a great assistant in the Greek kitchen.

BLENDER: Consider a blender to make dressings and sauces in an instant, especially the signature Greek *avgolemono* sauce—that tangy combination of frothy eggs and lemon.

MORTAR AND PESTLE: To combine a sauce or dip using just your strength, skip the electronic equipment and embrace the steadfast mortar and pestle.

PASTRY BRUSH: Pastry brushes are used to spread butter or olive oil on phyllo pies and brush the tops with egg wash. We use a premium-quality nylon paint-brush from the local hardware store to spread large swaths of liquid more quickly over the pastry sheets. Using nylon means easier cleanup: With a grease-cutting dish soap, such as Dawn, in the palm of your hand, swish the brush back and forth until it gets all lathered. Rinse thoroughly so your next phyllo dish doesn't taste soapy!

INSTANT-READ MEAT THERMOMETER: All ovens are different. While the cooking times for meats are specified in our recipes, it is best to take the temperature of the meat and fish to make sure it is cooked sufficiently and out of the temperature danger zone.

DUTCH OVEN: In more primitive times, the Greek home had a hearth with an open flame, and most cooking was done in communal ovens. Many Greek dishes utilize Dutch ovens because of this history—similar vessels were carried from the home to the village oven to bake. Now Dutch ovens can be used on a stove top or in a conventional oven.

GRILL: While most dishes can be adapted for the stove top or oven, grilling is at the heart of Greek cooking. Whether it is a smoky eggplant or souvlaki, cooking over a grill imparts authentic flavors. Traditionally, Greeks use *karvouna*, or mesquite charcoal briquettes, and a kebab-style grill with a rotisserie. Most grills are made of stainless steel and readily available if you Google "Greek grill."

STEAMER BASKET: A stainless steel steamer basket is easy to find, even in the utility section of a common grocery store. They are round, with holes and ½-inch feet to sit on the bottom of a pot. When using a steamer, put it into the bottom of any-size pan, pouring water just up to (but not covering) the holes in the steamer itself. Place the items to be steamed on top of the open steamer. Use over high heat so the water under the steamer boils. Covering the pan helps the steaming process happen more quickly and evenly.

Cooking Techniques

A variety of cooking techniques is used to create Greek dishes. Here are some of the most common.

BAKING: This is one of the most common techniques used in Greek cuisine. This dry-heat method is used to cook everything from breads to casseroles in the oven. Baking is commonly done at temperatures of 375°F and lower.

ROASTING: Another common dry-heat cooking technique using the oven, roasting is most commonly used to transform meat and vegetable dishes at a temperature of 400°F or higher in an open pan.

BRAISING: This wet cooking technique is commonly used for stews, with the ingredients lightly sautéed and cooked low and slow with liquid in a covered pot.

SEARING: This technique is commonly used in tandem with most other dry and wet cooking techniques. Sear meat and fish over high heat so a caramelized, flavorful crust develops.

GRILLING: This cooking method exposes ingredients to intense heat over a fire to cook them and impart a charred flavor. Mesquite briquettes provide the most Grecian flavor to your food.

TEMPERING: This technique involves bringing your ingredients to a desired temperature and is commonly used with eggs and chocolate. In Greek cooking, the *avgolemono* sauce is a staple of many dishes, including its namesake soup. So as not to scramble the eggs, temper them—bring them up to temperature—by whisking in hot broth and adding that mix back into your soup pot.

WORKING WITH PHYLLO: Phyllo, essentially a thin sheet of dough, is an indispensable ingredient in Greek pies and confections. Phyllo dough is typically packaged in 1-pound boxes containing 2 rolls of 24 sheets each, and can be found in the freezer section of your grocery store. To use, thaw overnight in the refrigerator, then bring to room temperature by placing the two (wrapped) rolls on the counter for an hour. Working with phyllo requires a certain finesse. To keep it from drying out when working with it, cover the unused sheets with a damp kitchen cloth. Most dishes require brushing each phyllo sheet with butter or olive oil. **Important:** If your recipe is made in a pan, such as Not Your Mother's Baklava (page 198) or Spanakopita (page 103), slice the finished recipe into individual servings *before* baking it.

ADDING SYRUPS TO PASTRIES: Many Greek pastries have two parts: the pastry and its syrup. The best way to get your pastry to fully absorb the syrup is to make the syrup ahead, cool it, and add it to the hot pastry when it's just out of the oven. This allows for maximum absorption—and those sizzling sounds coming off the pastry, let alone the smells . . . *moskovoliá*! (That's Greek for "smells super amazing!")

SEASONING: One of the most important techniques, seasoning helps develop flavors in dishes. Start building flavors by creating a blend of sea salt or kosher salt, freshly ground black pepper, Greek oregano (not Italian or Mexican—Greek!), fresh and dried herbs, and spices.

COOKING WITH OLIVE OIL: Most people don't realize that more than 70 percent of extra-virgin olive oil in grocery stores is adulterated with other oils, even though the label may say "extra-virgin olive oil." The FDA, admittedly, does not have time to police truth in labeling. This is why many food shows instruct you not to cook with it—never tell a Greek that! Adulterated oils smoke at low temperatures and become toxic, but *real* extra-virgin oils have a smoke point of almost 400°F. Greek varietal kalamata and Koroneiki cold pressed extra virgin olive oils can be found at many specialty grocery stores or online. Fresh, reputable olive oils should be fruity and tickle the back of your throat, never tasting heavy or having a peanut flavor. This savory liquid gold is on most every Greek table and, certainly, in every Greek kitchen.

A WORD ABOUT LEFTOVERS

We all love leftovers, and how long we keep them around is a personal thing. However, the Mayo Clinic recommends that leftover dishes be kept in the refrigerator for only up to three or four days. Keeping them around past that time increases the risk of food poisoning.

You can also freeze most dishes in covered containers, defrost them in the refrigerator, and reheat them so the internal temperature is at least 165°F. So, while we've tried to indicate storage instructions for our recipes, keep these guidelines in mind, as well.

About the Recipes

The best way to travel through Greece—without sailing through the islands, inhaling the aromas of her pine forests, or gazing up at the peak of Mount Olympus—is through the recipes in this book. Each dish harnesses the fundamentals of the Greek and Mediterranean way of life, most using olive oil as a backbone and filling out the rest with fresh produce and bold flavors.

Greeks indulge in every aspect of life. These recipes share that enthusiasm with you, for you to pass along enthusiastically to your "village." Traditions that once held a relative mystique even among our friends ("Oh, you're cooking Greek food tonight? What time is dinner?") can be created quite simply in your own kitchen and savored around an engaging table of family of friends. No matter where you call home, you can eat and live the way of the Greeks, who are some of the healthiest in the world, with lower rates of heart disease and diabetes, experiencing the gift of longevity and better quality of life in later years.

The recipes in this book were developed with you in mind. The ingredients are easily accessible at your local supermarket. Some recipes are updated using elements more accessible to us now than when the traditional Greek recipe was conceived. We've also simplified the recipes as much as possible to account for the hectic schedules of our Western lives. Historically, in the Greek kitchen, cooks had all day to prepare a feast. With the modern way of life, we have an hour if we're lucky. Take note of the cooking tips, where you can discover our secrets, making each dish even more accessible to you.

If there is one message we hope to leave you with, it's this: Enjoy yourself and those around you while you're eating; truly share in the day—turn your cell phones off and raise a glass to each other. The Greeks say *"yiamas"* (to us) or *"kali orexi"* (bon appétit). Then after dinner, turn on some Greek dance music, do a little dance, and say, "OPA!"

BREAKFAST

Feta cheese and Kalamata olives for breakfast? Yes, *kalimera* (good morning)! We didn't dedicate an entire chapter of this book to breakfast recipes because the *proino* (literally, "first meal") in Greece is usually super simple. Fresh fruit, yogurt with honey, a thick slice of toasted Greek bread with jam, and *paximadia* (biscotti-style coffee cookies) with warm goat's milk are all common. Thick Greek coffee, traditionally brewed in a long-handled open kettle, often comes mid- to late morning and, again, after the midday nap. When in Greece, an "American coffee" or frappé appeals to tourists, but traditional Greeks wait a few hours before imbibing caffeine.

A word about Greek yogurt: Commercially, the Fage (pronounced *fah-yay*; literally meaning "eat") Total brand is the original Greek varietal. A lot of yogurts call themselves "Greek," which means they are Greek *style*—thick and rich versus watery and sugary—but most contain thickening chemicals, sugar, and added flavorings. Yes, we're partial to the real thing; *the flavor and creaminess of true Greek yogurt make all the difference*! It never contains sugar.

Saturday mornings can get a little more special in the Greek kitchen. A *horiatiki* omelet is easily prepared combining Friday night's leftover potatoes and tiny chunks of feta cheese in a skillet generously coated with olive oil. Add a fresh, organic beaten egg and fry to golden perfection over medium-high heat, flipping once with a wide spatula (that's why you need the generous amount of olive oil). Freshly sliced tomatoes, Kalamata olives, and a drizzle of olive oil on the finished dish are a plus. This extravagant breakfast is a treat for lazy days, which are few and far between. The Greeks are always up to something!

TOMATO DIPLES, PAGE 38

CHAPTER THREE

Mezzethes

Entire meals of mezze (tapalike small plates) are relished in the Greek lifestyle, especially in summer when gardens are abundant and lighter meals simply make us all feel better. Recipes in this chapter can be made in advance—because it's far more pleasurable to sit at the table and talk, or dance with your loved ones, versus being stuck in the kitchen cooking. Imagine a party where all you need to do is pour the wine—OPA!

Den Ine Y Dika Sou Yiayia's Tzatziki
NOT YOUR YIAYIA'S TZATZIKI 23

Phyllo Krotides
PHYLLO CRACKERS 24

Strangisto Yiaourti Tiri
GREEK YOGURT CHEESE 26

Krema Spanaki
GREEK-Y CREAMED SPINACH 27

Kalamata Elia Mezze
KALAMATA OLIVE SPREAD 29

Melitzanosalata
EGGPLANT DIP 30

Htipiti
**ROASTED RED PEPPER
AND FETA CHEESE DIP** 32

Avocado *Skordalia*
AVOCADO GARLIC SPREAD 34

Feta-Kalamata Apogymnomena Avga
FETA-KALAMATA DEVILED EGGS 35

Throumpi Baklava
SAVORY BAKLAVA ROLLS 36

Tomato *Diples*
TOMATO FOLDOVER 38

NOT YOUR YIAYIA'S TZATZIKI

GLUTEN-FREE	SERVES 4	PREP TIME:	TOTAL TIME:
NUT-FREE		5 MINUTES	2 HOURS
VEGETARIAN			

Greeks are credited with creating tzatziki, but they actually made it popular as a topping for street food, such as gyros and grilled meats. Indian raita, with mint and yogurt, influenced the Greeks. Theo developed this contemporary version as an alternative to the traditional Greek version using yogurt, cucumber, garlic, and dill, making it a little heartier and more flavorful for use as a dip for *Phyllo Krotides* / Phyllo Crackers (page 24), an alternative to shrimp cocktail sauce, or a dip served with fried calamari.

1 cup whole-milk Greek yogurt

¼ cup Kalamata olives, pitted and very finely chopped

1 tablespoon minced fresh dill

1 tablespoon minced fresh Greek oregano

1 tablespoon minced fresh basil

2 teaspoons minced garlic

1. Start this recipe at least 2 hours ahead of when you want to serve it: Place a fine-mesh strainer inside a colander in the sink and add the yogurt to the strainer. Let the yogurt drain for about 2 hours, revealing a drier, creamier yogurt free of the natural liquids typically stirred back into the container. Transfer to a medium bowl.

2. Stir in the olives, dill, oregano, basil, and garlic. Serve immediately or cover and refrigerate for up to 3 days.

Variation tip: Fresh herbs make the final result look more appetizing and create a more interesting texture, but you can use dried herbs in half the quantity of fresh for about the same flavor. Make a larger container's worth of yogurt, using any leftovers for any and all dishes inspiring a Greek flavor. You and your guests will eat more of this than you'd like to think.

PER SERVING: Calories: 63; Total Fat: 2g; Saturated Fat: 1g; Protein: 7g; Total Carbs: 5g; Fiber: 1g; Sodium: 95mg

Phyllo Krotides
PHYLLO CRACKERS

NUT-FREE VEGETARIAN	SERVES 4	PREP TIME: 10 MINUTES	COOK TIME: 9 TO 12 MINUTES

This recipe came along as a mistake when Theo had sheets of raw phyllo left over. Noting how tasty leftover crumbs in a pan of baklava or spanakopita results in many hands scrambling for a few bits . . . well, now everyone can have their own crunchy bites. If you cut your roll of phyllo into 24 sheets, that makes 144 crackers! Store any extras in an airtight tin (not a plastic container) so they stay crisp.

5 sheets (from 1 roll) phyllo,
    at room temperature

3 tablespoons extra-virgin olive oil

1 egg white, beaten

1 tablespoon dried Greek oregano

2 teaspoons sea salt

¼ teaspoon ground nutmeg

½ cup grated *kasseri* cheese (optional)

1. Preheat the oven to 375°F.

2. Line a baking sheet with parchment paper.

3. Layer 4 sheets of phyllo, one at a time, flat onto the parchment paper, brushing each sheet lightly yet completely with olive oil before adding the next.

4. Lay the 5th sheet on top and brush it with egg white.

5. In a small bowl, mix together the oregano, salt, and nutmeg. Sprinkle the mixture evenly over the top layer of phyllo.

6. Top with the kasseri (if using).

7. Bake for 9 to 12 minutes until golden brown.

Substitution tip: Use any combination of dried herbs and spices to create your own unique cracker flavors. Another favorite combination is sea salt, black pepper, and red pepper flakes. Varietal crystalized salts, popular in specialty markets and online, make creative options infinite.

PER SERVING: Calories: 63; Total Fat: 2g; Saturated Fat: 1g; Protein: 7g; Total Carbs: 5g; Fiber: 1g; Sodium: 95mg

GREEK YOGURT CHEESE

GLUTEN-FREE NUT-FREE VEGETARIAN	SERVES 6	PREP TIME: 5 MINUTES	TOTAL TIME: 24 TO 48 HOURS

Greek yogurt has many applications. It is perfect on its own, mixed with honey, or used in place of sour cream to make any number of recipes healthier. You can use it to make a soft cheese as well. In this recipe, a perfect meld of Greek ingredients and Middle Eastern inspiration, thick Greek yogurt is strained through a cheesecloth. The result is a consistency much like traditional goat cheese, easy to roll into balls that can be studded with herbs and spices to taste and preserved in olive oil. This thick, tangy "cheese" is perfect on crostini and makes a stunning spread at parties.

1 (17.6-ounce) container 2% or whole-milk Greek yogurt

1 teaspoon kosher salt

2 tablespoons chopped fresh herbs and spices of choice, such as oregano, basil, thyme, chives, or red pepper flakes

1 cup extra-virgin olive oil, plus more as needed

1. Place a fine-mesh sieve over a large bowl and line it with cheesecloth.

2. In its original container, mix the yogurt with the salt. Spoon the yogurt into the cheesecloth-lined sieve. Bring up the sides of the cheesecloth to cover the yogurt, securing them with kitchen twine if needed. Place everything in the refrigerator and let the yogurt drain, emptying the bowl occasionally, until there is no more whey (the watery substance) draining into the bowl, up to 2 days. When no more whey is in the bowl, give the cheesecloth a final squeeze.

3. Roll the strained yogurt into 12 to 14 (1-inch) balls.

4. Sprinkle the herbs or spices onto the yogurt balls. Place them into a 7-cup glass container and cover with olive oil. These keep, covered and refrigerated, for up to 3 days.

PER SERVING: Calories: 355; Total Fat: 35g; Saturated Fat: 6g; Protein: 9g; Total Carbs: 4g; Fiber: 1g; Sodium: 415mg

Krema Spanaki
GREEK-Y CREAMED SPINACH

GLUTEN-FREE	SERVES 8	PREP TIME:	COOK TIME:
NUT-FREE		15 MINUTES	10 MINUTES
VEGETARIAN			

Mom said to eat your spinach! You will notice lots of recipes in this book calling for this healthy, leafy green. Spinach is a wonder green, containing strong components of calcium, iron, magnesium, fiber, and vitamins A, C, E, and K as well as potassium and even protein. It's just another one of the ingredients frequently used in this book that just might add to your own Greek-style longevity.

6 tablespoons extra-virgin olive oil, divided

1 medium onion, diced

2 garlic cloves, minced

2 teaspoons sea salt, divided

1 pound fresh spinach

3 eggs

1½ cups *mizithra* cheese, at room temperature

¼ teaspoon ground nutmeg

1. In a large skillet over medium-high heat, heat 2 tablespoons of olive oil.

2. Add the onion, garlic, and 1 teaspoon of salt. Cook for about 5 minutes, until the onions brown.

3. Add the spinach and the remaining 4 tablespoons of olive oil and salt. Cook for 1 to 2 minutes, stirring, until wilted. Reduce the heat to low.

4. In a medium bowl, whisk the eggs and cheese. Stir the egg-cheese mixture into the spinach until the sauce becomes smooth and thick. Remove from the heat.

5. Sprinkle with nutmeg and serve.

Substitution tip: If you can't find *mizithra*, which is a drier cheese, use ricotta cheese and reduce the eggs to 2 instead of 3.

PER SERVING: Calories: 174; Total Fat: 15g; Saturated Fat: 4g; Protein: 7g; Total Carbs: 5g; Fiber: 2g; Sodium: 556mg

Kalamata Elia Mezze

KALAMATA OLIVE SPREAD

| **GLUTEN-FREE** | **SERVES 4** | **PREP TIME:** |
| **VEGAN** | | 15 MINUTES |

Living in Santa Barbara wine country means lots of houseguests coming and going, enjoying premium weather year-round. Olives and nuts offer a metabolic means to absorb sugary carbs while satiating the hunger pangs associated with wine tasting. The ingredients make this a win-win for both flavor and health.

¼ cup raw almonds

1 cup Kalamata olives, pitted

¼ cup fresh basil

½ red bell pepper, seeded and cut into fourths

2 tablespoons extra-virgin olive oil

1 tablespoon dark balsamic vinegar

1 teaspoon lemon zest

1 teaspoon granulated garlic,
    or 2 teaspoons minced garlic

¼ teaspoon sea salt

¼ teaspoon dried Greek oregano

1. In a food processor, chop the almonds.

2. Add the olives, basil, bell pepper, olive oil, vinegar, lemon zest, garlic, salt, and oregano. Lightly blend to combine, keeping the mixture chunky and colorful.

Serving tip: Use as a topping for *Phyllo Krotides* / Phyllo Crackers (page 24), oven-roasted chicken or fish, or crusty bread.

Substitution tip: Pitted green olives or other peppers can be substituted in the same amounts for optional flavors. Canned artichoke hearts, drained and minced, can also be substituted for the olives—delish!

PER SERVING: Calories: 143; Total Fat: 14g; Saturated Fat: 2g; Protein: 2g; Total Carbs: 6g; Fiber: 2g; Sodium: 411mg

Melitzanosalata

EGGPLANT DIP

GLUTEN-FREE NUT-FREE VEGAN	MAKES 2 CUPS	PREP TIME: 25 MINUTES	COOK TIME: 20 TO 40 MINUTES

This dip is the perfect solution to summer's bounty of eggplant. We always have a container of it in the kitchen to bring out for an early evening snack or for drop-in guests. This recipe leans toward its Levantine influences, using tahini to add a rich layer of flavor. Start with the juice of two lemons. You can always add more as you go, but you can't take it away. Other variations of this recipe include omitting the tahini and adding mayonnaise in its place. A Macedonian Greek riff on this recipe, called *malidzano*, incorporates *sirenje* cheese and walnuts into the base recipe.

2 large globe eggplant

½ yellow onion

1 or 2 garlic cloves, smashed

¼ cup tahini

Juice of 2 lemons, plus more as needed

¼ cup fresh parsley leaves, plus more for garnish

¼ cup extra-virgin olive oil

1 teaspoon kosher salt

1 teaspoon freshly ground black pepper

1. Preheat a grill to medium heat, or the oven to 400°F.

2. With a fork, pierce holes all over the eggplant. Grill them for 20 to 30 minutes, turning every 10 minutes, until soft and the skin is dark but not too charred. Alternatively, place the eggplant on a baking sheet and bake for 30 to 40 minutes until they are deflated. Let the eggplant cool for 10 to 15 minutes.

3. Cut the tops off the eggplant and halve them lengthwise. Scoop the flesh into a strainer so the bitter juices can drain out. Discard the skins.

4. In a food processor, combine the onion, garlic, tahini, lemon juice, parsley, and drained eggplant flesh. Pulse to combine.

5. Once the ingredients are incorporated, turn the food processor to low speed and drizzle in the olive oil while it is running. Transfer the mixture to a bowl.

6. Taste and add additional lemon juice if needed. Add the salt and pepper. Serve immediately or refrigerate overnight to let the flavors develop.

7. Garnish with parsley and serve with toasted pita bread or raw vegetables. Cover and refrigerate leftovers for up to 3 days.

Cooking tip: Grilling the eggplant is key in this recipe. The char on the skin that comes from the grill imparts an extra layer of smoky flavor.

PER SERVING (½ CUP): Calories: 265; Total Fat: 21g; Saturated Fat: 3g; Protein: 5g; Total Carbs: 19g; Fiber: 10g; Sodium: 606mg

Htipiti

ROASTED RED PEPPER AND FETA CHEESE DIP

GLUTEN-FREE NUT-FREE VEGETARIAN	MAKES ABOUT 3 CUPS	PREP TIME: 15 MINUTES	COOK TIME: 50 MINUTES

The combination of sweet red peppers and creamy feta cheese is an essential addition to the Greek appetizer table. Not only is it a natural pairing with pita, but you can use it as a tangy spread for burgers and sandwiches. While you can enjoy it right after you make it, the texture thickens and the flavor improves if you refrigerate it overnight.

2 red bell peppers

½ yellow onion

2 garlic cloves

Juice of ½ lemon

10 ounces feta cheese (a creamy sheep's milk feta if you can find it)

2 tablespoons extra-virgin olive oil

½ teaspoon dried Greek oregano

1 teaspoon red pepper flakes, plus more as needed (optional)

1. Preheat the oven to 400°F.

2. Brush the peppers with olive oil and lay them on a greased baking sheet. Roast for 20 minutes. Turn them over and roast an additional 20 minutes, or until the skin is brown and wilted.

3. Pull the roasted peppers from the oven, put them in a paper bag, seal it, and let the peppers cool for 10 minutes. Once they are cooled, peel the skin off and slice them, removing the seeds and ribs.

4. In a food processor, combine the roasted peppers, onion, garlic, and lemon juice. Pulse to combine.

5. Add the feta, olive oil, oregano, and red pepper flakes and pulse until incorporated.

PER SERVING (½ CUP): Calories: 184; Total Fat: 15g; Saturated Fat: 8g; Protein: 7g; Total Carbs: 6g; Fiber: 1g; Sodium: 529mg

Avocado *Skordalia*

AVOCADO GARLIC SPREAD

GLUTEN-FREE VEGAN	SERVES 6	PREP TIME: 15 MINUTES

Here, Christina puts a California spin on a classic Greek dish. *Skordalia*, a pungent garlic (*skordo* in Greek) spread, is common throughout Greece. Spread on warm pita bread or use as an accompaniment to fish and vegetables. (It's also great for warding off vampires!) It's modernized here using avocados instead of starchy potatoes.

6 to 8 garlic cloves, smashed

½ cup blanched almonds

Juice of 1 lemon, plus more as needed

1 teaspoon kosher salt

3 Hass avocados, halved, pitted, and peeled

¼ cup extra-virgin olive oil

1. In a food processor, combine the garlic, almonds, lemon juice, and salt. Pulse until combined.

2. Add the avocado and pulse to combine.

3. Once combined, turn the food processor to low speed and slowly drizzle in the olive oil. Transfer to a serving bowl. Taste and add more lemon juice as needed.

Cooking tip: You can temper the assertiveness of the garlic by coating the whole cloves in olive oil and roasting them until they start to turn brown and become fragrant (don't let them burn). Christina usually does it in her toaster oven for 10 to 15 minutes, but you can roast them in aluminum foil in a 400°F oven for the same amount of time or until you get the desired results. Alternatively, let the chopped garlic sit in the lemon juice for 5 to 10 minutes before you blend everything together.

PER SERVING: Calories: 329; Total Fat: 32g; Saturated Fat: 6g; Protein: 4g; Total Carbs: 12g; Fiber: 8g; Sodium: 394mg

Feta-Kalamata Apogymnomena Avga

FETA-KALAMATA DEVILED EGGS

GLUTEN-FREE	SERVES 4	PREP TIME:
NUT-FREE		20 MINUTES
VEGETARIAN		

While this recipe may be able to trace its roots to thirteenth-century Andalusia (now southeastern Spain), the culinary term "deviled" first appeared only in the late 1700s in Great Britain, describing making food spicy. An 1896 Fannie Farmer recipe featured the deviled egg we know today, using mayonnaise as a binder. Deviled eggs frequently are the first party platter emptied, so the invention of a Greek-y version using olive oil instead of mayo seemed paramount. These don't disappoint and make a high-energy protein snack, perfect for picnics, too.

4 hard-boiled eggs, cooled and peeled (see Cooking tip)

¼ cup minced Kalamata olives

¼ cup crumbled feta cheese

2 tablespoons extra-virgin olive oil

1 tablespoon plus 1 teaspoon mustard

½ teaspoon sea salt

½ teaspoon dried Greek oregano

¼ teaspoon ground nutmeg

1. Halve the eggs. Carefully scoop the yolks into a small bowl, reserving the whites.

2. With a large fork, mash the egg yolks with the olives, feta, olive oil, mustard, salt, oregano, and nutmeg.

3. Scoop the mashed egg yolk mixture back into the empty whites, filling them. Serve immediately or chill.

Cooking tip: Eggs that are 1 to 2 weeks old peel more easily than fresh eggs after hard-boiling. For a perfectly boiled egg that is easy to peel: In a saucepan over high heat, bring 3 cups water, ½ teaspoon salt, and 2 tablespoons distilled white vinegar to a boil. Using a ladle or large spoon, carefully add the eggs to the pot, being careful not to crack them. Lower the heat to a gentle boil and cook for exactly 14 minutes. Immediately drain the hot water and place the eggs into a bowl of ice water. Cool completely before preparing the recipe.

PER SERVING (2 HALVES): Calories: 162; Total Fat: 15g; Saturated Fat: 4g; Protein: 7g; Total Carbs: 2g; Fiber: 1g; Sodium: 530mg

Throumpi Baklava
SAVORY BAKLAVA ROLLS

VEGETARIAN	MAKES 80 PIECES	PREP TIME: 1 HOUR	COOK TIME: 25 MINUTES

As a dessert, baklava dates back to second-century BCE Rome. This pretty, flavorful appetizer is a delicious update from Theo's kitchen. It can be made ahead and frozen raw, baked, and garnished just an hour before guests arrive (see Make-ahead tip). Savory, high-protein ingredients make this a healthy option. This mezze recipe is the most laborious one here, but worth it—try making them with a friend and a glass of wine.

1 cup minced pitted Kalamata olives

¼ cup minced red bell pepper

2 teaspoons dried Greek oregano

1 teaspoon granulated garlic

2 cups crushed pistachios

1 cup feta cheese crumbles

1 pound (2 rolls) phyllo, at room temperature

1½ cups extra-virgin olive oil

1. Preheat the oven to 350°F.

2. Line 2 baking sheets with parchment paper and set aside.

3. In a food processor, or by hand in a small bowl, mix the olives, red bell pepper, oregano, and garlic.

4. In a medium bowl, lightly toss together the pistachios and feta.

5. On a large clean cutting board, silicone pastry mat, or other protective counter cover, place 1 phyllo sheet with the short side facing you. Brush it with olive oil. Repeat with 4 more sheets, stacking and brushing each with olive oil.

6. Spread 1 heaping tablespoon of the olive–bell pepper mixture evenly onto the top layer. (It will be very thin and you'll see the phyllo through the mixture.)

7. Sprinkle ¼ cup of the pistachio-feta mixture over the top. (Again, you may see some phyllo through the mixture.)

8. Starting at the short edge closest to you, roll the stacked phyllo sheets tightly. Seal the roll with a light brushing of olive oil. Cut the roll into 8 equal pieces, placing them filling-side up on the prepared sheet. Repeat the process until all the phyllo is used.

9. Bake the rolls for 25 minutes, or until golden brown. Let cool and serve. Any leftover baked rolls should be wrapped in aluminum foil and will keep for 3 to 4 days in the refrigerator. Other storage styles will make the phyllo soggy.

Make-ahead tip: If prepping ahead of time, cut the rolls and place them side by side in a resealable plastic freezer bag to freeze them. When you're ready to bake, place the rolls on a parchment-lined sheet and add 1 minute to the baking time in the recipe.

Serving tip: For added flavor, blend equal parts fruit juice (orange, mango, or apple) with honey. Top each finished roll with ½ teaspoon of the mixture. Garnish with one tiny basil leaf or ⅛ teaspoon minced fresh basil.

Ingredient tip: If there is any, use leftover phyllo to make *Phyllo Krotides* / Phyllo Crackers (page 24).

PER SERVING (2 PIECES): Calories: 156; Total Fat: 13g; Saturated Fat: 2g; Protein: 2g; Total Carbs: 8g; Fiber: 1g; Sodium: 118mg

Tomato *Diples*

TOMATO FOLDOVER

NUT-FREE VEGETARIAN	SERVES 4	PREP TIME: 1 HOUR, 30 MINUTES	COOK TIME: 25 MINUTES

Greek palates prefer savory over spicy flavors. Greeks see the word *diples* and think of a folded-over phyllo dessert, fried, and smothered with honey and cinnamon. But our recipe uses a healthier version of piecrust that might remind you of a Danish pastry from its looks. The olive oil piecrust recipe does make a remarkable stand-in for dessert pies.

For the crust

2 cups sifted organic all-purpose flour, or pastry flour, plus more for flouring the work surface

½ teaspoon sea salt

1 teaspoon vanilla extract

⅓ cup extra-virgin olive oil

7 tablespoons very cold half-and-half

For the filling

1 egg, beaten

½ cup feta cheese, crumbled

2 medium Roma tomatoes, cut into ¼-inch slices, drained of excess liquid on paper towels

1 teaspoon minced garlic

½ teaspoon sea salt

½ teaspoon dried Greek oregano

2 teaspoons raw sesame seeds

To make the crust

1. In a medium bowl, use a fork to blend the flour and salt. Place the bowl in the freezer for 20 minutes.

2. Remove the flour from the freezer and make a well in the center.

3. In the well, add the vanilla, olive oil, and half-and-half. With a fork, mix just until the ingredients are blended—do not overmix. Form the dough into a ball, cover with plastic wrap, and refrigerate for about 30 minutes.

4. Preheat the oven to 325°F.

5. Roll the chilled dough out onto parchment paper (using a dusting of flour if needed) or a silicone mat into a 9-inch square.

To make the filling

1. Brush the entire crust with the beaten egg.

2. Sprinkle the feta over the crust.

3. Overlap the tomatoes in a spiral pattern, starting about 2 inches from the edge of the crust.

4. In a small bowl, mix the garlic, salt, and oregano. With a spoon, spread the mixture over the tomatoes.

5. Fold the crust edges up and over until they overlap onto the tomatoes.

6. Brush the crust edges with any leftover egg and sprinkle with sesame seeds. Place the finished pastry (it should look like a galette, but with thinner, pie-style crust) onto a sheet of parchment the size of your cookie sheet (see Baking tip).

7. Bake for 25 minutes, or until the crust is golden brown. Let it rest for 5 minutes before cutting. This is also delicious served at room temperature.

Substitution tip: Use ¼-inch zucchini slices, asparagus spears, or thin strips of sweet bell pepper in place of the tomatoes. Make sure any veggies you use are dry when you place them on top of the feta.

Baking tip: Before preheating the oven, place your baking sheet in the oven so the pan itself will heat up as the oven heats. You will place your pastry (which is on parchment paper) onto the hot pan. This helps the crust set more quickly without getting soggy, along with cooking the egg brushed on the crust more quickly, also keeping moisture out.

PER SERVING: Calories: 433; Total Fat: 20g; Saturated Fat: 8g; Protein: 12g; Total Carbs: 40g; Fiber: 6g; Sodium: 356mg

CHAPTER FOUR

Salads & Soups

Rarely does a meal in Greece begin without some type of salad. Whether it's the traditional village salad or something entirely different boasting fresh fruit and local cheese, these simple dishes pack a punch because of the freshness and locality of their ingredients. Soups are also a cornerstone of Greek cuisine. *Avgolemono*, by far the most ubiquitous, especially among the diaspora, is the Greek cure-all for any ailment. But with everything from fish to lamb and fresh vegetables, chicken soup only scratches the surface of the repertoire.

Drosistikos Karpouzi Soupa
REFRESHING WATERMELON SOUP 43

Horiatiki Gazpacho
GREEK GAZPACHO 44

Avgolemono
EGG-LEMON CHICKEN SOUP 46

Mock Magiritsa
EASTER LAMB SOUP 48

Psarosoupa
FISH SOUP 50

Fakes
LENTIL SOUP 52

Salata me Roka, Portokali, Maratho, kai Rodi
ARUGULA SALAD WITH ORANGES, FENNEL, AND POMEGRANATE 53

Horiatiki Salata
GREEK COUNTRY SALAD 55

Halloumi me Rodakino Kalokeri Salata
HALLOUMI AND PEACH SUMMER SALAD 56

Salata me Sparangi, Arakas, kai Avgo Pose
ASPARAGUS SALAD WITH PEAS AND POACHED EGG 58

Theo's Eliniki Salata Kipou
THEO'S GARDEN GREEK SALAD 60

Patata Salata
GREEK POTATO SALAD 62

Agapimeni Salata Tis Oikogeneias
FAMILY FAVORITE SALAD 64

Zesti Salata Synkomidis
WARM HARVEST SALAD 66

Drosistikos Karpouzi Soupa

REFRESHING WATERMELON SOUP

GLUTEN-FREE	SERVES 4	PREP TIME:
NUT-FREE		20 MINUTES
VEGETARIAN		

Theo grows seedless Sugar Baby watermelons that seem in endless supply at her Los Olivos, California, home and farm stand. There are only so many vodka-imbibed watermelon parties one can assemble! During the hottest months in your part of the country, make this cool, quick, healthy meal in a bowl with a Greek twist.

3 cups whole-milk Greek yogurt

2 cups cored, shredded cucumber

2 tablespoons chopped fresh mint leaves, plus 4 sprigs for garnish

2 tablespoons freshly squeezed lemon juice

1 teaspoon sea salt

1 small (6 to 7 inches diameter) seedless Sugar Baby watermelon, rind removed, cut into bite-size chunks

½ teaspoon freshly (finely) ground black pepper

1. In food processor or blender, combine the yogurt, cucumber, mint, lemon juice, and salt. Blend until smooth and creamy. Divide the yogurt evenly among 4 bowls.

2. Spoon watermelon chunks into the yogurt mixture.

3. Sprinkle with pepper and garnish with a mint sprig.

PER SERVING: Calories: 240; Total Fat: 3g; Saturated Fat: 2g; Protein: 20g; Total Carbs: 36g; Fiber: 2g; Sodium: 551mg

Horiatiki Gazpacho

GREEK GAZPACHO

GLUTEN-FREE NUT-FREE VEGETARIAN	SERVES 4 TO 6	PREP TIME: 5 MINUTES	COOK TIME: 5 TO 10 MINUTES

Gazpacho isn't just for the Greeks' Mediterranean counterparts in Spain. This dish is essentially a Greek village salad in soup form. It celebrates the best offerings of summer, when tomatoes are at their peak and picked warm off the vine. Contrast those rich, tangy flavors with cool, crisp cucumbers and deep olive oil that brings together all the flavors of the soup. Serve it cold or at room temperature, and chop extra vegetables to use as garnish along with feta cheese. It couldn't be easier—or more delicious.

3 pounds heirloom tomatoes, in season, roughly chopped

2 Persian cucumbers, roughly chopped

1 red or yellow bell pepper, seeded and roughly chopped

4 garlic cloves, roughly chopped

½ cup extra-virgin olive oil

¼ cup red wine vinegar or balsamic vinegar

1 teaspoon kosher salt, plus more as needed

1 teaspoon freshly ground black pepper, plus more as needed

½ cup feta cheese (optional)

1. In a blender or food processor, working in batches if needed, pulse together the tomatoes, cucumbers, bell pepper, and garlic.

2. Add the olive oil, vinegar, salt, and pepper. Purée to your desired consistency.

3. Strain (or leave chunky) and pour into a serving bowl, garnish with feta (if using), and serve seasoned with more salt and pepper, if desired.

Cooking tip: If you like your gazpacho extra smooth, after blending it, strain it through a fine-mesh sieve.

Ingredient tip: If you don't have access to a farmers' market or a garden for your tomatoes, choose organic heirloom tomatoes from your local supermarket.

PER SERVING: Calories: 318; Total Fat: 26g; Saturated Fat: 4g; Protein: 5g; Total Carbs: 22g; Fiber: 5g; Sodium: 603mg

Avgolemono

EGG-LEMON CHICKEN SOUP

NUT-FREE	SERVES 6	PREP TIME: 10 MINUTES	COOK TIME: 20 TO 30 MINUTES

This signature Greek chicken soup is also known as Greek penicillin. Not only are the broth and lemon restorative, but the egg in the sauce packs a protein punch. You can make this dish low carb by omitting the rice and pasta and adding extra chicken, and even some chopped celery, carrot, and onion. However, for a more indulgent experience, orzo adds starch to the broth, giving it a velvety texture.

For the soup

1½ pounds boneless skinless chicken thighs, cut into bite-size pieces

2 teaspoons kosher salt

2 teaspoons freshly ground black pepper, plus more as needed

1 tablespoon extra-virgin olive oil, plus more for garnish

¼ to ½ cup orzo or rice (optional)

8 cups chicken broth

For the sauce

3 eggs

Juice of 1 lemon

To make the soup

1. Season the chicken with salt and pepper.

2. Place a soup pot over medium-high heat and heat the olive oil.

3. Add the chicken and brown for 5 to 10 minutes.

4. Add the orzo (if using) and the chicken broth. Bring to a boil, reduce the heat to low, and simmer for 15 to 20 minutes.

To make the sauce

1. In a blender, or bowl if using a handheld mixer, blend the eggs until frothy.

2. Add the lemon juice and blend to combine.

3. Temper the sauce into the soup: With the blender on low speed (or while stirring), slowly add 1 cup of hot broth from the soup pot to the egg-lemon mixture. Fold the tempered sauce into the soup. Cook over low heat for 5 minutes more.

Time-saving tip: Ever wonder how to put a spin on a store-bought rotisserie chicken? This is the perfect vehicle. Just shred all the chicken and drop it into the broth.

Ingredient tip: You can use chicken breasts, but chicken thighs are more flavorful and hold up without drying out.

PER SERVING: Calories: 234; Total Fat: 11g; Saturated Fat: 3g; Protein: 31g; Total Carbs: 2g; Fiber: 0g; Sodium: 1,924mg

Mock Magiritsa
EASTER LAMB SOUP

GLUTEN-FREE NUT-FREE	SERVES 6 TO 8	PREP TIME: 10 MINUTES	COOK TIME: 1 HOUR, 25 MINUTES

Magiritsa is traditionally served at Easter to break the 40-day fast that Greek Orthodox Christians observe leading up to the holiday. At midnight on Holy Saturday, the priest announces that Christ has risen and follows that declaration with an hour-long (at least) Divine Liturgy, the breaking of red-dyed eggs, and a heaping bowl of *magiritsa*. Sometimes Christina and her husband can't wait the extra hour, and sneak out of church early to raid the kitchen for the first taste of this soup. For such a tasty dish, it's a shame that it's traditionally served only once a year, mainly because the standard recipe utilizes the offal from the lamb served on Easter Sunday. This easy recipe uses lamb shank, so you're now vindicated to make it and enjoy it at any time of year.

For the soup
2 lamb shanks, rinsed and excess fat trimmed
8 cups water
1 tablespoon extra-virgin olive oil
2 cups chopped celery (½-inch pieces)
1 fennel bulb, diced
1 tablespoon kosher salt
1 cup chopped scallion, white and green parts
½ cup long-grain rice, or basmati rice, rinsed
½ cup chopped fresh dill
Freshly ground black pepper

For the sauce
3 eggs
Juice of 1 lemon

To make the soup

1. Put the lamb shanks in a soup pot, cover with the water, and bring to a boil over high heat. Boil for 1 hour, uncovered. While the shanks boil, skim off any impurities that collect on top. With tongs, remove the meat from the pot, let it cool, and cut into bite-size cubes. Strain the broth into a large bowl.

2. In an 8-quart pot over medium-high heat, heat the olive oil.

3. Add the celery, fennel, and salt. Sauté for 5 minutes.

4. Add the scallion and sauté for 1 to 2 minutes more, or until the white parts are translucent.

5. Pour in the strained broth and add the lamb cubes and rice. Bring the mixture to a boil, reduce the heat to low, and simmer for 10 to 15 minutes, until the orzo is tender.

To make the sauce

1. In a blender, or bowl if using a handheld mixer, blend the eggs until frothy.

2. Add the lemon juice and blend to combine.

3. Temper the sauce into the soup: With the blender on low speed (or while stirring), slowly add 1 cup of hot broth from the soup pot to the egg-lemon mixture. Fold the tempered sauce into the soup. Cook over low heat for 5 minutes more.

4. Garnish with the dill and season with pepper before serving.

Time-saving tip: Cook the lamb shanks a day or two in advance and complete the rest of the soup the day you plan to serve it.

PER SERVING: Calories: 211; Total Fat: 9g; Saturated Fat: 3g; Protein: 13g; Total Carbs: 20g; Fiber: 3g; Sodium: 1,274mg

Psarosoupa
FISH SOUP

GLUTEN-FREE NUT-FREE	SERVES 6	PREP TIME: 30 MINUTES	COOK TIME: 50 MINUTES

Since the beginning of time, this soup has been a nourishing staple. Greek fishermen would make a soup with the heads and tails of fish after cleaning and selling the fillets. Fast-forward to when Theo was a young twentysomething—she lived on fish soup. This is a little-known secret of her personal history. It was cheap and satisfying, and she could make a big pot of it that would last for a few days. She hasn't made it for more than 30 years but resurrected the recipe for this book. Don't tell anyone, but she's living on it again!

4 Roma tomatoes

3 celery stalks, destringed

2 medium russet potatoes, cut into 1-inch pieces

1 bunch carrot tops or beet greens, or 1 pound kale

1 tablespoon minced garlic

¼ cup freshly squeezed lemon juice

2 teaspoons sea salt

1 teaspoon dried dill

½ teaspoon freshly ground black pepper

2 pounds white fish fillets, such as snapper, halibut, or cod, skin off

1 bunch scallions, white and green parts, finely sliced

6 cups spring water (see Cooking tip)

¼ cup extra-virgin olive oil

¼ cup fresh parsley leaves

1. In a large pot over high heat, combine the tomatoes, celery, potatoes, greens, garlic, lemon juice, salt, dill, and pepper. Add enough water to cover and bring to a boil. Reduce the heat to low and simmer for 15 to 20 minutes, until the potatoes are tender. Turn off the heat.

2. With a slotted spoon, transfer all the veggies to a large bowl. The skins on the tomatoes will have burst; peel them with a fork, being careful not to burn your fingers. They will peel easily. Put the tomato remains back into the pot. Discard the celery and greens. Return the potatoes to the pot.

3. Place the pot over medium heat and add the fish, scallions, spring water, and olive oil. Simmer for 20 to 30 minutes, until the fish is malleable and easily breaks apart into pieces. Remove from the heat. Serve piping hot garnished with parsley.

4. As Theo knows, a big pot lasts a few days. Cover and refrigerate any leftovers.

Substitution tip: Monkfish, shrimp, crabmeat, calamari, and lobster all add their own unique dimension to this versatile soup. This recipe also makes a nice vegan soup if you don't use the fish. Add 1 (12-ounce) can of great northern beans, drained and rinsed, to warm after the soup is made. Theo is against farmed fish, such as tilapia and salmon, because most are fed GMO corn feed—yuck! If you find a reliable sustainable-fish farmer and you see a blue-and-white seal on the package that says "Certified Sustainable Seafood MSC" (Marine Stewardship Council), it's as good and wholesome as farmed fish can get. Our advice: Use wild, line-caught fish whenever possible.

Cooking tip: Most traditional recipes for this *soupa* call for carrots, but Theo dislikes cooked carrots. Feel free to add about 3 medium carrots, chopped into ½-inch chunks, if you are so inspired. We use bottled spring water when making soup only because our tap water doesn't taste so great. Do you like your tap water? If yes, use it!

Serving tip: Add 1 tablespoon red pepper flakes during the final 10 minutes of cooking and serve with a heaping tablespoon of Greek yogurt for a zesty option.

PER SERVING: Calories: 343; Total Fat: 10g; Saturated Fat: 2g; Protein: 41g; Total Carbs: 24g; Fiber: 5g; Sodium: 436mg

Fakes

LENTIL SOUP

GLUTEN-FREE NUT-FREE	SERVES 4 TO 6	PREP TIME: 10 MINUTES	COOK TIME: 1 HOUR

Although this dish is extremely popular during the period of Great Lent, Greeks enjoy it any time of year. The key is having enough acid to give it a zing. If you decide it needs a little more, add vinegar to taste. The addition of cilantro at the end also brightens the flavor.

2 tablespoons extra-virgin olive oil, divided

1 onion, chopped

1 teaspoon kosher salt

2 garlic cloves, minced

3 celery stalks, chopped

2 carrots, chopped

1 tablespoon ground cumin

1 tablespoon dried Greek oregano

1 teaspoon freshly ground black pepper

1 pound green lentils

1 (14.5-ounce) can diced tomatoes, or 3 ripe tomatoes, grated

8 cups chicken broth

2 bay leaves

¼ cup red wine vinegar

¼ cup chopped fresh cilantro (optional)

1. In a soup pot over medium-high heat, heat 1 tablespoon of olive oil.

2. Add the onion and salt. Sauté for 5 minutes, or until the onion is translucent.

3. Add the garlic and sauté for about 1 minute, until fragrant.

4. Stir in the celery, carrots, cumin, oregano, and pepper. Sauté for 5 to 7 minutes more.

5. Stir in the lentils, tomatoes, chicken broth, and bay leaves. Cook for 30 to 45 minutes, until the lentils are tender.

6. Stir in the vinegar and cilantro (if using) and serve.

7. Cover and refrigerate leftovers for up to 3 days.

Cooking tip: With a bounty of different lentils widely available, experiment with different types to find your favorite.

PER SERVING: Calories: 600; Total Fat: 12g; Saturated Fat: 2g; Protein: 38g; Total Carbs: 86g; Fiber: 34g; Sodium: 2,151mg

ARUGULA SALAD WITH ORANGES, FENNEL, AND POMEGRANATE

GLUTEN-FREE NUT-FREE VEGAN	SERVES 6 TO 8	PREP TIME: 20 MINUTES

If you have the good fortune of taking a road trip through the Peloponnese, you may notice something similar to Southern California—endless stretches of orange groves. This salad celebrates the region's offerings, highlighting both navel oranges and blood oranges. The deep color and taste of the blood oranges beautifully contrast with the navel orange, all balanced by aromatic fennel and a pop of acid from the pomegranate seeds. It makes a gorgeous display.

For the salad

10 ounces fresh arugula

1 fennel bulb, quartered and thinly sliced

3 blood oranges, peeled and segmented

1 navel orange, peeled and segmented

1 cup pomegranate seeds

For the dressing

¼ cup balsamic vinegar or pomegranate balsamic, if possible

1 shallot, minced

1 teaspoon kosher salt

½ cup extra-virgin olive oil

To make the salad

In a large bowl, toss together the arugula, fennel, blood oranges, navel orange, and pomegranate seeds.

To make the dressing

1. In a medium bowl, combine the vinegar, shallot, and salt. Whisk in the olive oil until it emulsifies.

2. Dress the salad by adding a third of the dressing at a time, tossing as you go. Do not overdress.

PER SERVING: Calories: 276; Total Fat: 18g; Saturated Fat: 3g; Protein: 4g; Total Carbs: 29g; Fiber: 8g; Sodium: 431mg

Horiatiki Salata

GREEK COUNTRY SALAD

GLUTEN-FREE	**SERVES 4**	**PREP TIME:**
NUT-FREE		10 MINUTES
VEGETARIAN		

The plain old regular tomato, Early Girl, varietal works the best. Other times of year, thick-skinned Roma tomatoes will do fine. You can fancy things up with heirloom tomatoes for color and sass—but the simpler, the better. No other recipe is so frequently found on the menus of every Greek restaurant or Greek festival, at Greek funerals, and in every Greek kitchen.

4 large tomatoes, cut into chunks

1 medium cucumber, cut into ½-inch rounds, then halved

½ medium purple onion, thinly sliced into large half rings

6 ounces feta cheese, cut into 4 equal slices

20 Kalamata olives (see Serving tip)

12 tablespoons extra-virgin olive oil

3 teaspoons dried Greek oregano

1 teaspoon sea salt

1 teaspoon freshly ground black pepper

1. Divide the tomatoes and cucumber equally among 4 bowls.

2. Scatter onion pieces over each bowl.

3. Place 1 slice feta on top of each.

4. Divide and arrange the olives around the inside edge of each bowl.

5. Drizzle each with 3 tablespoons olive oil.

6. In a small bowl, mix the oregano, salt, and pepper. Sprinkle onto the salads and serve.

Serving tip: Kalamata Greek olives have pits. They taste different, too. Think of the difference between boneless chicken and bone-in chicken—both are good, but they're different, right? Have a big loaf of crusty bread to soak up the olive oil, vegetable juices, and seasoning amalgamation left in the bottom of the bowls. That's the best part! And, please, don't crumble the feta cheese! A nice slab over the top is not only beautiful but also lets the eater decide how much goat-y goodness goes into every bite.

PER SERVING: Calories: 552; Total Fat: 54g; Saturated Fat: 13g; Protein: 9g; Total Carbs: 15g; Fiber: 4g; Sodium: 1,146mg

HALLOUMI AND PEACH SUMMER SALAD

GLUTEN-FREE NUT-FREE VEGETARIAN	SERVES 4	PREP TIME: 10 MINUTES	COOK TIME: 10 TO 12 MINUTES

Halloumi is an unripened, briny cheese usually made from a combination of sheep's and goat's milk. This is Theo's favorite summertime salad, first sampled in Chania, Crete, at Apostolis Restaurant. She didn't ask them for their recipe but was able to re-create one with more dimension. Theirs was served chopped, in a bowl with a simple parsley sprig and red wine vinaigrette. A few attempts at the recipe during lavender-blooming season brought a more generous array of contemporary flavors to this simple-to-make salad.

For the salad

2 tablespoons extra-virgin olive oil

8 ounces halloumi cheese,
    cut into 16 equal pieces

6 cups fresh spinach

4 medium peaches, halved, pitted,
    and thinly sliced

1 tablespoon plus 1 teaspoon
    minced fresh parsley

For the dressing

¼ cup extra-virgin olive oil

¼ cup honey

¼ cup freshly squeezed lemon juice

½ teaspoon sea salt

½ teaspoon freshly ground black pepper

1 teaspoon culinary lavender, pulverized
    with a mortar and pestle (optional, for
    added flavor)

To make the salad

1. In a heavy-bottomed skillet over medium-high heat, heat the olive oil. Add the halloumi slices and fry for 5 to 7 minutes per side, until golden brown.

2. Arrange 1½ cups spinach on each of 4 serving plates.

3. Fan the peach slices in a circle on top of each salad, alternating with 4 pieces of fried cheese for each.

4. Sprinkle with the parsley.

To make the dressing

In a small bowl, whisk the olive oil, honey, lemon juice, salt, pepper, and lavender (if using). Pour equal amounts over each salad just before serving.

Cooking tip: Grill the peaches and halloumi on a gas or charcoal grill. Simply keep the cheese whole (as an 8-ounce chunk), halve the peaches, and brush with 2 tablespoons olive oil. Grill over a hot fire until the cheese and fruit have grill marks.

Substitution tip: Any fresh, ripe, soft fruit (such as apricots, strawberries, or plums) works beautifully in this salad, as does any summer melon.

PER SERVING: Calories: 525; Total Fat: 39g; Saturated Fat: 15g; Protein: 15g; Total Carbs: 35g; Fiber: 4g; Sodium: 566mg

Salata me Sparangi, Arakas, kai Avgo Pose

ASPARAGUS SALAD WITH PEAS AND POACHED EGG

GLUTEN-FREE NUT-FREE VEGETARIAN	SERVES 4 TO 6	PREP TIME: 10 TO 15 MINUTES	COOK TIME: 10 MINUTES

Christina's mom would always tell her stories about how her *papou* (grandfather) used to forage for the tastiest wild asparagus, growing in a field outside his house in North Chicago, and some version of this salad would always hit the table in spring. While foraging opportunities for asparagus are limited these days, this fresh, bright green salad is the perfect manifestation of spring vegetables found at the farmers' market or in your grocery store.

12 ounces asparagus, trimmed and cut into 1-inch pieces

1 cup peas

1 egg

1 tablespoon white wine or white vinegar

2 garlic cloves, minced

1 teaspoon kosher salt

1 teaspoon freshly ground black pepper

Juice of 2 large lemons

½ cup extra-virgin olive oil

½ cup chopped fresh dill

1. In a large pot of boiling water, blanch the asparagus and peas for 1 minute. With a large slotted spoon, remove them from the boiling water and immediately shock in an ice water bath. Drain and let them cool completely.

2. Bring a small pot of water to a simmer (not a boil) and add the vinegar.

3. Crack the egg into a ramekin or small bowl.

4. With a spoon, stir the simmering water. While it is still swirling, gently release the egg into the water as close to the surface as possible.

5. Let the egg poach for 5 minutes, then remove with a slotted spoon.

6. In a small mixing bowl, combine the garlic, salt, pepper, and lemon juice. Let the mixture sit for 5 minutes.

7. Whisk the olive oil into the lemon-garlic mixture until it emulsifies.

8. Place the cooled vegetables in a large mixing bowl. Toss with the dill and dressing. Serve on a large platter topped with the poached egg.

Serving tip: This dish is extremely versatile. Serve it on its own as a salad, add more poached eggs for a beautiful brunch main course, or toss it with pasta, gnocchi, or orzo for a beautiful, fresh pasta dish.

PER SERVING: Calories: 300; Total Fat: 27g; Saturated Fat: 4g; Protein: 7g; Total Carbs: 13g; Fiber: 5g; Sodium: 613mg

THEO'S GARDEN GREEK SALAD

GLUTEN-FREE NUT-FREE VEGETARIAN	SERVES 4	PREP TIME: 40 MINUTES	COOK TIME: 15 MINUTES

There's something indescribable about pairing these six foods together—it's like a food-and-wine pairing in a bowl but without the wine! One thing we can't live without is avocados, and we are grateful to live in California where they are plentiful. Theo grows everything on this ingredient list in her year-round garden—even the Kalamata olives. This salad includes "healthy Greek fat" as sumptuous taste bud partners (the theme of our book!), so we thought we'd have a little fun creating this colorful, modern Greek salad.

3 medium (about 3 inches diameter) beets, cut into 1-inch chunks

1 tablespoon apple cider vinegar, distilled, or wine vinegar

1 avocado

2 hard-boiled eggs (see Cooking tip, page 35), peeled and quartered

12 Kalamata olives

4 fresh figs, quartered

4 ounces feta cheese, crumbled

1 tablespoon lemon zest

1 teaspoon sea salt

1 teaspoon freshly ground black pepper

12 large basil leaves, cut into chiffonade (see page 14)

4 tablespoons extra-virgin olive oil

1. Fill a medium saucepan with water, place it over high heat, and bring to a boil. Add the beets and vinegar and boil for 15 to 20 minutes, making sure not to over-boil. A fork should easily go to the middle of a test piece but not break it apart. Drain the beets when done and divide them among 4 small bowls.

2. Quarter the avocado and slice each quarter lengthwise into 3 equal segments from one end to about ¼ inch from the other end, keeping one end solid for fanning. Carefully scoop the avocado fruit away from the skin. Fan the avocado over the beets.

3. Arrange the eggs, olives, and figs around the outside of the avocado slices, alternating for color.

4. Top with feta, and sprinkle each bowl with ¼ tablespoon lemon zest, ¼ teaspoon salt, and ¼ teaspoon pepper.

5. Distribute the basil over the salads.

6. Drizzle each bowl with 1 tablespoon of olive oil.

Cooking tip: Boiling beets with vinegar (or lemon juice) keeps them from bleeding. If you use fancy beets, such as the striped Chioggia variety, this trick comes in handy.

Serving tip: Boil the beets and eggs 1 day to 2 hours before serving and chill. This salad is best served chilled.

PER SERVING: Calories: 419; Total Fat: 34g; Saturated Fat: 9g; Protein: 10g; Total Carbs: 29g; Fiber: 7g; Sodium: 1,042mg

Patata Salata

GREEK POTATO SALAD

GLUTEN-FREE NUT-FREE VEGAN	SERVES 8	PREP TIME: 15 MINUTES	COOK TIME: 15 MINUTES

The earliest potato salads were created by the Spanish in the sixteenth century, with the potatoes boiled in vinegar and spices. (Note to self—must try!) Potato salad became popular in America during the early 1960s, and Theo's mom made this salad for countless picnic potlucks. The bowl never came home with leftovers. The only difference here is her mom used Crisco oil. In the 1960s a lot of Greeks, and other immigrants, tried to assimilate themselves into American culture in almost every way—and the ads were convincing! This is one of those comfort salads that tastes so much better with really fresh extra-virgin olive oil. Momma Helen would be so proud, and we think she would agree to removing her Crisco from today's modern Greek kitchen.

4 large potatoes, such as Yukon Gold, or red potatoes (some red potatoes can be small so increase the quantity to equal 4 large potatoes), cut into 1-inch chunks

1 cup chopped green bell pepper

1 cup sliced destringed celery (¼-inch-thick slices)

½ cup sliced scallion, using most of the greens (¼-inch-thick slices)

¼ cup minced pitted Kalamata olives

½ cup extra-virgin olive oil

1 tablespoon lemon zest

1 tablespoon minced garlic

2½ teaspoons sea salt

1 teaspoon freshly ground black pepper

1 teaspoon dried Greek oregano

1. Fill a medium saucepan with water, place it over high heat, and bring to a boil. Add the potatoes and boil for about 15 minutes. A fork should easily go to the middle of a test piece but not split it. Drain when done and let them cool.

2. In a large bowl, combine the cooled potatoes, bell pepper, celery, scallion, olives, olive oil, lemon zest, garlic, salt, pepper, and oregano. Mix well and serve.

3. If you're lucky enough to have leftovers, cover and refrigerate for up to 3 days.

Cooking tip: Double this recipe! People love it and you will want those leftovers.

Substitution tip: Add some extra protein to this meal by adding hard-boiled eggs to the salad or, Theo's favorite way to eat it, a poached or soft-centered fried egg on top for each person. Add chopped bacon if you want to Americanize this salad. Yesterday's leftover steak or salmon works great, too.

PER SERVING: Calories: 254; Total Fat: 13g; Saturated Fat: 2g; Protein: 4g; Total Carbs: 32g; Fiber: 4g; Sodium: 488mg

FAMILY FAVORITE SALAD

GLUTEN-FREE NUT-FREE VEGETARIAN	SERVES 4	PREP TIME: 20 MINUTES	COOK TIME: 6 MINUTES

Greeks love their *fruta* (fruit) and *tiri* (cheese). This salad combines the best of both worlds for a quick, original dinner full of interesting texture and flavors. We love making entire meals around salads and a glass of Santorini white wine. Simple, elegant, and satiating—you get your bread and eat it, too!

For the salad

4 (1½-inch-thick) slices Greek bread or crusty dense bread

¼ cup extra-virgin olive oil, plus more as needed (see Cooking tip)

2 large heads romaine lettuce, outer leaves removed, cut into chiffonade (see page 14)

2 cups cubed cantaloupe (1-inch cubes)

6 ounces kasseri cheese, cut into ½-inch cubes

1 cup fresh strawberries, sliced

For the dressing

8 large strawberries

¼ cup fresh Greek oregano

3 tablespoons extra-virgin olive oil

1 teaspoon sea salt

To make the salad

1. Before turning on the stove, pat each piece of bread with a drizzle of olive oil; most of the oil will be absorbed, but not all—you do not want your bread soaked in oil.

2. In a large skillet (big enough to fit all 4 pieces of bread) over medium heat, heat any remaining olive oil, or add a bit more if needed.

3. Add the bread and toast for 2 to 3 minutes per side. Remove from the heat.

4. Place 2 cups of lettuce on each of 4 plates.

5. Equally divide the cantaloupe, cheese, and sliced strawberries among the plates.

To make the dressing

1. In a small food processor or blender, blend the large strawberries, oregano, olive oil, and salt. Pour the dressing over the salads.

2. With a serrated knife, cut each slice of toasted bread into 1-inch chunks and toss them on top.

Ingredient tip: Kasseri cheese is typically found near the Asiago or Parmesan cheese in most cheese cases.

Substitution tip: Raspberries can be substituted for the strawberries, and peaches for the cantaloupe. Fresh basil or mint may be substituted for the oregano.

Cooking tip: You may need to add a little more olive oil to your skillet before toasting the bread if you soaked up every drop in step 1.

PER SERVING: Calories: 621; Total Fat: 41g; Saturated Fat: 11g; Protein: 21g; Total Carbs: 49g; Fiber: 5g; Sodium: 1,160mg

Zesti Salata Synkomidís

WARM HARVEST SALAD

GLUTEN-FREE VEGETARIAN	SERVES 4	PREP TIME: 15 MINUTES	COOK TIME: 1 HOUR

Sometimes a warm salad hits the spot on a cool day. We love making this hearty salad during the fall season, when pistachio kernels are freshly harvested and sweet potatoes evoke the coming of winter.

2 large sweet potatoes, pierced 6 to 8 times with a fork

6 tablespoons extra-virgin olive oil, divided

8 ounces organic cremini mushrooms, quartered, brown bottoms trimmed from the stems

1 medium onion, chopped

1 teaspoon sea salt, divided

1 pound dandelion greens, alligator kale, or fresh spinach

4 tablespoons *mizithra* cheese

4 tablespoons roasted pistachios

4 tablespoons chopped fresh parsley

1. Preheat the oven to 400°F.

2. Bake the sweet potatoes (you may want to put a piece of aluminum foil underneath to catch any drips) for 1 hour.

3. In the meantime, when the sweet potatoes have cooked for about 30 minutes, place a large skillet over medium-high heat, add 2 tablespoons of olive oil, the mushrooms, onion, and ½ teaspoon of salt. Sauté for 3 to 4 minutes, keeping the mushrooms firm. Transfer to a medium bowl.

4. Return the skillet to medium heat. Add the remaining 4 tablespoons of olive oil and stir in the greens until wilted, about 3 minutes.

5. Stir in the mushroom and onion mixture.

6. Remove the sweet potatoes from the oven and cut each crosswise into 8 slices. As you slice them, the peels should slip away; discard the peels. Arrange 4 sweet potato slices on each of 4 plates. Sprinkle evenly with the remaining ½ teaspoon of salt.

7. Scoop the warm greens, mushroom, and onion mixture over the warm sweet potatoes.

8. Top each with 1 tablespoon of cheese, pistachios, and parsley.

Substitution tip: Use Greek yogurt or feta instead of the *mizithra* cheese.

PER SERVING: Calories: 361; Total Fat: 24g; Saturated Fat: 4g; Protein: 9g; Total Carbs: 32g; Fiber: 5g; Sodium: 599mg

CHAPTER FIVE

Beans, Rice & Pasta

Greeks have always known how to stretch a meal, and beans, rice, and pastas are not only an economical way to do it—they are also extremely delicious. This collection of dishes contains some of the most revered in Greek cuisine. *Pastitsio*, with its layers of spiced beef and creamy béchamel sauce, is among the most decadent, while *manestra* is simple and crave-worthy at the same time. *Spanakorizo* is a healthy combination of spinach, tomatoes, and fresh herbs that, even when made vegan, is so flavorful you'll be stacking your plate with seconds.

Gigandes Plaki
**BRAISED GIANT BEANS
IN TOMATO SAUCE** 71

Skioufikta me Manitaria kai Kotopoulo
**SKIOUFIKTA WITH WILD MUSHROOMS
AND CHICKEN** 74

Makaronia me Domates, Garida, kai Vasilikos
**SPAGHETTI WITH TOMATO,
SHRIMP, AND BASIL** 75

Kolokythiaki kai Fountoukia
**BUTTERNUT SQUASH
AND HAZELNUT PASTA** 77

Makaronada
PASTA WITH MEAT SAUCE 79

Pastitsio
BAKED PASTA WITH MEAT SAUCE 80

Salata me Kritharaki, Domates, Elies, kai Feta
**PASTA SALAD WITH ORZO,
TOMATO, OLIVES, AND FETA** 83

Manestra
ORZO PASTA WITH TOMATO 84

Spanakorizo
SPINACH RICE 85

Pilaffi me Fides
RICE PILAF WITH VERMICELLI 86

Gigandes Plaki

BRAISED GIANT BEANS IN TOMATO SAUCE

GLUTEN-FREE NUT-FREE VEGAN	SERVES 6 TO 8	PREP TIME: 8 TO 10 HOURS	COOK TIME: 2 HOURS

This is technically the Greek version of baked beans (similar dishes abound in Turkey and the Middle East), but instead of bacon and brown sugar, you use a rich tomato sauce and spices to flavor the dish. Don't let the prep time deter you. It's something you can manage a few days ahead; keep the rehydrated beans in your refrigerator until you're ready to bake them in the sauce.

1½ cups dried gigandes or large lima beans

½ teaspoon baking soda, as needed

1 tablespoon extra-virgin olive oil, plus more for garnishing (optional)

1 large yellow onion, chopped

1 teaspoon kosher salt

3 garlic cloves, minced

1 tablespoon dried Greek oregano

2 celery stalks, minced

1 carrot, minced

1 (14.5-ounce) can diced tomatoes

¼ cup chopped fresh parsley, for garnishing (optional)

1. In a large bowl or pot, combine the beans and enough water to cover by about 2 inches. Soak the beans in the water overnight.

2. Drain, rinse, and place the beans in a large soup pot. Cover the beans with fresh water, bring to a boil over high heat, reduce heat to low, and simmer for 1 hour. Check the beans after 45 minutes. If they are still hard and mealy, add the baking soda to the water. Continue to cook until the beans are soft. Drain.

3. Preheat the oven to 350°F.

4. In a large skillet over medium-high heat, heat the olive oil.

5. Add the onion and salt. Cook for 3 to 5 minutes, until the onion is translucent.

(CONTINUED)

6. Add the garlic. Cook for about 1 minute, until fragrant.

7. Add the oregano, celery, and carrot. Cook for 5 to 7 minutes more.

8. Stir in the tomatoes, reduce the heat to low, and simmer for 15 minutes.

9. Transfer the beans and the sauce to a 9-by-13-inch baking dish. Bake for 30 minutes.

10. Garnish with the parsley and olive oil (if using), and serve.

Cooking tip: If you want a thicker sauce, process ¼ to ½ cup of the beans through a food mill (or mash them) and mix into the pan before baking.

PER SERVING: Calories: 96; Total Fat: 3g; Saturated Fat: 1g; Protein: 4g; Total Carbs: 15g; Fiber: 4g; Sodium: 511mg

Skioufikta me Manitaria kai Kotopoulo

SKIOUFIKTA WITH WILD MUSHROOMS AND CHICKEN

NUT-FREE	SERVES 6 TO 8	PREP TIME: 15 MINUTES	COOK TIME: 25 MINUTES

This is the perfect one-pot dish for a chilly night, when you want to indulge in earthy comfort food. The combination of the mushrooms and the pasta cooked in a rich, creamy sauce rather than water says everything. *Skioufikta* is a traditional pasta from Crete that has a similar shape to cavatelli or strozzapreti. If neither one is readily available, the shape of orecchiette pasta also lends itself to this dish.

1½ pounds boneless skinless chicken thighs

1 teaspoon kosher salt

1 teaspoon freshly ground black pepper

2 tablespoons extra-virgin olive oil

1 medium onion, chopped

4 garlic cloves, minced

1 pound cremini mushrooms, roughly chopped

12 ounces pasta, such as cavatelli, strozzapreti, or orecchiette

1 bunch fresh thyme, tied with kitchen twine

2 cups chicken broth

1 cup heavy (whipping) cream or soy cream

½ cup (or more) grated hard salty cheese, such as *kefalotiri* or Romano

1. Cut the chicken into cubes and season with the salt and pepper.

2. Heat a Dutch oven over medium-high heat.

3. Add the olive oil and chicken. Cook for 7 to 10 minutes, until the chicken is brown.

4. Add the onion. Cook for 3 to 5 minutes, until translucent.

5. Add the garlic. Cook for 30 seconds.

6. Add the mushrooms to the mix and cook for 5 to 7 minutes, until they soften.

7. Stir in the pasta, thyme, broth, and cream. Simmer for 8 to 10 minutes, until the pasta is cooked.

8. Remove and discard the thyme stems, and garnish with the cheese.

PER SERVING: Calories: 721; Total Fat: 22g; Saturated Fat: 9g; Protein: 43g; Total Carbs: 91g; Fiber: 5g; Sodium: 941mg

Makaronia me Domates, Garida, kai Vasilikos

SPAGHETTI WITH TOMATO, SHRIMP, AND BASIL

NUT-FREE	SERVES 6	PREP TIME: 15 MINUTES	COOK TIME: 25 MINUTES

This simple pasta dish takes you straight to the Greek islands, where seafood and fresh tomatoes are just as common as whitewashed buildings overlooking the sea.

1 pound large shrimp, peeled and deveined

1 teaspoon lemon zest

6 tablespoons extra-virgin olive oil, divided

Sea salt

Freshly ground black pepper

1 pound cherry tomatoes, halved

4 garlic cloves, minced

½ cup dry white wine or water

1 pound spaghetti or linguini

½ cup fresh basil, cut into chiffonade (see page 14)

Juice of 1 lemon

1. In a small bowl, combine the shrimp, lemon zest, and 2 tablespoons of olive oil. Season with salt and pepper. Let it rest while you make the sauce.

2. In a large skillet over medium heat, heat 2 tablespoons of olive oil. Stir in the tomatoes.

3. Wait 1 minute and add the garlic. Season with salt and pepper. Cook for 5 minutes.

4. Add the wine and continue to cook for about 15 minutes, until the tomatoes start to dissolve and the sauce is reduced.

5. During the last 5 minutes of cooking, add the shrimp and cook until pink.

6. While the sauce cooks, boil the spaghetti for 1 minute less than the package instructions indicate. Reserve 1 cup of pasta water. Drain the spaghetti.

7. In the pasta pot over medium heat, heat the remaining 2 tablespoons of olive oil.

8. Add the drained spaghetti and sauce and stir to combine, adding some of the pasta water if the mixture seems too dry. Sprinkle with the basil and the lemon juice, and serve.

PER SERVING: Calories: 476; Total Fat: 13g; Saturated Fat: 2g; Protein: 25g; Total Carbs: 62g; Fiber: 3g; Sodium: 143mg

Kolokythiaki kai Fountoukia

BUTTERNUT SQUASH AND HAZELNUT PASTA

VEGETARIAN	SERVES 6 TO 8	PREP TIME: 15 MINUTES	COOK TIME: 30 MINUTES

Squash is a staple of the Greek diet, and butternut squash, particularly, has been gaining popularity in Greece over the last few years. In this recipe, the sweet squash teams with another favorite Greek ingredient—hazelnuts—which are often served on their own to accompany wine or spirits, as has been the practice since ancient times. Greek yogurt stands in for butter and cream in this pasta dish, lightening it and making it healthier overall.

1½ pounds butternut squash, peeled and cubed

½ red onion, sliced

6 garlic cloves

2 tablespoons extra-virgin olive oil

2 tablespoons kosher salt, plus 1 teaspoon, divided

1 teaspoon freshly ground black pepper

½ teaspoon ground nutmeg

½ cup Greek yogurt (2% or whole milk)

1 cup milk

1 cup hazelnuts, peeled and blanched, half of them smashed or processed into small pieces

1 pound pasta, such as fettuccini or pappardelle

1. Preheat the oven to 400°F.

2. On a rimmed sheet pan, toss the butternut squash, onion, and garlic with the olive oil, 1 teaspoon of salt, and the pepper. Bake for 20 to 30 minutes, shaking the tray halfway through cooking, and being careful not to let the onion and garlic burn.

3. While the squash bakes, prepare the pasta according to the package directions, adding the remaining 2 tablespoons of salt to the cooking water. Reserve 1 cup of cooking water and drain the pasta.

4. Transfer the contents of the baking sheet to a blender or food processor. Add the yogurt, milk, and the whole (unsmashed) hazelnuts, and process thoroughly.

(CONTINUED)

5. Put the pasta back into the cooking pot.

6. Add the butternut squash sauce and turn on the burner to the lowest setting possible. Combine the pasta with the sauce, adding some pasta water if the mixture seems too dry. Serve garnished with the smashed hazelnuts.

Ingredient tip: Add a few tablespoons of fresh herbs (such as thyme and/or sage) to the sauce.

PER SERVING: Calories: 542; Total Fat: 21g; Saturated Fat: 3g; Protein: 17g; Total Carbs: 78g; Fiber: 8g; Sodium: 805mg

Makaronada
PASTA WITH MEAT SAUCE

NUT-FREE	SERVES 6	PREP TIME: 10 MINUTES	COOK TIME: 30 MINUTES

This rich dish is like the Greek version of bolognese—with a twist. Cinnamon and allspice come into play with savory meat in a slowly simmered pasta sauce. While you can wrap it up in about a half hour, the longer you simmer the sauce, the more flavor will develop and the richer it will be. Misko No. 2 noodles are the preferred noodle in Greek dishes such as *makaronada* and *pastitsio*. They are narrow, hollow, strawlike noodles similar to bucatini. If you can't find either one, try linguini.

1 teaspoon extra-virgin olive oil

1 pound ground beef

1 onion, chopped

3 garlic cloves, minced

2 teaspoons kosher salt

1 teaspoon ground cinnamon

½ teaspoon ground allspice

1 (6-ounce) can tomato paste

1 (14.5-ounce) can diced tomatoes

½ cup red wine

1 teaspoon freshly ground black pepper

1 pound Misko No. 2 noodles, bucatini, or linguini

½ cup grated *kefalotiri*, Parmesan, or Romano cheese

1. In a large skillet over medium-high heat, heat the olive oil.

2. Add the beef. Cook for 5 to 7 minutes, breaking it up with the back of a spoon, until brown. Drain off the fat and return the skillet and beef to the heat.

3. Add the onion, garlic, and salt. Cook for 5 minutes, until the onion is translucent.

4. Add the cinnamon, allspice, and tomato paste. Cook for 3 minutes more.

5. Stir in the tomatoes, red wine, and pepper. Cover the skillet, reduce the heat to low, and simmer for 15 minutes.

6. While the sauce simmers, cook the pasta according to the package instructions. Reserve 1 cup of pasta water, drain the pasta, and return it to the pot.

7. Add the sauce to the pasta pot and stir to incorporate it into the pasta, adding some pasta water if the mixture seems too dry. Garnish with the cheese and serve.

PER SERVING: Calories: 598; Total Fat: 27g; Saturated Fat: 10g; Protein: 29g; Total Carbs: 60g; Fiber: 13g; Sodium: 966mg

BAKED PASTA WITH MEAT SAUCE

NUT-FREE	SERVES 12	PREP TIME: 30 MINUTES	COOK TIME: 2 HOURS

Greeks put this dish in context by saying it's a Greek version of lasagna, but it is so much more. A warmly spiced, meaty tomato sauce is layered with pasta and a rich béchamel. When it's time to indulge, the Greeks really know how to do it right!

For the béchamel
1 cup (2 sticks) butter

1 cup all-purpose flour

6 cups milk, heated, divided

¼ teaspoon ground nutmeg

Sea salt

Freshly ground black pepper

6 eggs

½ cup grated *kefalotiri* or Romano cheese

For the meat filling
2 tablespoons extra-virgin olive oil

2 pounds ground beef

2 medium onions, minced

3 garlic cloves, minced

Sea salt

4 celery stalks, minced

3 carrots, minced

½ teaspoon ground cinnamon

¼ teaspoon ground allspice

¼ teaspoon ground nutmeg

1 (6-ounce) can tomato paste

1 (14.5-ounce) can diced tomatoes

½ cup red wine

For the pasta
1 pound Misko No. 2 noodles or penne

2 tablespoons butter

1 cup grated *kefalotiri* or
    Romano cheese, divided

To make the béchamel

1. In a heavy saucepan over medium/medium-low heat, melt the butter.

2. Add the flour and cook for about 10 minutes, stirring constantly.

3. Slowly add 4 cups of heated milk, whisking constantly.

4. Add the nutmeg, season with salt and pepper, and remove from the heat.

5. In a blender, beat the eggs until frothy. Temper the egg mixture into the sauce: Add the remaining 2 cups of heated milk to the eggs to bring them up to temperature. Slowly add the mixture from the blender back into the saucepan, stirring constantly until thickened.

6. Stir in the cheese.

To make the meat filling

1. In a large skillet over medium-high heat, heat the olive oil.

2. Add the beef. Cook for 5 to 7 minutes, breaking it up with the back of a spoon, until brown. Drain off the fat and return the skillet and beef to the heat.

3. Add the onions and garlic and season with salt. Cook for 5 minutes, until the onion is translucent.

4. Add the celery and carrots. Cook for 5 minutes more.

5. Add the cinnamon, allspice, nutmeg, and tomato paste. Cook for 3 minutes more.

6. Stir in the tomatoes and red wine. Cover the skillet, reduce the heat to low, and simmer for 15 minutes.

To make the pasta

1. Preheat the oven to 375°F.

2. While the meat filling cooks, cook the pasta according to the package directions. Drain and return the pasta to the pot.

3. Add the butter, ¾ cup of cheese, and 2 cups of the béchamel. Stir to combine. Transfer the pasta to a large baking pan, spreading it in an even layer.

4. Spread the meat sauce in an even layer over the pasta.

5. Top with the remaining béchamel and sprinkle with the remaining ¼ cup of cheese.

6. Bake for 45 minutes to 1 hour, until the top is golden brown. Remove from the oven and let it stand for at least 15 minutes before serving.

PER SERVING: Calories: 743; Total Fat: 47g; Saturated Fat: 22g; Protein: 33g; Total Carbs: 48g; Fiber: 5g; Sodium: 489mg

Salata me Kritharaki, Domates, Elies, kai Feta

PASTA SALAD WITH ORZO, TOMATO, OLIVES, AND FETA

NUT-FREE **VEGETARIAN**	**SERVES 6**	**PREP TIME:** 15 MINUTES

This riff on a traditional Greek salad adds orzo to the mix. It's the perfect dish for a summer barbecue, and, because it's served cold or room temperature, it's wonderful for leftovers.

For the dressing

¼ to ⅓ cup extra-virgin olive oil, as desired

¼ cup red wine vinegar

For the salad

½ pound orzo, cooked according to the package directions, still warm

1 pound cherry tomatoes, halved

3 medium Persian cucumbers, sliced

1 red or orange bell pepper, julienned

½ red onion, sliced

½ cup Kalamata olives, pitted and chopped

1 tablespoon dried Greek oregano

1 teaspoon sea salt

1 teaspoon freshly ground black pepper

1 cup feta cheese, cubed (optional)

¼ cup capers (optional)

To make the dressing

In a small bowl, whisk the olive oil into the vinegar until emulsified. Set aside.

To make the salad

1. In a large bowl, combine the cooked orzo, tomatoes, cucumbers, bell pepper, red onion, olives, oregano, salt, and pepper. Give it all a good stir to combine everything.

2. Add the dressing and toss to coat.

3. Garnish with the feta cheese and capers (if using).

Serving tip: This dish is perfect on its own but is also a great accompaniment to grilled chicken breast, shrimp, or salmon.

PER SERVING: Calories: 300; Total Fat: 14g; Saturated Fat: 2g; Protein: 7g; Total Carbs: 40g; Fiber: 4g; Sodium: 418mg

Manestra

ORZO PASTA WITH TOMATO

GLUTEN-FREE NUT-FREE VEGAN	SERVES 4 TO 6	PREP TIME: 10 MINUTES	COOK TIME: 15 MINUTES

This simple, comforting dish has reached cult status throughout Greece and the diaspora. One of Christina's favorite memories of it was when she lived in Athens and used to make her way down to the city's central market after a night out with friends. The meat and produce stalls were all closed, but a tantalizing aroma sailed on the cool night breeze. Within the market was a food stand that served stick-to-your-bones dishes, such as *manestra,* into the early hours of the morning. This is her version of it.

2 tablespoons extra-virgin olive oil

1 yellow onion, chopped

1 ½ teaspoons kosher salt, divided

2 garlic cloves, minced

1 (14.5-ounce) can diced tomatoes

½ pound orzo

1 tablespoon dried Greek oregano

3 cups water, plus more as needed

1. In a large pot over medium-high heat, heat the olive oil.

2. Add the onion and 1 teaspoon of salt. Cook for 3 to 5 minutes, until translucent.

3. Add the garlic. Cook for 30 seconds to 1 minute, until fragrant.

4. Stir in the tomatoes, orzo, oregano, the remaining ½ teaspoon of salt, and 3 cups of water. Bring the mixture to a simmer and cook for 9 minutes, stirring frequently. If the orzo becomes too thick, add more water to thin it out.

5. Cover and refrigerate any leftovers for up to 3 days.

Cooking tip: This dish is perfect on its own, but can also accommodate easy additions like chicken breasts, thighs, or legs. You can also garnish it with *kefalotiri,* Parmesan, or Romano cheese.

PER SERVING: Calories: 305; Total Fat: 8g; Saturated Fat: 1g; Protein: 8g; Total Carbs: 50g; Fiber: 4g; Sodium: 1,169mg

Spanakorizo

SPINACH RICE

GLUTEN-FREE NUT-FREE VEGAN	SERVES 6	PREP TIME: 15 MINUTES	COOK TIME: 35 TO 45 MINUTES

When she wasn't rolling spanakopita triangles in the church community center, a young Christina was at her stove making this dish for her family. It's hearty and healthy and simple enough to use as a base recipe and riff on the ingredients, like doubling the spinach or omitting the tomatoes.

2 tablespoons extra-virgin olive oil

1 onion, minced

2 teaspoons kosher salt, divided

2 garlic cloves, minced

3 celery stalks, minced

2 carrots, minced

2 medium tomatoes, chopped, or 8 to 10 ounces cherry tomatoes, halved

10 ounces frozen spinach, thawed and drained, or 1 pound fresh spinach, wilted and drained

1 cup rice

2 cups water

½ cup chopped fresh dill

2 teaspoons freshly ground black pepper

1. In a large lidded pan over medium heat, heat the olive oil.

2. Add the onion and 1 teaspoon of salt. Sweat the onion for 3 to 5 minutes, until translucent.

3. Add the garlic. Cook for about 30 seconds, until fragrant.

4. Add the celery and carrots. Cook for 5 minutes more.

5. Stir in the tomatoes and cook for 2 to 3 minutes, until they start to release some of their juice.

6. Add the spinach, rice, water, and dill. Mix thoroughly to combine and cover the pot. Bring to a boil and immediately reduce the heat to low. Simmer for 20 to 30 minutes.

7. Once the rice is cooked, let the dish sit for 10 minutes. Fluff with a fork and serve. Cover and refrigerate any leftovers for up to 3 days.

PER SERVING: Calories: 221; Total Fat: 6g; Saturated Fat: 1g; Protein: 8g; Total Carbs: 36g; Fiber: 4g; Sodium: 1,123mg

Pilaffi me Fides
RICE PILAF WITH VERMICELLI

SERVES 4 TO 6	**PREP TIME:** 15 MINUTES	**COOK TIME:** 30 MINUTES

This is an extremely simple dish but one that was a staple in Christina's house while growing up. She still asks her mom to make it for her when she visits. This pairs well with anything from roasted chicken to souvlaki.

3 tablespoons extra-virgin olive oil

1 cup chopped scallion, white and green parts

1 teaspoon kosher salt

1 cup basmati rice, rinsed

½ cup vermicelli noodles, broken

2½ cups chicken broth or vegetable broth

1 teaspoon freshly ground black pepper

½ cup toasted pine nuts or almonds (optional)

1. In a medium saucepan over medium-high heat, heat the olive oil.

2. Add the scallion and salt. Sauté for 3 to 5 minutes, until the scallion becomes soft.

3. Add the rice and vermicelli. Sauté for 5 minutes more.

4. Pour in the broth and bring the mixture to a boil, stirring occasionally. Reduce the heat to low and simmer for 20 minutes. Remove from the heat and let it stand, covered, for 5 minutes.

5. Stir in the pepper and pine nuts (if using).

Ingredient tip: All rice is not created equal. Basmati rice is a variety of long-grain rice that is easy to cook and clumps less than short-grain or medium-grain rice and therefore is one of the best choices to use in a dish like this.

PER SERVING: Calories: 335; Total Fat: 12g; Saturated Fat: 2g; Protein: 8g; Total Carbs: 49g; Fiber: 1g; Sodium: 1,065mg

CHAPTER SIX

Vegetable Mains

Vegetables are the core of the Greek diet. Cooking with fresh vegetables helps us live stronger and keeps our *yiayias* aging beautifully and our *papous* climbing mountains. Even fasting times are proven good times with these beloved dishes to enjoy; nobody feels like they are even giving anything up, and we really aren't. The true richness of vegetables isn't brought out with sugar, like a lot of chefs seem to think—it's salt and olive oil.

Fasolakia me Patates
GREEN BEANS WITH POTATOES 91

Chortofagos Moussaka
VEGETABLE MOUSSAKA 92

Yemista me Kinoa Pligouri
STUFFED TOMATOES WITH QUINOA 95

Kolokithokeftedes
BAKED ZUCCHINI PATTIES 96

Tourlou
VEGETABLE MEDLEY 98

Melitzana Papoutsakia
EGGPLANT SLIPPERS 100

Spanakopita
SPINACH PIE 103

Psiti Melitzana kai Kolokythia me Revithia, Xinomizithra, kai Vasilikos
ROASTED EGGPLANT AND ZUCCHINI WITH CRUNCHY SPICED CHICKPEAS, XINOMIZITHRA, AND BASIL 106

Dolmathes me Frankostafyla kai Koukounari
GRAPE LEAVES STUFFED WITH CURRANTS AND PINE NUTS 108

Aginares me Patates sto Fourno
ROASTED ARTICHOKES AND POTATOES 111

Melizantes kai Kolokithakia Tiganites
CRISPY GREEK FRIED EGGPLANT AND ZUCCHINI 112

Lemoni Krimidi Pita
LEMONY ONION PIE 115

I Efkoli Elliniki
THE EASY GREEK 117

Lahanodolmades
CABBAGE ROLLS GREEK STYLE 118

Horiatiki Frittata
VILLAGE FRITTATA 120

Fasolakia me Patates

GREEN BEANS WITH POTATOES

GLUTEN-FREE NUT-FREE VEGAN	SERVES 4	PREP TIME: 10 MINUTES	COOK TIME: 10 TO 15 MINUTES

Traditional *fasolakia* is a hearty green bean stew with tomato sauce and potatoes. This is Christina's fresh update on the nostalgic favorite that replaces stewed limp beans with ones that are crisp and bright green, along with other bright and clean flavors from the tomatoes and fresh lemon juice.

1 pound baby potatoes

1 pound green beans, ends trimmed, or haricots verts

Juice of 2 lemons

1 shallot, minced

1 garlic clove, minced

½ cup extra-virgin olive oil

10 ounces cherry tomatoes, halved

¼ cup chopped fresh dill

1. In a medium pot over high heat, boil the potatoes for 10 to 15 minutes, until they are easily pierced with a fork. Drain.

2. In another medium pot over high heat, blanch the green beans in boiling water for 1 minute. Drain.

3. In a medium bowl, combine the lemon juice, shallot, and garlic.

4. Whisk in the olive oil until emulsified.

5. In a large bowl, add the green beans, potatoes, and tomatoes. Add the dressing and dill and toss to coat.

6. Serve with crusty bread for soaking up the extra dressing, if desired. Refrigerated leftovers will keep for up to 3 days.

Cooking tip: To make a lower-carb version of this dish, omit the potatoes and add more tomatoes and beans.

Substitution tip: Cherry tomatoes are the right size for this dish and are flavorful year-round. Fresh, in-season tomatoes chopped to the size of a halved cherry tomato also work for this dish.

PER SERVING: Calories: 341; Total Fat: 26g; Saturated Fat: 4g; Protein: 3g; Total Carbs: 28g; Fiber: 8g; Sodium: 28mg

Chortofagos Moussaka

VEGETABLE MOUSSAKA

GLUTEN-FREE NUT-FREE VEGETARIAN	SERVES 12	PREP TIME: 45 MINUTES	COOK TIME: 1 HOUR, 15 MINUTES

Moussaka is a decadent baked dish of eggplant, ground beef, and béchamel that is common throughout Greece. This is Christina's lighter, vegetable-focused riff on a classic Greek dish. Instead of ground beef or lamb, the recipe weaves a rich sauce of mushrooms and chickpeas with tangy tomatoes. For the top that is traditionally a béchamel, a cauliflower purée steps in, not only increasing the dish's nutritional value but also making it gluten-free.

For the base

3 eggplant, cut into ¼-inch rounds

1 tablespoon kosher salt

¼ cup extra-virgin olive oil

For the top

1 cauliflower head, cut into florets, or 1 pound cauliflower florets

1 teaspoon kosher salt

1 teaspoon freshly ground black pepper

¼ cup Greek yogurt

¼ cup shredded or grated *kefalotiri* or Parmesan cheese

1 egg

¼ cup extra-virgin olive oil

For the filling

1 tablespoon extra-virgin olive oil, plus more for assembling the moussaka

1 onion, chopped

2 teaspoons kosher salt

4 garlic cloves, chopped

12 ounces cremini mushrooms, stemmed and roughly chopped

1 teaspoon freshly ground black pepper

½ teaspoon ground cinnamon

¼ teaspoon ground nutmeg

2 tablespoons tomato paste

1 (28-ounce) can diced tomatoes

1 (15.5-ounce) can chickpeas

To make the base

1. Spread the eggplant on 2 baking sheets and dust with the salt. Let them stand for 30 minutes. This draws out the bitter moisture in the eggplant. After 30 minutes, blot the eggplant with paper towels to remove any moisture.

2. Preheat the oven to 400°F.

3. Grease the baking sheets and brush the eggplant slices with olive oil. Bake for 15 minutes, or until golden brown. Flip and bake for 15 minutes more.

4. Remove from the oven and let them cool.

To make the top

1. While the eggplant bakes, steam the cauliflower for about 10 minutes, until it yields to the tip of a knife (see Cooking tip). Drain, reserving 1 cup of the steaming liquid, and transfer the cauliflower to a food processor.

2. Add the salt, pepper, yogurt, cheese, and egg. Pulse to combine.

3. With the food processor on low speed, drizzle in the olive oil. If the mixture is lumpy, add some of the reserved steaming water, a few tablespoons at a time, until you get a smooth purée. Set aside.

To make the filling

1. Reduce the oven temperature to 350°F.

2. In a large, deep skillet over medium-high heat, heat the olive oil.

3. Add the onion and salt. Sauté for 3 to 5 minutes, until the onion is translucent.

4. Add the garlic. Cook for 30 seconds to 1 minute, until fragrant.

5. Add the mushrooms and cook for 7 to 10 minutes, until they soften.

6. Stir in the pepper, cinnamon, allspice, and tomato paste. Cook for 2 minutes.

7. Stir in the tomatoes and chickpeas. Cover the pot, reduce the heat to low, and simmer for 15 minutes.

(CONTINUED)

Vegetable Moussaka, continued

To assemble the moussaka

1. Grease a 9-by-13-inch baking pan with olive oil.

2. Lay the base, using all the eggplant slices.

3. Layer in the filling, spreading it evenly.

4. Top with the cauliflower purée.

5. Bake for 30 to 45 minutes, until the top is golden brown. Cover and refrigerate any leftovers for up to 3 days.

Time-saving tip: This is a great dish to practice multitasking. While the eggplant bakes, simultaneously cook the filling and create the cauliflower purée. Just keep track of where you are in the process so you don't overcook your components.

Cooking tip: Use any pot that can be fitted with a steamer basket. Add at least 3 inches of water to the pot. Place the cauliflower in the steamer basket and put the basket in the pot. Cover the pot and bring to a boil over medium-high heat. Once it boils, reduce the heat to low. Check often to make sure there's still water in the pot. When the florets can be easily pierced with a knife, turn off the heat.

Alternatively, put the cauliflower florets in a microwave-safe bowl. Add 3 tablespoons water. Cover tightly with plastic wrap and microwave on high power for 3 minutes. Carefully remove the lid (watch out for the steam!). If the florets are not easily pierced with a knife, re-cover and continue to microwave in 1-minute increments, checking after each.

PER SERVING: Calories: 227; Total Fat: 12g; Saturated Fat: 2g; Protein: 9g; Total Carbs: 25g; Fiber: 8g; Sodium: 1,342mg

Yemista me Kinoa Pligouri

STUFFED TOMATOES WITH QUINOA

NUT-FREE VEGAN	SERVES 8	PREP TIME: 20 MINUTES	COOK TIME: 45 MINUTES

Pligouri is a traditional Greek salad of tomatoes, onions, cucumbers, and bulgur wheat—similar to tabbouleh. This is a riff on that salad stuffed into a tomato and substituting nutrient-rich quinoa for the bulgur, and zucchini for the cucumbers.

1 onion, chopped

1 teaspoon sea salt

1 teaspoon freshly ground black pepper

2 garlic cloves, minced

¾ cup quinoa, rinsed

8 large tomatoes, cored, pulp scooped out and reserved

8 ounces cherry tomatoes, halved

1 zucchini, quartered and chopped

1 cup water

¼ cup minced fresh parsley, or 2 tablespoons dried parsley

¼ cup minced fresh mint, or 2 tablespoons dried mint

1. Heat a saucepan or lidded skillet over medium-high heat.

2. Add the onion, salt, and pepper. Cook for 3 to 5 minutes until the onion is translucent.

3. Add garlic and quinoa. Cook for 2 minutes more.

4. Mix in the tomato pulp, cherry tomatoes, and zucchini. Cook for 3 minutes.

5. Preheat the oven to 350°F.

6. Add the water to the pan. Cover the pan, reduce the heat to low, and simmer for about 15 minutes, until the liquid evaporates. Let stand for 5 minutes.

7. Fluff the quinoa mixture with a fork and stir in the parsley and mint.

8. Fill the tomato shells with the quinoa mixture, place them in a large baking dish, and bake for 20 minutes.

PER SERVING: Calories: 115; Total Fat: 2g; Saturated Fat: 0g; Protein: 5g; Total Carbs: 22g; Fiber: 5g; Sodium: 250mg

Kolokithokeftedes

BAKED ZUCCHINI PATTIES

NUT-FREE VEGETARIAN	SERVES 4	PREP TIME: 40 MINUTES	COOK TIME: 30 MINUTES

Zucchini grow in abundance during the summer in Greece, and this dish is a perfect way to use them. Normally these patties are fried and served as an appetizer or main course. This recipe, for a healthier version of the favorite, calls for baking instead of frying.

3 zucchini (about 1½ pounds), grated

1 teaspoon kosher salt

½ cup chopped scallion, white and green parts

1 garlic clove, grated

1 cup bread crumbs

1 cup feta cheese

¼ cup shredded *kefalotiri*, Parmesan, or Romano cheese

2 eggs, beaten

2 tablespoons finely chopped fresh dill

1. Place the zucchini in a fine-mesh strainer, sprinkle with the salt, mix thoroughly, and let it drain in the sink for 30 minutes. Squeeze out as much liquid as possible.

2. Preheat the oven to 375°F.

3. Line a baking sheet with parchment paper.

4. In a medium bowl, combine the zucchini, scallion, garlic, bread crumbs, feta and *kefalotiri* cheeses, eggs, and dill. Form the zucchini mixture into 1-inch balls. Lightly smash the balls into patties and place on the prepared baking sheet.

5. Bake for 30 minutes, turning once halfway through cooking. Cover and refrigerate leftovers for up to 3 days.

Serving tip: These are perfect served with *Den Ine Y Dika Sou Yiayia's Tzatziki* / Not Your *Yiayia's* Tzatziki (page 23) or over pasta with a basic tomato sauce.

Substitution tip: Substitute almond flour for the bread crumbs to make this recipe gluten-free.

PER SERVING: Calories: 297; Total Fat: 14g; Saturated Fat: 8g; Protein: 16g; Total Carbs: 28g; Fiber: 3g; Sodium: 1,333mg

Tourlou
VEGETABLE MEDLEY

GLUTEN-FREE NUT-FREE VEGAN	SERVES 8	PREP TIME: 35 MINUTES	COOK TIME: 40 MINUTES

The French have ratatouille, the Greeks, *tourlou* ... but, alas, the French get credit for both. In Greek, *tourlou* literally means "all mixed up," and *trelee* means a mixed-up person—please don't confuse the two!

Greek babies cut their teeth on this vegan classic. Theo's girls used to race into their *yiayia's* home to see if she was making it for their visit. There's something about *tourlou's* amalgamation of flavors you don't forget once you've tasted it. We have enjoyed this dish as a main during fasting seasons but also on pasta with feta or kasseri oozing through the medley of noodles and veggies. It even makes a distinctive pizza sauce—with Greek cheese of any kind, or without.

1 large globe eggplant, chopped into 1-inch chunks

1 tablespoon sea salt, plus 1 teaspoon, divided

1 medium onion, chopped

¾ cup extra-virgin olive oil, plus 2 tablespoons, divided

2 medium zucchini, sliced into ¼-inch rounds

2 yellow squash, such as crookneck or patty pan, sliced into ¼-inch rounds

1 large red bell pepper, seeded and cut into 1-inch pieces

1 teaspoon freshly ground black pepper

1 large (28-ounce) can whole tomatoes, broken into chunks with a knife while still in the can

3 garlic cloves, minced

1 teaspoon ground nutmeg

1. Rinse the eggplant in a colander. Sprinkle with 1 tablespoon of salt and let it sit in the colander in the sink for 15 to 20 minutes. This process leaches out any bitterness from the eggplant. Rinse and pat dry with paper towels.

2. Preheat the oven to 350°F.

3. In a medium bowl, toss the eggplant chunks with ¼ cup of olive oil and the remaining 1 teaspoon of salt.

4. In a large, heavy-bottomed skillet over medium-high heat, add 2 tablespoons of olive oil, the eggplant, and the onion. Cook for 12 to 15 minutes, letting the eggplant brown before stirring occasionally and scraping up any browned bits (*fond*) from the bottom of the skillet.

5. Add the zucchini, yellow squash, and bell pepper.

6. Pour the remaining ½ cup of olive oil evenly over the vegetables and mix together so all the vegetables are coated.

7. Pour the tomatoes over the oiled vegetables. Stir to combine.

8. Arrange the vegetables in a 9-by-13-inch baking dish. Sprinkle with the nutmeg.

9. Bake for 22 to 25 minutes.

10. Cover and refrigerate any leftovers for up to 3 days—just like lasagna, it gets better and better.

Substitution tip: Use any type of pepper for this dish. *Pasilla* peppers will make it spicier. Carrots, whole mushrooms, and potatoes are also good, and any kind of canned tomatoes will work. If you do add potatoes, parboil them first so they cook completely with the other vegetables.

Cooking tip: Use a Dutch oven to cook this dish on the stove top, over medium-high heat for the same amount of time as the baking time, stirring frequently to make sure nothing sticks to the bottom of the pot. The vegetables are likely to fall apart from stirring, however.

Serving tip: If you want more of a vegetable stew consistency, add an additional can of tomatoes. Serve over rice or noodles for a heartier main dish.

PER SERVING: Calories: 275; Total Fat: 25g; Saturated Fat: 4g; Protein: 3g; Total Carbs: 14g; Fiber: 5g; Sodium: 953mg

Melitzana Papoutsakia

EGGPLANT SLIPPERS

NUT-FREE VEGETARIAN	SERVES 4	PREP TIME: 45 MINUTES	COOK TIME: 40 MINUTES

Eggplant is a popular vegetable in Greece, in case you haven't noticed from all the recipes featuring it in this book. We have converted many eggplant haters to eggplant lovers, primarily by not telling them they are eating eggplant until they compliment us on the dish—*then* we tell them! This is a favorite go-to from Theo's garden. It's so easy and makes a perfect appetizer or main dish. There are many versions of *papoutsakia* on Greek restaurant menus. Basically, it translates into something that is stuffed. We always recommend trying *papoutsakias* if you enjoy comfort food, as cheese is usually a main ingredient.

2 medium globe eggplant, halved lengthwise

2 teaspoons sea salt, divided

2 eggs, beaten

¾ cup shredded kasseri cheese

3 garlic cloves, minced

½ teaspoon freshly ground black pepper

1 (12-ounce) can tomato paste

4 tablespoons extra-virgin olive oil, divided

½ teaspoon ground nutmeg

½ cup herbed bread crumbs

1 pound fresh spinach

2 tablespoons freshly squeezed lemon juice

1 tablespoon coarsely chopped fresh parsley

¼ teaspoon dried Greek oregano

1. Rub each eggplant half with ½ teaspoon of salt. Let sit for 15 to 20 minutes. This leaches out any bitterness from the eggplant. After about 20 minutes, rinse off the salt.

2. Preheat the oven to 350°F.

3. Line a baking sheet with parchment paper and set aside.

4. Scoop out the eggplant flesh with a spoon, leaving about ½ inch on the skins, and put the scooped eggplant flesh into a vegetable steamer. In a 6-quart pot over medium-high heat, heat 2 cups water. Place the steamer in the pot and steam the eggplant, uncovered, for 10 minutes until soft.

5. Transfer the eggplant to a large bowl and add the eggs, cheese, garlic, 1 teaspoon of salt, and the pepper, mashing the ingredients together.

6. In a small bowl, blend the tomato paste, remaining ½ teaspoon of salt, and 2 tablespoons of olive oil.

7. Place the eggplant halves cut-side up on the prepared sheet, and stuff each half with equal amounts of the mashed eggplant mixture.

8. Spoon the tomato-paste-and-olive-oil blend equally over each stuffed eggplant half.

9. Sprinkle each with nutmeg and bread crumbs.

10. Bake for 25 to 30 minutes until golden brown.

11. Ten minutes before serving, steam the spinach (you can steam it quickly by placing a colander in a sink, adding the spinach, and pouring 4 cups boiling water over it) and drain. Drizzle with the lemon juice and remaining 2 tablespoons of olive oil and sprinkle with the parsley and oregano.

12. Place an equal amount of spinach on each of 4 serving plates next to 1 stuffed eggplant half.

Serving tip: You can serve the finished stuffed eggplant as a side dish without the spinach, but the combination of flavors that the spinach and its dressing create with the eggplant is a premium symbiosis.

PER SERVING: Calories: 352; Total Fat: 19g; Saturated Fat: 4g; Protein: 14g; Total Carbs: 40g; Fiber: 16g; Sodium: 723mg

Spanakopita

SPINACH PIE

NUT-FREE VEGETARIAN	SERVES 12	PREP TIME: 30 TO 45 MINUTES	COOK TIME: 45 MINUTES TO 1 HOUR

You will rarely encounter a Greek holiday or celebration without *spanakopita*. In Greece, these pies of flaky phyllo filled with spinach, onion, herbs, and cheese are in plentiful supply, making it the logical choice for breakfast, lunch, or dinner. For Christina, the perfect spanakopita involves beautiful wilted spinach, woven with a variety of cheeses. In Greece, cooks typically use a nice salty *kefalotiri*, but you can also use Parmesan, Romano, pecorino, or a mix. Along with feta cheese, this recipe also calls for cream cheese, which is not used in Greece, but Christina loves how it binds the whole pie together with a satisfying flavor and texture. Fresh herbs make the entire mix pop, so splurge on those.

For the filling

2 pounds fresh spinach, or 2 (12-ounce) bags

3 bunches scallions, white and green parts, chopped

2 tablespoons extra-virgin olive oil

4 ounces feta cheese

2 cups grated *kefalotiri*, Parmesan, or Romano cheese, plus more as needed

8 ounces cream cheese

⅓ cup chopped fresh dill

⅓ cup chopped fresh mint

⅓ cup chopped fresh flat-leaf parsley

2 teaspoons freshly ground black pepper

2 eggs, beaten

2 tablespoons Cream of Wheat or farina, plus more as needed

For the pie

1 pound (2 rolls) phyllo, at room temperature

8 to 12 tablespoons (1 to 1½ sticks) butter, divided

1 egg yolk, beaten with 1 tablespoon water

(CONTINUED)

Spinach Pie, continued

To make the filling

1. In a large pan over medium-high heat, wilt the spinach for about 4 minutes. Transfer it to a colander or, better, a salad spinner to drain any excess water.

2. Return the pan to medium-high heat and add the scallions and olive oil. Sauté for about 4 minutes.

3. Stir in the spinach to combine. Transfer the mixture to a large bowl.

4. Add the feta, *kefalotiri*, cream cheese, dill, mint, parsley, pepper, eggs, and Cream of Wheat. Mix well (Christina uses her hands). The mixture should hold together at this point. If it's watery, add more Cream of Wheat and/or cheese. Set the filling aside.

To assemble the pie

1. Preheat the oven to 400°F.

2. Unroll the phyllo so it is in one rectangular pile.

3. In a small pan over low heat, melt 8 tablespoons (1 stick) of butter.

4. Dip a pastry brush in the melted butter and brush a 9-by-13-inch baking pan.

5. Pick up 1 phyllo sheet and lay it in the baking pan. Brush the phyllo with butter. Repeat layering and buttering each of 11 more phyllo sheets, until you have a layer of 12 sheets.

6. Top the phyllo with the filling, distributing it evenly.

7. Make your top crust by adding 1 phyllo sheet, buttering it, and repeating the process until you have 15 buttered sheets on top. If any phyllo overhangs your pan, trim the excess and neatly tuck in the edges. Score the pie into 12 square pieces with a very sharp nonserrated knife, making sure to cut all the way through (because it's really hard to remove if you don't).

8. Brush the beaten egg yolk over the top. Bake for 45 minutes to 1 hour, until the top is brown.

9. Cover and refrigerate any leftovers for up to 3 days.

Time-saving tip: Make it ahead. Spanakopita is the perfect dish to have on hand for last-minute company or a future event. Assemble the pie up until the egg wash. Wrap it tightly in plastic wrap and freeze for up to 1 month. When ready to cook, you can take it directly from the freezer, put the egg wash on top, and bake it in a 400°F oven for about 1 hour, or until the top is golden brown.

PER SERVING: Calories: 434; Total Fat: 30g; Saturated Fat: 17g; Protein: 16g; Total Carbs: 28g; Fiber: 4g; Sodium: 680mg

Psiti Melitzana kai Kolokythia me Revithia, Xinomizithra, kai Vasilikos

ROASTED EGGPLANT AND ZUCCHINI WITH CRUNCHY SPICED CHICKPEAS, XINOMIZITHRA, AND BASIL

NUT-FREE VEGETARIAN	SERVES 6	PREP TIME: 15 MINUTES	COOK TIME: 1 HOUR

Roasting eggplant and zucchini together makes for a delicious, hearty vegetarian main dish. Spiced crispy chickpeas complete the dish by adding a zing of flavor and contrast with crunch. You may even want to double the recipe for the chickpeas because they are an addictive snack on their own.

1 (15.5-ounce) can chickpeas, drained and dried with paper towels, absorbing as much moisture as possible

4 tablespoons extra-virgin olive oil, divided

3 teaspoons kosher salt, divided

1 teaspoon ground cumin

1 pound eggplant, cut into 1-inch chunks

1 pound zucchini, halved and cut into 1-inch chunks

1 teaspoon freshly ground black pepper

¼ cup good-quality balsamic vinegar

1 cup fresh basil, cut into chiffonade (see page 14)

1 cup *xinomizithra,* a rich sheep's-milk, ricotta cheese, or crème fraîche

1. Preheat the oven to 400°F.

2. Line a baking sheet with parchment paper.

3. In a medium bowl, toss the chickpeas with 2 tablespoons of olive oil. Spread the chickpeas on the prepared sheet and bake for 30 minutes until crispy/crunchy.

4. Transfer to a clean medium bowl and, while hot, toss with 1 teaspoon of salt and the cumin. Set aside.

5. When the chickpeas are done, in a large bowl, toss the eggplant and zucchini with 1 teaspoon of salt, the pepper, and the remaining 1 tablespoon olive oil. Spread the vegetables onto a rimmed sheet pan and bake for 30 minutes until tender.

6. Remove from the oven and turn the vegetables into a large bowl.

7. To the vegetables, add the vinegar, the remaining 1 teaspoon of salt, and the basil. Toss to combine. Transfer to a serving platter and top with the crispy chickpeas and dollops of *xinomizithra*.

8. Cover and refrigerate any leftovers for up to 3 days.

Time-saving tip: Crunchy chickpeas are a snack sold all over Greece and are just starting to show up in US grocery stores. They're addictive. If you are short on time, pick up a bag at your local supermarket.

PER SERVING: Calories: 252; Total Fat: 13g; Saturated Fat: 3g; Protein: 8g; Total Carbs: 28g; Fiber: 7g; Sodium: 1,429mg

Dolmathes me Frankostafyla kai Koukounari

GRAPE LEAVES STUFFED WITH CURRANTS AND PINE NUTS

GLUTEN-FREE VEGAN	MAKES 36 TO 48 ROLLS	PREP TIME: 30 MINUTES	COOK TIME: 1 HOUR, 30 MINUTES

One of Christina's earliest memories is of her *yiayia* telling her to go out to the backyard and pick grape leaves off the fence. This was the first time she watched her make the traditional dish of grape leaves stuffed with a variety of fillings, such as rice, or a combination of meat and rice, and so on. This recipe lightens things up and uses a mixture of rice, currants, and pine nuts for the stuffing.

1 (1-pound) jar grape leaves, drained, rinsed, stems trimmed

½ cup extra-virgin olive oil

2 cups sliced scallion, white and green parts

1 teaspoon kosher salt

1 cup rice

¼ cup finely chopped fresh dill

¼ cup finely chopped fresh mint

½ cup currants

½ cup pine nuts, toasted

4 cups water, divided

¼ cup freshly squeezed lemon juice

1. Select 5 of the larger grape leaves and use them to line a lidded 7- to 8-quart stockpot or Dutch oven. This helps keep the finished rolls from sticking to the bottom of the pot.

2. In a large skillet over medium-high heat, heat the olive oil.

3. Add the scallion and salt. Sauté for 5 minutes.

4. Add the rice, dill, mint, currants, pine nuts, and 2 cups of water. Cover the skillet and simmer for 15 minutes. Remove from the heat and set aside to cool.

(CONTINUED)

5. Assemble the rolls: Spread out 1 grape leaf, shiny-side down. Place 1 teaspoon of the rice mixture near the bottom center of the leaf. Fold the bottom up over the filling. Fold in the sides and continue to roll up. Place the roll into the lined pot. Repeat with the remaining leaves and filling, placing them in the lined pot in an even layer and stacking layers as you go.

6. In a small bowl, mix the remaining 2 cups of water with the lemon juice. Pour over the rolls in the pot. If you have any grape leaves left, cover the top layer with them. Lay a plate on top of the stacked rolls, cover the pot, and place it over medium-high heat. When the water boils, reduce the heat to low and simmer for 1 hour, adding more water if necessary.

7. To serve, discard the excess grape leaves and place the rolls on a serving platter.

PER SERVING (2 ROLLS) : Calories: 125; Total Fat: 9g; Saturated Fat: 1g; Protein: 2g; Total Carbs: 12g; Fiber: 1g; Sodium: 361mg

Aginares me Patates sto Fourno

ROASTED ARTICHOKES AND POTATOES

NUT-FREE **VEGETARIAN**	**SERVES 4**	**PREP TIME:** 10 MINUTES	**COOK TIME:** 1 HOUR

One of Christina's favorite Greek kitchens is in Gramvousa, on the way to Balos Beach on the northwestern coast of Crete. The alfresco restaurant uses a wood-fired oven to expertly roast local meats and vegetables. Their version of this dish arrives at your table with sizzling roasted potatoes and tender lemony artichokes topped with local *staka* cheese—a gooey, decadent Cretan cheese made from the milk solids of butter. It's hard to find anything close to *staka* outside of that part of Crete, so crème fraîche, *xinomizithra*, or a rich sheep's-milk ricotta are adequate substitutions. You can also keep it vegan by omitting the cheese.

1 pound baby Dutch potatoes, halved

12 tablespoons extra-virgin olive oil, divided

2 teaspoons kosher salt, divided

2 teaspoons freshly ground black pepper, divided

1 pound frozen artichoke hearts, thawed and halved

Juice of 1 lemon

1 cup crème fraîche, *xinomizithra*, or sheep's-milk ricotta

1. Preheat the oven to 350°F.

2. In a medium bowl, toss together the potatoes, 6 tablespoons of olive oil, 1 teaspoon of salt, and 1 teaspoon of pepper. Transfer to a large baking dish and roast for 1 hour.

3. Once the potatoes have been roasting for 30 minutes, in the same bowl, toss together the artichokes and the remaining 6 tablespoons of olive oil, salt, and pepper. Add them to the potatoes and continue to roast for 30 minutes more.

4. Remove from oven, sprinkle with the lemon juice, top with the crème fraîche, and serve.

Ingredient tip: You can also make this dish using fresh artichokes. Clean and halve the hearts, add them to the baking dish with the potatoes, and roast them for the full hour.

PER SERVING: Calories: 580; Total Fat: 47g; Saturated Fat: 9g; Protein: 13g; Total Carbs: 34g; Fiber: 9g; Sodium: 1,352mg

Melizantes kai Kolokithakia Tiganites

CRISPY GREEK FRIED EGGPLANT AND ZUCCHINI

NUT-FREE VEGETARIAN	SERVES 4	PREP TIME: 1 HOUR	COOK TIME: 30 MINUTES

Mom said eat your vegetables—and we promise nobody will turn these away. Fried treats are best served in small batches for groups of 4 to 6, not when entertaining large groups. You don't need a deep fryer for this recipe, just a heavy-bottomed skillet—cast iron is perfect—and some fresh extra-virgin olive oil. If your oil is not fresh, it could smoke at the frying point, between 350°F and 375°F, which will ruin this dish. If you have a fryer handy, it is typically preset to 365°F—perfect for fresh extra-virgin olive oil. Unless you are able to jet off to Greece for a few hours to sit at a seaside *taverna*, these are a fun alternative to make for a small group . . . imagining the boats gliding by as you munch away mindlessly.

1 medium eggplant, cut evenly into ¼-inch slices

2 medium zucchini, cut evenly into ¼-inch slices

1 tablespoon sea salt, plus 2 teaspoons, divided

¾ cup all-purpose flour, sifted

¾ cup fine bread crumbs

½ teaspoon freshly ground black pepper

½ teaspoon dried dill

2 eggs, beaten in a shallow dish

¼ cup milk

1 cup extra-virgin olive oil

1 lemon, quartered

¼ cup chopped fresh Greek basil

1. Place eggplant and zucchini slices in a colander and toss with 1 tablespoon of salt. Let stand for 45 minutes in the sink to leach out excess water and bitterness. Rinse off the salt. Drain on paper towels until dry. Make sure the vegetables are completely dry before proceeding.

2. In a shallow dish, with a fork, mix the flour, bread crumbs, remaining 2 teaspoons of salt, the pepper, and the dill.

3. Beat the eggs together with the milk. Then, using a fork, dip each vegetable slice into the mixture, coating both sides, then lift it out, allowing any excess egg to drain back into the dish.

4. Dip each egg-coated vegetable into the flour/bread crumb mixture, coating both sides. Place the coated vegetables on a plate. Set aside, covered with paper towels.

5. In a large, heavy-bottomed or cast-iron skillet over medium-high heat, heat the olive oil; it should be about ¼ inch deep. The oil is hot enough when a tiny amount of flour is dropped into the pan and it sizzles.

6. Carefully add the coated eggplant to the hot oil in batches, without the pieces touching each other. Fry for 2 to 3 minutes per side, until golden brown. Drain on paper towels, making sure the towels do not become soaked with oil.

7. Repeat with the zucchini slices.

8. Serve hot to retain crispness, with quartered lemons and a sprinkling of fresh basil.

Cooking tip: Fry all the pieces of one vegetable variety first, then the other, for even cooking; this is why it's important to slice the vegetables evenly. When deep-frying food, make sure you have only enough oil in a deep skillet to come up to about half the height of whatever you are frying when the oil is bubbling—do not cover the food with oil. You will need to reduce the heat under the skillet the more you fry, so the oil doesn't smoke. Frying with extra-virgin olive oil is tricky, but so worth it! If you do burn a batch, we promise you'll have the touch and won't do it again. Every cooktop is different. Just pay attention and find a partner in the kitchen to assist in turning the fried vegetables and removing them to drain so you don't get distracted from the frying.

Serving tip: Served with *Den Ine Y Dika Sou Yiayia's Tzatziki* / Not Your *Yiayia's* Tzatziki (page 23) or Avocado *Skordalia* / Avocado Garlic Spread (page 34).

PER SERVING: Calories: 299; Total Fat: 16g; Saturated Fat: 3g; Protein: 9g; Total Carbs: 33g; Fiber: 6g; Sodium: 562mg

Lemoni Krimidi Pita

LEMONY ONION PIE

NUT-FREE VEGETARIAN	SERVES 8	PREP TIME: 30 MINUTES, PLUS 40 MINUTES TO 1 HOUR TO COOL	COOK TIME: 1 HOUR

The first time Theo visited her *Thea* Katina in Bitola, Macedonia, she had a pita pie called *zelnik*. It was filled with fermented cabbage and herbs—and was a little too intense for her to eat more than a very small portion. An abundance of sweet onions delivered from a neighbor encouraged her to experiment, coming up with her own, quicker version using different ingredients to create this protein-rich meal in a pan.

1 large onion, diced

1 cup diced baby leeks, white and light green parts

4 tablespoons extra-virgin olive oil, divided

½ pound (1 roll) phyllo, at room temperature

4 eggs, beaten

1 cup shredded *kefalotiri*, Parmesan, or Asiago cheese

2 tablespoons lemon zest

½ teaspoon sea salt

½ teaspoon freshly ground black pepper

½ teaspoon dried Greek oregano

½ teaspoon granulated garlic

1. In a large skillet over medium-high heat, combine the onion, leeks, and 3 tablespoons of olive oil. Cook for 8 to 10 minutes, until the onion browns. Remove from the heat and let cool.

2. Preheat the oven to 375°F.

3. Brush the bottom of a 9-by-13-inch baking dish with olive oil. Place 1 sheet of phyllo in the dish, brush it with some of the remaining 1 tablespoon of olive oil, and repeat layering and brushing with 10 more phyllo leaves.

4. In a large bowl, mix the beaten eggs with the onion and leek mixture, cheese, lemon zest, salt, pepper, oregano, and garlic. Pour over the phyllo.

(CONTINUED)

5. Top with the remaining phyllo sheets, layering and brushing with olive oil 1 sheet at a time. When finished, fold over any overlapping phyllo dough onto the top of the pie.

6. With a very sharp nonserrated knife, cut the pie into 8 equal pieces before baking for 45 minutes, until golden brown. Let cool for 40 minutes to 1 hour, allowing the flavors to blend, before serving.

7. Cover and refrigerate any leftovers for up to 3 days. I like to heat the leftovers in a conventional oven or toaster oven instead of a microwave so they don't get soggy.

Serving tip: This also serves well at room temperature. *Den Ine Y Dika Sou Yiayia's Tzatziki* / Not Your *Yiayia's* Tzatziki (page 23) is a perfect accompaniment.

Cooking tip: You can make this in a round springform pan, alternating the layers, not exactly over each other, but askew, creating an interesting overlap design.

Substitution tip: Add shiitake, cremini, or portobello mushrooms, cooking them with the onion and leeks. Swap kasseri or feta cheese for the *kefalotiri,* but Theo thinks the *kefalotiri* flavor profile works best for this recipe.

PER SERVING: Calories: 243; Total Fat: 15g; Saturated Fat: 5g; Protein: 9g; Total Carbs: 19g; Fiber: 1g; Sodium: 460mg

I Efkoli Elliniki

THE EASY GREEK

GLUTEN-FREE VEGETARIAN	SERVES 4	PREP TIME: 20 MINUTES	COOK TIME: 30 MINUTES

Theo's favorite vegetarian flavor combination is a quick, high-protein flavor feast during fasting seasons or when she's on the go and doesn't have a lot of time to prepare dinner. The main ingredients in this dish create good texture and lively character on the taste buds.

4 medium artichokes

6 eggs, beaten

¼ cup feta cheese, crumbled

7 tablespoons extra-virgin olive oil, divided

½ teaspoon sea salt

1 cup organic canned fava beans, drained and rinsed

Juice of 1 lemon

12 Kalamata olives

1 tablespoon plus 1 teaspoon chopped fresh Greek basil

1. In a large pot over high heat, set a steamer basket and add 2 cups water. Place the artichokes in the basket, cover the pot, and steam the artichokes for about 25 minutes, until you can pierce through to the middle with the tip of a sharp knife. Remove from the heat and let cool. Cut away the outer leaves, being careful toward the core to keep the artichoke heart intact.

2. In medium bowl, mix the eggs and feta.

3. In a large skillet over medium heat, heat 3 tablespoons of olive oil.

4. Add the egg and feta mixture. Scramble lightly for about 2 minutes, making sure not to overcook them.

5. Place one artichoke heart in the center of each of 4 small plates. Sprinkle with the salt. Surround each artichoke heart with some scrambled eggs. Create an outer ring on the dish with the fava beans.

6. In a small bowl, whisk the remaining 4 tablespoons of olive oil and the lemon juice. Drizzle over the artichoke hearts and fava beans.

7. Arrange 3 olives on each plate and sprinkle the basil over the beans.

PER SERVING: Calories: 470; Total Fat: 35g; Saturated Fat: 7g; Protein: 19g; Total Carbs: 29g; Fiber: 11g; Sodium: 692mg

CABBAGE ROLLS GREEK STYLE

GLUTEN-FREE VEGETARIAN	SERVES 8	PREP TIME: 1 HOUR	COOK TIME: 30 MINUTES

Cabbage rolls are said to be of Romanian origin, but almost every northern and eastern European nation has its own version. And, since Theo has never been one to follow the rules, her own version is presented here. Recipes abound for traditional meat-and-rice-stuffed cabbage rolls with *avgolemono* sauce (see page 46). Her mom and sister make succulent, cigar-size cabbage rolls with a tomato sauce, common in northern Greece/Macedonia, where her family is from. One day, Theo was craving her mom's cabbage rolls and didn't have ground meat or rice in her food stash. So she used what was in the fridge (as she often does), creating her own Greek-style tradition.

4 large Yukon Gold or red potatoes, cut into 1-inch pieces

4 teaspoons sea salt, divided

1 pound fresh spinach

2 teaspoons freshly ground black pepper, divided

1 head green cabbage, any dirty or cracked outer leaves removed

¼ cup extra-virgin olive oil

1 (28-ounce) can organic fire-roasted tomatoes

1 head elephant garlic, cloves thinly sliced

1 teaspoon sugar

1 teaspoon dried Greek oregano

Ground nutmeg, for dusting

1. Bring a large pot of water to a boil over high heat. Add the potatoes and 1 teaspoon of salt. Boil for about 15 minutes, until cooked, being careful not to overcook them.

2. Place the spinach in a colander. With a slotted spoon, transfer the potatoes into the colander, letting the hot potatoes wilt the spinach. Stir together in the colander to continue to wilt the spinach. Season with 1 teaspoon of salt and 1 teaspoon of pepper. Transfer to a large bowl.

3. Return the pot with the water to high heat and bring to a boil.

4. Insert a sturdy meat fork or a fork with long tines into the core of the cabbage. Immerse the cabbage in the boiling water for 90 seconds until the outer leaves turn green and translucent. Remove from the water and place in a colander, gently peeling away the blanched leaves. Repeat the blanching/peeling process until you reach the core. You may have some yellowish leaves toward the center of the core; this is normal—use them! Lay the cabbage leaves in a large pan and cover with clean kitchen towels to absorb excess water. Turn off the heat, discard the cabbage water, and set a vegetable steamer in the pot with enough water to cover it.

5. To the bowl of potatoes and spinach, add the olive oil, 1 teaspoon of salt, the remaining 1 teaspoon of pepper, and the oregano.

6. In a small bowl, stir together the tomatoes, elephant garlic, and remaining 1 teaspoon of salt.

7. Into the center of each cabbage leaf, spoon some of the spinach mixture, leaving enough cabbage on the sides to fold the leaf over the stuffing. Starting with the narrow end, fold the leaf over the mixture,

then fold the wide end over, finishing with the sides. Place the roll seam-side down in the steamer. (Do not turn on the stove until the pot is filled with rolls.) Repeat with the remaining cabbage leaves and filling.

8. After each layer of cabbage rolls is in place, drizzle about ¼ of the tomato mixture over it and dust very lightly with nutmeg.

9. Spoon any remaining tomato sauce over the top.

10. Turn on the heat to medium-high, get the water boiling under the steamer, and steam the cabbage rolls for 10 minutes.

Substitution tip: Use blanched romaine lettuce leaves instead of cabbage.

Serving tip: This may sound odd, but try this for breakfast with 2 soft-fried eggs. The Greeks call soft-fried eggs *matia,* which means "eyes."

PER SERVING: Calories: 219; Total Fat: 7g; Saturated Fat: 1g; Protein: 6g; Total Carbs: 37g; Fiber: 8g; Sodium: 855mg

Horiatiki Frittata

VILLAGE FRITTATA

GLUTEN-FREE VEGETARIAN	SERVES 8	PREP TIME: 45 MINUTES	COOK TIME: 40 MINUTES

Okay, okay, so frittatas are basically Italian pan meals that have been around for centuries. Some sources say the word frittata means something messy—or even someone who is a bit zany and mixed up. We love to make frittatas for dinner, although you might see them on breakfast menus. The great thing about this one is that it's like a cooked-up Greek salad in one pan—no muss, no fuss, quick, and healthy. You see a lot of frittata recipes calling for cast-iron pans, but we say, why put yourself under that kind of stress? Using a nonstick pan is a no-brainer every time, turning out a perfect crustless egg pie onto your cutting board instead of the possibility of a stuck-on pan and an assemblage of crusty ingredients that don't make for a pretty plate. Go for the nonstick pan, pour yourself a glass of Santorini white wine, and forget about everything else—this recipe is that easy.

11 tablespoons extra-virgin olive oil, divided

½ cup chopped onion

12 eggs

½ cup whole-milk Greek yogurt

1 cup feta cheese, crumbled

1½ cups diced tomatoes

1 teaspoon dried Greek oregano

1 teaspoon sea salt

½ teaspoon freshly ground black pepper

½ cup grated kasseri cheese

2 avocados, halved, pitted, peeled, and sliced

½ cup chopped (½-inch chunks) cucumber

¼ cup finely chopped pitted Kalamata olives

1. Preheat the oven to 350°F.

2. In a 10-inch skillet over medium-high heat, heat 1 tablespoon of olive oil. Add the onion. Cook for 8 to 10 minutes until brown.

3. In a large bowl, beat together the eggs and yogurt until blended.

4. Stir the feta cheese into the eggs along with tomatoes, oregano, salt, and pepper.

5. Drizzle 2 tablespoons of olive oil over the onions in the skillet, making sure the entire pan is coated evenly with olive oil.

6. Pour the egg mixture into the skillet and cook for 2 minutes, just until the egg mixture looks like it's cooking around the edges only. Remove from the heat and place the pan into the oven. Bake for 15 minutes. The frittata should just be turning a light brown around the edges (not golden brown!). Don't worry it if it's not browning. The center should be jiggly.

7. Sprinkle the kasseri cheese on top of the frittata and return it to oven for 10 minutes more.

8. When it's done, slide the frittata out of the skillet onto a silicone baking sheet or cutting board. Slice into 8 equal pieces. Top with the avocado, cucumber, and olives. Drizzle 1 tablespoon of olive oil over each serving. You can also serve this at room temperature. Leftovers keep, covered, for 24 hours in the refrigerator.

Substitution tip: You can use sour cream instead of Greek yogurt, but we like the custardy quality of the finished frittata best when using the yogurt.

PER SERVING: Calories: 468; Total Fat: 43g; Saturated Fat: 11g; Protein: 15g; Total Carbs: 9g; Fiber: 4g; Sodium: 650mg

FETA CRAB CAKES, PAGE 146

CHAPTER SEVEN

Seafood Mains

Greece boasts 8,498 miles of coastline, and Greeks are, by nature, a nautical people. They've revered the sea and its offerings since ancient times, when they would paint frescos and pottery with images of octopus and fish. Greeks don't need to finesse their fish that much to make it shine. These recipes are, for the most part, simple in nature and let the fresh ingredients stand out.

Lavraki Skara
GRILLED WHOLE SEA BASS 125

Psarakia Spetsiota
PAN-COOKED FISH WITH TOMATOES 126

Psari ston Atmo me Domata, Maratho, kai Eiles
**FISH STEAMED IN PARCHMENT WITH
TOMATO, FENNEL, AND OLIVES** 128

Hifias Souvlaki
SWORDFISH SOUVLAKI 130

Gemisto Monacho Psari
STUFFED MONKFISH 131

Garides Santorini
SHRIMP SANTORINI 133

Elliniko Kokteil Garides
GREEK-STYLE SHRIMP COCKTAIL 136

Kalamari Tiganites
FRIED CALAMARI 137

Kalamari Gemeista
STUFFED SQUID 139

Htapodi me Syka kai Rodákina
OCTOPUS WITH FIGS AND PEACHES 141

Htapodi me Patates
OCTOPUS WITH POTATOES 143

Feta Keik Kavourion
FETA CRAB CAKES 146

Atmismena Mydia me Aspri Crassi kai Maratho
**STEAMED MUSSELS WITH
WHITE WINE AND FENNEL** 148

Rizi me Thalassina
SEAFOOD RICE 151

Meikta Thalassina me Krasi kai Kapari
**MIXED SEAFOOD WITH
WINE AND CAPERS** 153

Lavraki Skara

GRILLED WHOLE SEA BASS

GLUTEN-FREE NUT-FREE	SERVES 2	PREP TIME: 5 MINUTES	COOK TIME: 15 MINUTES

Although the name *lavraki* might not be familiar to you, the sea bass that thrives off the shores of Greece is more commonly known by its Italian moniker—branzino. This fish is prized for its delicate taste and texture, and one of the best ways to draw out its qualities is to grill it whole.

1 (1-pound) whole *lavraki*, gutted, scaled, and patted dry

¼ cup extra-virgin olive oil

Sea salt

Freshly ground black pepper

1 bunch fresh thyme

¼ cup chopped fresh parsley

2 teaspoons minced garlic

1 small lemon, cut into ¼-inch rounds

1. Preheat a grill to high heat.

2. Rub the olive oil all over the fish's surface and in its middle cavity.

3. Season liberally with salt and pepper.

4. Stuff the inner cavity with the thyme, parsley, garlic, and lemon slices.

5. Set the *lavraki* on the grill (see Cooking tip). Cook for 6 minutes per side.

6. Remove the head, backbone, and tail. Carve 2 fillets from each side for serving.

Cooking tip: If you don't have a grill, you can also broil your sea bass. Follow the recipe instructions up to step 4, but broil your fish for 4 minutes per side and then finish it off in a preheated 400°F oven for 3 minutes.

PER SERVING: Calories: 480; Total Fat: 34g; Saturated Fat: 5g; Protein: 43g; Total Carbs: 1g; Fiber: 0g; Sodium: 279mg

Psarakia Spetsiota

PAN-COOKED FISH WITH TOMATOES

NUT-FREE	SERVES 6 TO 8	PREP TIME: 20 MINUTES	COOK TIME: 45 MINUTES

This simple one-pan meal originates from the Greek island of Spetses, a historical naval and commercial fishing region of the Saronic Islands. During many Fridays of Great Lent, this dish reminds us that we can fast and still eat phenomenal flavors. This was not so popular when we were little. Being from south-central Ohio, we didn't get the best fish; but with fresh fish now widely available, the prep time on this dish is about 20 minutes—so there's no excuse for not making a gourmet Greek meal for you and your friends more often.

1½ cups extra-virgin olive oil

1½ cups tomato juice

2 (12-ounce) cans organic tomato paste

2 teaspoons sea salt

2 teaspoons cane sugar

1 teaspoon freshly ground black pepper

1 teaspoon dried Greek oregano

3 pounds fresh white fish fillets, such as cod or sustainably raised tilapia or sea bass

2 large sweet onions, thinly sliced

1 cup white wine, such as sauvignon blanc

1½ cups bread crumbs, toasted

4 garlic cloves, sliced into rounds

½ cup coarsely chopped fresh parsley

4 large, firm tomatoes, in season, thinly sliced

1. Preheat the oven to 325°F.

2. In a large bowl, stir together the olive oil, tomato juice, tomato paste, salt, sugar, pepper, and oregano. Brush a small amount of the mixture onto the bottom of 9-by-13-inch roasting pan.

3. Lay the fresh fish fillets side by side on top of the tomato mixture.

4. Cover with the onion slices, overlapping them.

5. Sprinkle the wine evenly over each piece of fish.

6. Pour half of the tomato and olive oil mixture over the fish.

7. In a small bowl, stir together the bread crumbs, garlic, and parsley. Spread over the fish.

8. Lay the tomato slices, overlapping them, over the fish. Pour the remaining tomato mixture over the top.

9. Bake for 40 to 45 minutes.

10. Leftovers should be used within 24 hours; make a quick, open-faced fish sandwich on toasted bread, adding 1 tablespoon olive oil to each piece of toast.

Substitution tip: If fresh tomatoes aren't in season, use 8 to 10 Roma tomatoes, which are typically available year-round, or 2 (28-ounce) cans of whole tomatoes.

Cooking tip: You can make delicious bread crumbs by toasting leftover bread of any kind—even the heels—and then crushing the toast with a rolling pin or in a food processor.

Serving tip: Mix leftovers together into bite-size pieces, adding 1 tablespoon mayonnaise per cup to make delicious cold fish sandwiches on toasted bread . . . a Greek-y version of tuna salad without the tuna!

PER SERVING: Calories: 908; Total Fat: 55g; Saturated Fat: 8g; Protein: 51g; Total Carbs: 57g; Fiber: 9g; Sodium: 1,334mg

Psari ston Atmo me Domata, Maratho, kai Eiles

FISH STEAMED IN PARCHMENT WITH TOMATO, FENNEL, AND OLIVES

GLUTEN-FREE NUT-FREE	SERVES 4	PREP TIME: 15 MINUTES, PLUS 10 MINUTES TO MARINATE	COOK TIME: 20 MINUTES

Steaming this delicate dish is perfect for bringing out the flavor of not only the fish but also all the other ingredients included in the parchment with it. The parchment packets are easy to assemble and cook at the same time, making this the perfect main course for a dinner party.

Juice of 2 lemons

4 tablespoons extra-virgin olive oil, divided

2 teaspoons sea salt

1 teaspoon freshly ground black pepper

4 (6- to 8-ounce) fish fillets, such as sea bass, cod, or halibut

½ pound tomatoes, chopped

½ cup chopped scallion, white and green parts

¼ cup chopped Kalamata olives

1 tablespoon capers, drained

¼ cup white wine vinegar

2 garlic cloves, minced

1 fennel bulb, quartered and thinly sliced

1. Preheat the oven to 375°F.

2. In a large bowl, whisk the lemon juice, 2 tablespoons of olive oil, salt, and pepper.

3. Add the fish and marinate in the refrigerator for 10 minutes.

4. In a medium bowl, combine the tomatoes, scallion, olives, capers, vinegar, remaining 2 tablespoons of olive oil, and garlic.

5. Fold 4 (12-by-16-inch) pieces of parchment paper in half and cut out a half heart shape, keeping as much of the parchment as possible. Unfold the hearts and place ¼ of the fennel close to the center crease to make a bed for the fish. Top with 1 fish fillet and ¼ of the tomato mixture.

6. Fold the parchment back over the fish and, starting at the bottom end, start folding the edges, overlapping to seal the packet. Bake for 20 minutes.

7. Refrigerate any leftovers in the parchment in an airtight container for up to 3 days.

Cooking tip: You can scramble an egg and brush the edges of the parchment with it before you start your overlapping folds. This helps create a seal so none of the steam escapes.

PER SERVING: Calories: 277; Total Fat: 16g; Saturated Fat: 2g; Protein: 27g; Total Carbs: 9g; Fiber: 3g; Sodium: 1,514mg

Hifias Souvlaki

SWORDFISH SOUVLAKI

GLUTEN-FREE NUT-FREE	SERVES 4	PREP TIME: 15 MINUTES, PLUS 10 MINUTES TO MARINATE	COOK TIME: 10 MINUTES

Swordfish are common in the waters of the southern Aegean and are fished mainly in the spring and summer. This firm, oily fish has the perfect texture for souvlaki—it stays on the skewer and holds up on the grill.

½ cup freshly squeezed lemon juice

½ cup extra-virgin olive oil

1 teaspoon kosher salt

1 teaspoon freshly ground black pepper

1 teaspoon dried Greek oregano

2 pounds swordfish steaks,
    cut into 1-inch cubes

8 ounces cherry tomatoes

1 red onion, quartered

1. In a medium bowl, whisk the lemon juice, olive oil, salt, pepper, and oregano.

2. Add the fish and marinate in the refrigerator for 10 to 15 minutes.

3. Heat a grill to medium-high heat.

4. Skewer the swordfish, tomatoes, and red onion, alternating 1 to 2 pieces of fish for each tomato and onion quarter. Grill the kebabs for 5 minutes per side.

5. Alternatively, broil the skewers carefully for 3 to 5 minutes per side, checking frequently.

6. Serve with a squeeze of lemon and Avocado *Skordalia* / Avocado Garlic Spread (page 34).

7. If you have leftovers, disassemble the souvlaki, put them in an airtight container, and refrigerate for up to 3 days. The great thing about swordfish is that it is sturdy and reheats beautifully.

Ingredient tip: If you notice your swordfish fillet has a dark red section, that is the bloodline. It has a strong flavor and you may, or may not, want to eat it. If not, ask your fishmonger to remove it.

PER SERVING: Calories: 493; Total Fat: 34g; Saturated Fat: 6g; Protein: 42g; Total Carbs: 6g; Fiber: 2g; Sodium: 774mg

Gemisto Monacho Psari

STUFFED MONKFISH

GLUTEN-FREE NUT-FREE	SERVES 4	PREP TIME: 20 MINUTES	COOK TIME: 8 MINUTES

We like to use monkfish for this recipe because of its lobsterlike flavor, but sometimes it's difficult to find fresh. Halibut, sea bass, sustainably farmed tilapia, cod—really, any good fresh white fish will work! The first time Theo made this recipe was when she was 23 and lived across from a seafood restaurant and market in Dayton, Ohio. She took it over to their French general manager. He tasted it, took a swig of Vouvray she had suggested as a pairing, polished off the plate, handed it back to her, winked, and told her it was "too rich." There's a Greek word for wise guys like that—but we won't share it here!

4 (6-ounce) fresh white fish fillets

6 tablespoons extra-virgin olive oil, divided

½ teaspoon sea salt

½ teaspoon freshly ground black pepper

¼ cup feta cheese

¼ cup minced green olives

¼ cup minced orange pulp

1 tablespoon orange zest

½ teaspoon dried dill

¼ cup chopped fresh Greek basil

1. In a medium bowl, combine the fish with 2 tablespoons of olive oil, salt, and pepper.

2. In another bowl, mix together the feta, olives, and orange pulp. Spoon the mixture onto the fish fillets and spread it to coat them. Roll the fillets, inserting 2 toothpicks through to the other side to hold them together.

3. In heavy-bottomed skillet over medium-high heat, heat the remaining olive oil for about 15 seconds.

(CONTINUED)

4. Add the rolled fillets and cook for 6 to 8 minutes, depending on their thickness, rolling onto each side as they cook, until white in the center.

5. Top each piece with the orange zest, dill, and basil, equally divided.

6. I love leftover fish when I'm lucky enough to get some, but it should be used within 24 hours. Mash leftovers together with a fork, adding 1 tablespoon olive oil for every serving, and place atop fresh greens—it sure beats canned tuna fish!

Cooking tip: You will be able to tell when the fish is cooked by making certain the center part is bright white and no translucency remains. The finished fish will be golden brown on the outside.

Substitution tip: Use lemon, blood orange, or your favorite citrus, matching the zest with whatever fruit pulp you choose.

PER SERVING: Calories: 365; Total Fat: 25g; Saturated Fat: 5g; Protein: 29g; Total Carbs: 7g; Fiber: 2g; Sodium: 541mg

Garides Santorini

SHRIMP SANTORINI

GLUTEN-FREE NUT-FREE	SERVES 4	PREP TIME: 20 MINUTES	COOK TIME: 30 MINUTES

Christina's first time enjoying this dish was at an open-air restaurant in Fira, the main city on the island of Santorini. Under a beautiful sunset she noshed on succulent shrimp accompanied by rich, tangy tomatoes topped with feta cheese. The Greeks have been teaming seafood with cheese for thousands of years, so the old adage of not combining the two need not apply here.

1 pound shrimp, peeled and deveined

5 tablespoons extra-virgin olive oil, divided

2 teaspoons kosher salt, plus more for seasoning the onion

2 teaspoons freshly ground black pepper, plus more for seasoning the shrimp

1 onion, chopped

4 garlic cloves, minced

2 pounds tomatoes, chopped or grated

½ teaspoon red pepper flakes

½ teaspoon dried Greek oregano

Handful Kalamata olives, pitted (optional)

6 ounces feta cheese

3 tablespoons chopped fresh parsley

1. Preheat the oven to 400°F.

2. In a large bowl, toss the shrimp with 1 tablespoon of olive oil and the salt, and season with black pepper.

3. In a medium oven-safe skillet over medium heat, heat the remaining 4 tablespoons of olive oil.

4. Add the onion and season with salt. Cook for 3 to 5 minutes, until translucent.

5. Add the garlic and black pepper. Cook for 3 to 5 minutes, stirring, until soft.

6. Add the tomatoes, red pepper flakes, and oregano. Sauté for 10 minutes. (If your skillet isn't oven-safe, you can turn the tomato mixture into a 9-by-13-inch baking dish.)

(CONTINUED)

7. Arrange the shrimp and olives (if using) over the tomato mixture in one layer.

8. Crumble the feta over the surface.

9. Bake for 10 to 12 minutes, until the shrimp are a medium-pinkish color and the cheese is a bit browned. Don't over-cook the shrimp.

10. Remove from the oven and garnish with parsley.

Ingredient tip: You have many options when it comes to tomatoes. You can grate full-size tomatoes into a bowl or use halved cherry tomatoes. If you don't have fresh tomatoes, use a 28-ounce can of good-quality tomatoes. Try to get fresh tomatoes at your local farmers' market when they are in season, or buy organic tomatoes at your supermarket.

Serving tip: Serve with crusty bread for dipping, or over rice or orzo as a main dish.

PER SERVING: Calories: 458; Total Fat: 29g; Saturated Fat: 10g; Protein: 35g; Total Carbs: 17g; Fiber: 4g; Sodium: 1,929mg

Elliniko Kokteil Garides

GREEK-STYLE SHRIMP COCKTAIL

GLUTEN-FREE	SERVES 4	PREP TIME: 15 MINUTES	COOK TIME: 5 MINUTES

Shrimp are plentiful on Greek restaurant menus. We often eat them boiled with the heads on, eating the shells and all! If you can't stomach that (and, indeed, you need super-fresh shrimp for the heads to taste good), it's really the dipping sauce that matters here. Theo created this Greek-style aioli one night because she didn't have traditional cocktail sauce for boiled shrimp. I don't think we'll ever go back to the boring red stuff again.

1 pound (20- to 30-count) wild shrimp, peeled and deveined

1 egg

1 tablespoon finely chopped fresh Greek oregano or dill

2 teaspoons minced Kalamata olives

1 garlic clove, minced

1 teaspoon mustard

½ cup walnut oil

¼ teaspoon sea salt

¼ teaspoon freshly ground black pepper

1. In a large pot over high heat, bring 8 cups of water to a boil.

2. Add the shrimp and boil for 2 to 3 minutes, until pink. Drain and cool.

3. In a food processor, combine the egg, oregano, olives, garlic, and mustard. Blend to combine.

4. With the processor running on low speed, very gradually add the walnut oil through the feed tube on your food processor.

5. When it has thickened to a mayonnaise-like texture, blend in the salt and pepper. Serve immediately with the shrimp, or use within 1 day.

Substitution tip: Substitute extra-virgin olive oil for the walnut oil here. You can also substitute farmed shrimp, but the flavor will not resonate like wild-caught shrimp. We also don't like using farm-raised shrimp because most of it is farmed in Thailand using unfair labor practices.

PER SERVING: Calories: 257; Total Fat: 13g; Saturated Fat: 2g; Protein: 31g; Total Carbs: 5g; Fiber: 2g; Sodium: 422mg

Kalamari Tiganites

FRIED CALAMARI

GLUTEN-FREE NUT-FREE	SERVES 4 TO 6	PREP TIME: 20 MINUTES	COOK TIME: 2 MINUTES

Market squid has been fished in the Pacific for almost 200 years. The Chinese originated the culinary use of squid, followed by the Mediterranean countries. They have a short life span and lay huge numbers of eggs, which has made them a historically sustainable commercial seafood.

You can easily escape to Greece with this easy recipe. And the first time Theo took her then-husband there, he wandered through a gorgeous little fishing village one morning by himself looking for coffee, saying, "Calamari, calamari . . ." What he really meant was *kalimera*, which means "good morning." He came back to the room and asked, "Why is everyone looking at me funny when I say good morning to them?"

This recipe is a staple on seaside menus all over the Mediterranean. Just don't confuse it with "good morning!"

2 eggs

1 cup organic cornmeal

1 teaspoon sea salt

½ teaspoon dried dill

1 pound calamari rings and tentacles

½ cup Kalamata olives, pitted

1 lemon, cut into wedges and seeded

2 cups extra-virgin olive oil

(CONTINUED)

Fried Calamari, continued

1. Beat the eggs in a flat shallow dish with a fork.

2. In another flat shallow dish, mix the cornmeal, salt, and dill with a fork.

3. Prepare the calamari, olives, and lemon slices for frying by lightly coating each piece with egg and dredging through the seasoned cornmeal.

4. In a large skillet over medium heat, heat the olive oil until it sizzles when a smattering of flour is tossed into it. Do not overheat! The oil should be about 350°F.

5. Add the calamari, lemon, and olives to the pan; it's okay if the items touch. Fry for about 2 minutes, until golden brown, adjusting the heat so the oil doesn't get too hot.

6. Remove the items with a slotted spoon and place on paper towel to drain any excess oil.

7. This dish is best eaten immediately. Leftovers will become soggy and lose flavor with refrigeration—but then again, we never have leftovers!

Serving tip: Tastes great using *Den Ine Y Dika Sou Yiayia's Tzatziki* / Not Your *Yiayia's* Tzatziki (page 23) or *skordalia* as a dip. Christina's Avocado *Skordalia* / Avocado Garlic Spread (page 34) is a wonderful accompaniment. Fresh lemon juice combined with minced garlic and Greek basil makes a nice drizzling option, too.

Substitution tip: Swap any kind of seafood for calamari in this recipe. You can also use flour instead of organic cornmeal, but it will be heavier and greasier when finished. Theo suggests organic cornmeal versus regular cornmeal because of the GMOs found in nonorganic varieties.

PER SERVING: Calories: 374; Total Fat: 19g; Saturated Fat: 3g; Protein: 23g; Total Carbs: 28g; Fiber: 3g; Sodium: 706mg

Kalamari Gemeista

STUFFED SQUID

| **GLUTEN-FREE** | **SERVES 4** | **PREP TIME:** 20 MINUTES | **COOK TIME:** 30 TO 45 MINUTES |

There is more than one way to cook a squid. And although fried cala-mari is synonymous with squid, the cephalopod's tubular shape just screams for stuffing. This is a basic recipe. You can omit the sauce altogether and, instead, grill the squid and bathe it in equal parts olive oil and lemon juice, or riff on the stuffing, using ground meat or sausage instead of the rice.

For the squid

1 tablespoon extra-virgin olive oil

1 onion, chopped

1 teaspoon sea salt

1 teaspoon freshly ground black pepper

3 garlic cloves, minced

1 pound small (3 to 4 inches) squid, cleaned

½ pound cherry tomatoes, halved

¼ cup basmati or long-grain rice, rinsed

¼ cup pine nuts, toasted

¼ cup fresh basil, cut into chiffonade (see page 14)

For the sauce

¼ cup extra-virgin olive oil

1 onion, chopped

1 teaspoon sea salt

1 teaspoon freshly ground black pepper

2 garlic cloves, chopped

¼ cup dry white wine

1 (28-ounce) can diced tomatoes

¼ cup fresh basil, cut into chiffonade (see page 14)

Juice of 1 lemon

Lemon slices, for serving

(CONTINUED)

Stuffed Squid, continued

To make the squid

1. In a large pot over medium-high heat, heat the olive oil.

2. Add the onion, salt, and pepper. Cook for 3 to 5 minutes until translucent.

3. Add the garlic. Cook for 1 minute until fragrant.

4. If the squid came with tentacles, chop them up and put them in the pot now.

5. Add the cherry tomatoes, rice, and pine nuts. Cook for about 3 minutes, until the tomatoes become soft.

6. Fold the fresh basil into the mixture.

7. Prick the squid bodies all over with a toothpick and snip off the very end of the cavity.

8. Stuff each squid with filling so it is ¼-to-½ full. The rice will expand when the squid cooks in the sauce, so make sure there's room.

To make the sauce and cook the squid

1. In the same pot in which you cooked the stuffing, heat the olive oil over medium-high heat.

2. Add the onion, salt, and pepper. Cook for 3 to 5 minutes, until translucent.

3. Add the garlic. Cook for about 1 minute.

4. Add the white wine to deglaze the pan, scraping up any browned bits (*fond*) from the bottom of the pan.

5. Stir in the tomatoes. Cook for 10 minutes.

6. Add the basil.

7. Add the stuffed squid in even layers to the pot. Cover the pot and simmer for 30 minutes. Check the squid by piercing it with a knife—if there is too much resistance, cook for 15 minutes more.

8. When the squid is cooked through, squeeze the lemon into the pot and serve with additional lemon slices. Cover and refrigerate any leftovers for up to 3 days.

Cooking tip: Small squid can be tricky to stuff. Use a demitasse spoon for best results.

PER SERVING: Calories: 429; Total Fat: 25g; Saturated Fat: 3g; Protein: 22g; Total Carbs: 28g; Fiber: 4g; Sodium: 1,000mg

Htapodi me Syka kai Rodákina

OCTOPUS WITH FIGS AND PEACHES

| GLUTEN-FREE NUT-FREE | SERVES 4 | PREP TIME: 15 MINUTES, PLUS 2 HOURS TO MARINATE | COOK TIME: 10 MINUTES |

Theo has been making balsamic fruit vinegars since 1998; you can find her Global Gardens brand at globalgardensonline.com or at her Los Olivos, California, farm stand. Be careful not to use any that contain high fructose corn syrup or sugar. If you do, the sugar will burn during the cooking process. Cooking with vinegar may be new to you, but Theo has been doing it for years with great success since she started experimenting with acidity in various dishes. It's all about cooking quickly, which is great for you, too—delicious dinner in minutes!

1 pound fresh or frozen octopus tentacles, cut into ¼-inch-thick rounds

¼ cup extra-virgin olive oil

1 teaspoon sea salt

1 teaspoon freshly ground black pepper

1 teaspoon granulated garlic

½ teaspoon dried Greek oregano

1 cup fig balsamic vinegar

6 fresh figs, halved

2 large peaches, quartered

¼ cup chopped fresh parsley

1. In a large bowl, thoroughly mix the octopus, olive oil, salt, pepper, garlic, and oregano to coat well. Marinate in the refrigerator for 2 hours. Bring to room temperature before cooking.

2. In an 8- to 10-inch heavy-bottomed deep skillet over medium-high heat, bring the fig balsamic vinegar to a boil. Reduce the heat to a rolling simmer. Stir with the flat side of a metal spatula so any thickened vinegar is mixed into the liquid instead of sticking to the pan. After about 4 minutes, when the vinegar is foamy on top, add the octopus and stir quickly, cooking for only 2 to 3 minutes, until the meat is firm and coated with caramelized vinegar. With a fork, transfer to a serving bowl.

(CONTINUED)

3. Add the figs and peaches to the vinegar remaining in the skillet. Cook for about 1 minute, stirring them into the caramelized vinegar just until coated and soft. Transfer to the serving bowl and gently stir to combine.

4. Top with the parsley.

5. This dish will keep, covered and refrigerated, for up to 2 days if you discard the fruit, as it ferments quickly, ruining any leftovers. Cold, leftover octopus from this recipe can be sliced into small chunks and arranged over greens, tomatoes, or any vegetables for added flavor.

Substitution tip: This recipe is delicious with shrimp, calamari, or mixed seafood.

Cooking tip: If you have a grill, use it for this recipe for grill marks and charred flavor. Theo prefers large octopus tentacles for texture; they work best with this marinade style. If you use frozen octopus, completely thaw it and squeeze out all excess water. Dry on paper towels for 10 minutes before marinating. If the vinegar starts to caramelize too rapidly, add 2 tablespoons water at a time and use a metal spatula to stir up the caramelization from the bottom of the pan, mixing it with the octopus.

PER SERVING: Calories: 304; Total Fat: 14g; Saturated Fat: 2g; Protein: 21g; Total Carbs: 23g; Fiber: 4g; Sodium: 474mg

Htapodi me Patates
OCTOPUS WITH POTATOES

GLUTEN-FREE NUT-FREE	SERVES 4	PREP TIME: 10 MINUTES	COOK TIME: 35 MINUTES

Don't let the prospect of cooking octopus intimidate you. It's easy to overcome the pitfall of rubbery octopus by simmering it before grilling—and you don't even need to use a wine cork. Just load your pot with aromatics, like the ones listed here, and add the octopus. Simmer until you can easily pierce the thickest part of the cephalopod, where the head meets the tentacles—cooking time increases with the weight of the octopus. When it gives, it's time to remove it from the pot.

2 pounds octopus, cleaned

1 pound baby potatoes

1 fennel bulb, quartered

1 bay leaf

10 peppercorns

Juice of 2 lemons

¼ cup extra-virgin olive oil

1 teaspoon kosher salt

1 teaspoon freshly ground black pepper

3 garlic cloves, minced

1 cup chopped scallions, white and green parts

¼ cup chopped fresh parsley

1. In an 8-quart pot over medium-high heat, combine the octopus, potatoes, fennel, bay leaf, and peppercorns. Cover with water. Cover the pot, bring to a boil, reduce the heat to low, and simmer until the thickest part of the octopus yields to the tip of a knife. Start checking after 15 minutes for an octopus that's around 1 pound and after 25 to 30 minutes for an octopus that's 2 pounds. Don't overcook the octopus or it will be rubbery.

2. Preheat a grill to high heat.

(CONTINUED)

3. Remove the octopus and cut it into 2- to 3-inch pieces and place them on the grill for 1 to 2 minutes per side.

4. In a medium bowl, whisk the lemon juice, olive oil, salt, pepper, and garlic.

5. Remove the potatoes from the pot and add to the dressing, along with the scallions and parsley, and toss to combine.

6. Add the grilled octopus to the bowl and toss with the rest of the ingredients. Turn out onto a platter and serve. Cover and refrigerate any leftovers for up to 3 days.

Ingredient tip: Although most octopus in Greece is pulled fresh from the sea and dried on lines before it's grilled, it's OK to buy frozen octopus. Any octopus that is frozen will most often come cleaned as well, so that's less work for you.

PER SERVING: Calories: 392; Total Fat: 15g; Saturated Fat: 2g; Protein: 43g; Total Carbs: 22g; Fiber: 6g; Sodium: 630mg

FETA CRAB CAKES

NUT-FREE	SERVES 4	PREP TIME: 30 MINUTES	COOK TIME: 15 MINUTES

Theo created the Caliterranean Café for one year while building her Los Olivos, California, farm stand. The café was a combination of her love for the California/Mediterranean lifestyle, a true "bucket list" venture where some of these recipes were refined. Without a doubt, her crab cakes were the most popular item, selling out when fresh Dungeness crab from Santa Barbara's Channel Islands was in season. You can use canned crab or even imitation crab if you're on a budget—but nothing beats the flavor of fresh!

1 pound crabmeat

½ cup minced scallion, green parts only

⅓ cup bread crumbs

¼ cup feta cheese, crumbled

2 eggs, beaten

2 garlic cloves, minced

1 small Anaheim or *pasilla* chile (if you want a little spice) or 1 small red bell pepper, seeded and cut into ⅛-inch pieces

1 medium firm tomato, cut into ¼-inch pieces, drained of excess liquid

2 tablespoons minced fresh fennel

2 tablespoons minced fresh parsley

½ teaspoon dried dill

½ teaspoon dried Greek oregano

½ teaspoon sea salt

½ teaspoon freshly ground black pepper

¼ teaspoon ground nutmeg

3 tablespoons extra-virgin olive oil

1. In a large bowl, combine the crabmeat, scallion, bread crumbs, feta, eggs, garlic, chile, tomato, fennel, parsley, dill, oregano, salt, pepper, and nutmeg. Mix thoroughly. Divide the mixture into 8 equal portions and form each into a 2½-inch patty about ½ inch thick, creating a definitive edge for easier flipping when cooking.

2. In a large skillet over medium-high heat, heat the olive oil. Place the crab cakes in the heated pan and brown for 7 to 8 minutes per side.

Cooking tip: This recipe is a lot of fun to make ahead of time; freeze the patties on a parchment paper–covered baking sheet and then store them in a zipper freezer bag. They come in handy on busy evenings or when you want to invite friends over but not do the prep work—it will be done and delicious! Cook them frozen, using the same method as above. They are actually easier to cook when frozen!

Serving tip: Serve as a sandwich on a sourdough bun, using 2 patties topped with mayonnaise, lettuce, sliced tomato, pickles, and onion. Alternatively, serve over steamed kale, spinach, or brown rice. An easy salad dressing can be made using equal parts olive oil and lemon juice, with 1 teaspoon minced garlic.

PER SERVING: Calories: 315; Total Fat: 16g; Saturated Fat: 4g; Protein: 15g; Total Carbs: 30g; Fiber: 3g; Sodium: 1,396mg

Atmismena Mydia me Aspri Crassi kai Maratho

STEAMED MUSSELS WITH WHITE WINE AND FENNEL

GLUTEN-FREE NUT-FREE	SERVES 4	PREP TIME: 20 MINUTES	COOK TIME: 30 MINUTES

Mussels thrive off the coast of mainland Greece and in the Greek islands. The Greeks steam them, stuff them, and serve them *saganaki*-style with tomatoes and feta. This simple, clean dish utilizes the aromatics of fennel, another revered Greek ingredient, to team with the earthiness of the bivalves and the acid of wine. Serve with a side of rice or grilled bread brushed with olive oil.

¼ cup extra-virgin olive oil

1 onion, chopped

1 teaspoon sea salt

4 garlic cloves, minced

1 teaspoon red pepper flakes (optional)

1 fennel bulb, chopped, leaves reserved

1 cup dry white wine

4 pounds mussels, scrubbed and debearded (see Ingredient tip)

Juice of 2 lemons

1. In an 8-quart pot over medium-high heat, heat the olive oil.

2. Add the onion and salt. Cook for 5 minutes, until translucent.

3. Add garlic and red pepper flakes. Cook for 1 minute.

4. Stir in the chopped fennel. Cook for 3 minutes.

5. Stir in the wine and simmer for about 7 minutes.

6. Carefully pour the mussels into the pot. Reduce the heat to medium, give everything a good stir, cover the pot, and cook for 5 to 7 minutes.

(CONTINUED)

7. Remove the opened mussels and divide them among 4 bowls. Re-cover the pot and cook any unopened mussels for 3 minutes more. Divide any additional opened mussels among the bowls. Discard any unopened mussels. Evenly distribute the broth into the bowls. Garnish with the fennel leaves.

8. If you have leftovers, remove the mussels from their shells, cover, and refrigerate for up to 3 days.

Ingredient tip: Don't be intimidated by handling and cooking mussels. They're surprisingly easy and very quick to cook. When you clean the mussels, discard any that have broken shells. If you find mussels that have already opened, give them a good tap. If they close after a minute or two, keep them and discard any that stay open. After cooking mussels, discard the ones that don't open.

PER SERVING: Calories: 578; Total Fat: 23g; Saturated Fat: 4g; Protein: 55g; Total Carbs: 26g; Fiber: 3g; Sodium: 1,790mg

Rizi me Thalassina
SEAFOOD RICE

GLUTEN-FREE NUT-FREE	SERVES 6	PREP TIME: 10 MINUTES	COOK TIME: 35 TO 40 MINUTES

This dish is almost like a Greek version of paella. You can customize it to whatever seafood is accessible to you. It's perfect with just shrimp or with a mixture of shrimp, squid, and/or mussels. You can even add fish fillets if that suits your taste. Normally you can cook those at the beginning, like you cook the squid, and set them aside to be added in at the end. If you use mussels, steam them at the end with the shrimp.

1 tablespoon extra-virgin olive oil, plus 1 teaspoon, divided

1½ pounds seafood (squid, cut into rounds, large shrimp, and mussels)

1 onion, chopped

1 teaspoon sea salt

4 garlic cloves, minced

1 cup chopped celery

2 medium tomatoes, chopped, or 8 ounces cherry tomatoes

½ cup dry white wine

2 cups arborio rice

¼ cup chopped fresh parsley

¼ cup chopped fresh dill

4¼ cups chicken, vegetable, or fish broth, divided

Lemon wedges, for serving

1. In a large skillet over medium-high heat, heat 1 tablespoon of olive oil.

2. Add the squid and cook for about 2 minutes. Remove the squid and set aside.

3. Add the remaining 1 teaspoon of olive oil to the skillet to heat.

4. Add the onion and salt. Cook for 5 minutes, until translucent.

5. Add the garlic and cook for 1 minute more.

6. Add the celery and tomatoes. Cook for 3 minutes.

7. Pour in the wine and cook for about 3 minutes, stirring frequently.

(CONTINUED)

8. Stir in the rice, parsley, dill, and 4 cups of broth. Cover the skillet and simmer for 15 minutes. After 15 minutes, most of the liquid should be absorbed, but there should still be a little left. If there isn't, add the remaining broth.

9. Top the rice mixture with the shrimp and mussels, cover the skillet, and simmer for 5 minutes more, until the shrimp are just cooked.

10. Return the squid to the skillet. Discard any unopened mussels. Serve with the lemon wedges on the side.

11. Cover and refrigerate any leftovers for up to 3 days.

Ingredient tip: You will rarely see seafood served in Greece without lemon wedges. That tradition goes for this dish as well. A squeeze or two of lemon will add a burst of acidity to an already flavorful dish.

PER SERVING: Calories: 246; Total Fat: 5g; Saturated Fat: 1g; Protein: 28g; Total Carbs: 18g; Fiber: 2g; Sodium: 875mg

Meikta Thalassina me Krasi kai Kapari

MIXED SEAFOOD WITH WINE AND CAPERS

GLUTEN-FREE NUT-FREE	SERVES 4	PREP TIME: 25 MINUTES	COOK TIME: 10 MINUTES

Super easy, super healthy, super delicious, and always on the list of everyone's favorite vacation dinners. (Yes, we usually rent homes with real kitchens on vacation so we can cook with local farm-fresh products, no matter the time of year; yes, we still have fun; yes, we eat better food than any restaurant can serve to us!)

1 (1-pound) bag frozen mixed seafood

½ cup white wine, such as sauvignon blanc or chardonnay

¼ cup extra-virgin olive oil

½ teaspoon sea salt

½ teaspoon freshly ground black pepper

½ cup capers, drained

¼ cup chopped fresh parsley

1. Thaw the frozen seafood by rinsing in a colander under cold running water for several minutes, turning so that it will thaw evenly. Let it sit for 5 minutes, then squeeze out the excess water completely.

2. In a small bowl, whisk the white wine, olive oil, salt, and pepper.

3. In a 10-inch skillet over medium-high heat, bring the white wine mixture to a simmer.

4. Add the seafood and stir in the capers. Cook for about 5 minutes, until cooked through.

5. Sprinkle with the parsley and serve.

6. Cover and refrigerate any leftovers for up to 2 days. I like to make a cold seafood salad by arranging them over salad greens with fresh lemon wedges, basil, and 1 tablespoon olive oil per serving.

Serving tip: Serve over steamed spinach, brown rice, or noodles, with lemon wedges.

Cooking tip: You can cook with any white wine. We prefer a wine that goes well with seafood, so frequently we use whatever wine we'll drink with the meal.

PER SERVING: Calories: 235; Total Fat: 14g; Saturated Fat: 3g; Protein: 17g; Total Carbs: 4g; Fiber: 1g; Sodium: 1,097mg

CHAPTER EIGHT

Meat Mains

There is a funny line in the movie *My Big Fat Greek Wedding* when the American fiancé tells his Greek girlfriend's aunt he's a vegetarian. "Good," she replies, "I'll make you lamb." Yes, we are omnivores—and traditional Greeks eat every inch of the animal, no waste—but we'll spare you recipes for goat's eyeballs and cow's intestine soup here. Theo has a great story about encountering the latter, high atop a Macedonian mountain after a night of reveling into the wee hours of the dawn; ask her!

Paidakia Skara
GRILLED RACK OF LAMB 157

Gemisto Podi Arniou
STUFFED LEG OF LAMB 158

Arni Psito
ROASTED LEG OF LAMB 161

Youvetsi
**BRAISED LAMB OR BEEF
WITH SPICED TOMATO SAUCE** 163

Stifado
BEEF STEW 165

Keftedes
MEATBALLS 167

Souvlaki
PORK SOUVLAKI 169

Hirino me Damaskina kai Syka
**BRAISED PORK SHOULDER
WITH PLUMS AND FIGS** 170

Hirino Kreas me Glyko
**PORK TENDERLOIN WITH
SWEET FRUIT GLAZE** 172

Cretan Kreatopita
MEAT PIE 174

Ellinika Biftekia
GREEK BURGERS 177

Horiatiki Stroma Piato
COUNTRY-STYLE LAYERED DISH 179

Gemisto Olokliro Kotopoulo
STUFFED WHOLE CHICKEN 182

Stithos Kotopoulo Gemisto me Spanaki kai Feta
**SPINACH AND FETA STUFFED
CHICKEN BREASTS** 185

Kotopoulo Kapama
**BRAISED CHICKEN WITH
TOMATO SAUCE AND SPICES** 186

Paidakia Skara
GRILLED RACK OF LAMB

| GLUTEN-FREE NUT-FREE | SERVES 2 | PREP TIME: 5 MINUTES | COOK TIME: 15 MINUTES |

A simple rack of lamb tastes luxurious, and really only requires the right amount of seasoning and cooking time to get it there. This simple recipe combines rosemary and garlic to complement the richness of the lamb. After carving the finished piece of meat into lamb chops, finish with a simple squeeze of lemon and serve with anything from *Pilaffi me Fides* / Rice Pilaf with Vermicelli (page 86) to *Gigandes Plaki* / Braised Giant Beans in Tomato Sauce (page 71) to *Aginares me Patates sto Fourno* / Roasted Artichokes and Potatoes (page 111).

1 (1-pound) rack of lamb

1 tablespoon extra-virgin olive oil

1 tablespoon kosher salt

1 tablespoon freshly ground pepper

1 tablespoon chopped fresh rosemary

2 garlic cloves, minced

1. Preheat the grill to medium-low (see Cooking tip).

2. Rub the rack of lamb with the olive oil, salt, pepper, rosemary, and garlic.

3. Sear the rack, meat-side down, for 5 minutes, moving it around frequently to sear the surface of the meat evenly all over.

4. Flip, move to indirect heat, and continue to grill, covered, for 8 to 10 minutes, until the internal temperature reaches 135°F to 140°F.

5. Remove the lamb from the heat and let rest for 10 minutes. Cut into chops and serve.

Cooking tip: Medium to low heat is best when dealing with this cut of meat. Alternatively, you can bake this in a 450°F oven for 20 to 30 minutes. Remove, cover with aluminum foil, and let sit for 10 minutes. Carve into individual or double-cut chops.

PER SERVING: Calories: 458; Total Fat: 27g; Saturated Fat: 8g; Protein: 47g; Total Carbs: 4g; Fiber: 2g; Sodium: 3,651mg

Gemisto Podi Arniou
STUFFED LEG OF LAMB

GLUTEN-FREE NUT-FREE	SERVES 8	PREP TIME: 30 MINUTES	COOK TIME: 50 MINUTES

Lamb is simply delicious. If you are a carnivore and don't like lamb, it's probably because you haven't had good young spring lamb, or you're eating mutton. Australian leg of lamb can be found in the big-box stores, reasonably priced, and usually very good quality. Better yet, if you have local lamb farmers, go there! There's nothing like eating food grown as close to home as possible. It owns a finish that conveys a certain *terroir* that is elemental and unique to your region. If you can, have your butcher debone your lamb leg to get a "leg up" on your recipe prep. If not, insert a long, narrow knife into the center of the meat, feeling the knife along the bone, slicing the meat along one entire length so you can "unwrap" the bone away from the meat.

1 whole (before deboning, about 5-pound) leg of young spring lamb, deboned and excess fat trimmed

2 large garlic cloves, thinly sliced

¼ cup extra-virgin olive oil

1 tablespoon sea salt

1 teaspoon dried Greek oregano

1 teaspoon freshly ground black pepper

¼ teaspoon ground cloves

1 (12-ounce) package frozen spinach, thawed and squeezed to remove excess water

1 cup jarred roasted red bell peppers, such as Mezzetta brand, drained and cut into ¼-inch chunks

1. Preheat the oven to 375°F.

2. Using the flat side of a meat cleaver or a rolling pin, pound the meat to make it all about 2 inches thick. With the tip of a sharp knife, make small incisions all over the leg, just long enough to stuff the garlic slices into.

3. Thoroughly rub the olive oil over the meat.

4. In a small bowl, combine the salt, oregano, pepper, and cloves. Rub the spices over the oiled meat.

(CONTINUED)

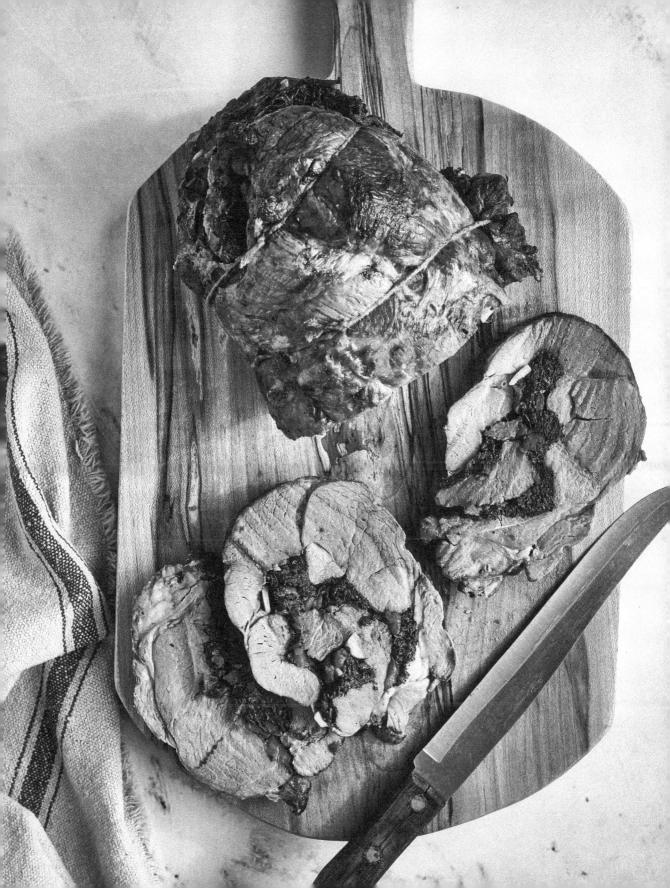

5. Spread the spinach onto the spiced meat with your hand.

6. Sprinkle the red bell pepper pieces over the spinach.

7. Starting at one end, roll up the meat, and tie the finished roll with kitchen twine 2 inches from both ends and in the middle of the roll. Place the roll on a rack set inside a large roasting pan. Bake for 10 minutes per pound, or until an instant-read thermometer reads 135°F (medium rare) to 150°F (medium). Do not overcook. The meat will continue to cook once removed from the oven. Let stand for 10 minutes before cutting into 1-inch slices.

Cooking tip: The most important part of this recipe is draining the spinach thoroughly and squeezing out all excess water.

PER SERVING: Calories: 545; Total Fat: 29g; Saturated Fat: 1g; Protein: 58g; Total Carbs: 7g; Fiber: 1g; Sodium: 737mg

Arni Psito

ROASTED LEG OF LAMB

GLUTEN-FREE NUT-FREE	SERVES 8 TO 10	PREP TIME: 20 MINUTES, PLUS 30 MINUTES RESTING TIME	COOK TIME: 2 HOURS

Roasted lamb is the traditional centerpiece of a Greek Easter feast, symbolizing Jesus Christ as the Lamb of God. Christina loves the tradition of roasting a whole lamb on the spit—so much so that at her wedding she hired Theo's nephew to cook two for her. For smaller celebrations, roasted leg of lamb offers a similar satisfaction with a fraction of the work. In this recipe, an herbed garlic paste spread over the lamb creates a beautiful dimension of flavor. This recipe starts out at high heat to brown the outside of the leg and finishes cooking at a low temperature to ensure even cooking throughout the leg. Don't throw all your hard work away at the end. Make sure to let the lamb rest for 30 minutes to allow the juices that have gravitated to the center of the leg to redistribute.

1 (6- to 8-pound) leg of lamb, Frenched, thigh bone removed

15 garlic cloves, divided

10 fresh rosemary sprigs, divided

½ cup extra-virgin olive oil, divided

2 tablespoons kosher salt, divided

2 tablespoons freshly ground black pepper, divided

½ cup fresh mint, cut into chiffonade (see page 14)

Juice and zest of 1 lemon

1. Make 5 slits in the leg of lamb and stuff each with 1 garlic clove.

2. Insert 3 rosemary sprigs where the meat meets the bone at the top of the leg and 3 more near the bone in the bottom back.

3. Slather ¼ cup of olive oil over the leg of lamb and sprinkle with 1 tablespoon of salt and 1 tablespoon of pepper.

(CONTINUED)

4. Using a mortar and pestle, or in a food processor, grind the mint, lemon juice, lemon zest, and remaining 10 garlic cloves, 4 rosemary sprigs (leaves only), 1 tablespoon of salt and 1 tablespoon of pepper, and the remaining olive oil until it becomes a paste. Rub it into the meat.

5. Place the lamb in a large roasting pan and roast for 30 minutes at 425°F.

6. Reduce the temperature to 325°F and roast the lamb for another hour to 1½ hours, or until the internal temperature reaches 135°F.

7. Remove from the oven, cover with aluminum foil, and let rest for at least 30 minutes to let the juices redistribute.

8. Cover and refrigerate any leftovers for up to 3 days.

Ingredient tip: Rosemary, garlic, and mint all marry well together, but so do other herbs. Experiment with your own combinations with additions of thyme, parsley, or basil.

PER SERVING: Calories: 580; Total Fat: 35g; Saturated Fat: 2g; Protein: 55g; Total Carbs: 6g; Fiber: 1g; Sodium: 1,747mg

Youvetsi

BRAISED LAMB OR BEEF WITH SPICED TOMATO SAUCE

GLUETEN-FREE NUT-FREE	SERVES 4 TO 6	PREP TIME: 30 MINUTES	COOK TIME: 3 HOURS

While this dish is common throughout Greece, it is thought that the name is derived from the Turkish word *güveç*, the earthenware pot in which the dish is cooked. Christina loves throwing dinner parties in Los Angeles, and during the cooler months, a rich *youvetsi* braise gets the crowd salivating. This specific recipe particularly lends itself to lamb shoulder or beef short ribs. The richness of the meat is cut with the acidity from the tomatoes and tomato paste, and the end result is extremely comforting with the addition of warming spices, such as cinnamon, nutmeg, and cloves. Serve with simple rice or orzo pasta.

1 tablespoon extra-virgin olive oil, plus more as needed

2 pounds boneless lamb shoulder or beef short ribs

3 teaspoons kosher salt, divided

3 teaspoons freshly ground black pepper, divided

1 onion, chopped

2 garlic cloves, minced

3 celery stalks, chopped

3 carrots, chopped

1 teaspoon ground cinnamon, or two cinnamon sticks

1 teaspoon ground nutmeg

1 cup red wine

1 (14.5-ounce) can diced tomatoes

1 (6-ounce) can tomato paste

2 to 3 cups chicken broth

1. Preheat the oven to 325°F.

2. In a 7- to 9-quart Dutch oven over medium-high heat, heat the olive oil.

3. Season the lamb or beef with 1½ teaspoons salt and 1½ teaspoons pepper. Working in batches if necessary, add the meat to the pot and cook for 5 to 7 minutes per side to brown. Transfer the meat to a plate. Drain any excess fat and return the pot to the heat.

4. Add the onion and remaining 1½ teaspoons of salt and pepper to the pot with a little more olive oil if needed. Cook for about 5 minutes, scraping any browned bits (*fond*) from the bottom of the pot, until soft.

(CONTINUED)

5. Add the garlic. Cook for 1 minute to soften.

6. Add the celery, carrots, cinnamon, and nutmeg. Cook for 5 minutes more.

7. Stir in the wine, tomatoes, and tomato paste. Cook for 5 to 7 minutes, until reduced by half.

8. Return the meat to the pot, add enough chicken broth to cover it, cover the pot, and place it in the oven. Braise for 2 hours.

9. Cover and refrigerate any leftovers for up to 3 days. The flavor is even better after it sits for a day.

Ingredient tip: Bone-in cuts of short rib or lamb shoulder also work well for this recipe. You will have to use more meat, about 4 pounds, to account for the weight of the bone.

PER SERVING: Calories: 492; Total Fat: 29g; Saturated Fat: 12g; Protein: 25g; Total Carbs: 23g; Fiber: 5g; Sodium: 1,987mg

Stifado
BEEF STEW

GLUTEN-FREE NUT-FREE	SERVES 4	PREP TIME: 30 MINUTES	COOK TIME: 3 HOURS

This has become a wintertime staple at Theo's house. The first time she made it, she dreaded the time it would take and wondered if it would be worth it. The recipe *does* take time—like some of the other meat recipes in this chapter—but they are not difficult and you don't want to rush it and miss a step. The resulting aroma from the pot of beef permeates the kitchen, guaranteeing everyone a happy tummy. She usually makes this on a holiday when her farm stand is closed and she can open a nice bottle of *Amethystos* to complement her time in the kitchen.

6 tablespoons extra-virgin olive oil, divided

½ cup pearl onions, peeled

1 celery stalk, chopped into ¼-inch pieces

3 large garlic cloves, sliced

2 pounds beef stew meat

2 teaspoons sea salt

1 teaspoon freshly ground black pepper

1 teaspoon dried Greek oregano

2 cups red wine

2 cups beef broth

1 (28-ounce) can whole tomatoes

½ teaspoon ground cinnamon

½ teaspoon ground nutmeg

1 pound fingerling potatoes

2 bay leaves

8 ounces cremini or shiitake mushrooms

2 red bell peppers, quartered

¼ cup fresh basil, cut into chiffonade (see page 14)

1. In a large Dutch oven over medium-high heat, add 2 tablespoons of olive oil, the onions, and celery. Cook for about 8 minutes, until the onions are translucent, letting some pieces stick to the bottom and stirring them up with a metal spatula back into the mixture. Remove from the heat and transfer to a large bowl, removing most of this mixture from the bottom of the pot. Make sure the bowl is big enough to add the meat.

2. Return the pot to the heat and add 2 tablespoons of olive oil and the garlic. Cook for about 3 minutes, using the same browning and stirring procedure as step 1. Keep the toasted garlic in the pot.

(CONTINUED)

3. Add the remaining 2 tablespoons of olive oil and the meat, salt, pepper, and oregano. Stir to coat with the oil and spices. Let the meat brown, by allowing it to stick slightly with the now-caramelized garlic for about 3 minutes per side of meat. Keep that metal spatula handy so you can get under the meat and browned garlic bits in the bottom of the pan.

4. Transfer the meat and garlic to the celery and onion mixture in the bowl. Some charred bits of garlic, celery, and onion or even some tiny bits of meat will be left in the bottom of the pot—that's a beautiful thing!

5. Return the pot to the heat. Pour the wine into the hot pan to deglaze it, stirring up any browned bits (*fond*) on the bottom. Let the wine boil and reduce for about 20 minutes.

6. Preheat the oven to 275°F.

7. Stir in the beef broth, tomatoes, cinnamon, and nutmeg. Cooking for 20 minutes, using your spatula to cut the tomatoes into chunks, while reducing the liquids in the pot into a rich broth. The "reduction" will be about 75 percent of the amount of liquid you started with; it won't be a heavy, thick broth, but it will be a rich, dark liquid with a heavenly smell.

8. Remove from the heat and return all the meat, garlic, celery, and onions to the pot.

9. Add the potatoes and bay leaves, and bury them along with the meat under the broth. Arrange the mushrooms and bell peppers on top.

10. Cover the pot, place it in the oven, and cook for 2 hours, checking after 20 minutes to make certain the broth in the pot is just simmering. If it is boiling, reduce the heat by 25 degrees.

11. Serve garnished with the basil. Cover and refrigerate any leftovers for up to 3 days.

Serving tip: Serve just out of the oven with fresh slabs of warm bread brushed (not soaked!) with olive oil to soak up the meat juices. Can also be served with Greek rice, *manestra*, or egg noodles. The next day, remove any fat that has gathered on top of the stew. Toasted sandwiches using the residual sauce/gravy from the bottom of the pot as a spread under the stew make memorable leftovers. Or for breakfast, served open-faced on a toasted English muffin, topped with one poached egg per muffin slice.

PER SERVING: Calories: 789; Total Fat: 35g; Saturated Fat: 7g; Protein: 58g; Total Carbs: 46g; Fiber: 8g; Sodium: 1,611mg

Keftedes

MEATBALLS

NUT-FREE	MAKES 12 TO 15 MEATBALLS	PREP TIME: 15 MINUTES	COOK TIME: 20 MINUTES

Delicious, herbaceous *keftedes* are a staple of Greek dinner parties and family dinners. What really makes these stand out is the addition of fresh mint. It lightens the mixture and brings in another element of flavor. They're easy to make as well. Serve them with *Den Ine Y Dika Sou Yiayia's Tzatziki* / Not Your *Yiayia's* Tzatziki (page 23) as part of an appetizer spread or indulge in a dish of them for a main course.

1 pound ground beef or ground lamb

1 small onion, grated

½ cup fresh mint, cut into chiffonade (see page 14)

½ cup bread crumbs

2 garlic cloves, grated

1 egg

1 tablespoons red wine vinegar

1 teaspoon ground Greek oregano

1 teaspoon kosher salt

1 teaspoon freshly ground pepper

1. Preheat the broiler.

2. Line a baking sheet with parchment paper or aluminum foil.

3. In a medium bowl, mix the ground beef, onion, mint, bread crumbs, garlic, egg, vinegar, oregano, salt, and pepper. Do not overmix or your meatballs can become tough. Using a fork to mix the ingredients helps with this.

4. Scoop out 1 tablespoon of meat mixture at a time, form into a ball, and place the meatballs on the prepared sheet.

5. Broil for 20 minutes, turning once halfway through cooking, until browned.

6. If you have any leftovers (not likely!), cover and refrigerate for up to 3 days.

Substitution tip: Use almond flour in place of the bread crumbs to make these meatballs gluten-free. You can also experiment with different meats. This recipe works well with everything from ground lamb to ground turkey or chicken.

PER SERVING (1 MEATBALL): Calories: 69; Total Fat: 4g; Saturated Fat: 1g; Protein: 5g; Total Carbs: 4g; Fiber: 1g; Sodium: 246mg

Souvlaki

PORK SOUVLAKI

GLUTEN-FREE NUT-FREE	SERVES 6	PREP TIME: 20 MINUTES	COOK TIME: 15 MINUTES

Greece's favorite street food is the perfect centerpiece for a backyard barbecue. Lemony, herbed pieces of pork are skewered with sweet red onions and bell peppers. Although this selection of vegetables holds up to cooking, if you want to be completely precise, you can skewer all the meat together and all the vegetables together and serve as one beautiful platter where each component is cooked to its optimal temperature. This helps you avoid burning your vegetables and undercooking your meat.

3 pounds pork tenderloin, halved lengthwise and cut into 1½-inch cubes

⅓ cup freshly squeezed lemon juice

⅓ cup extra-virgin olive oil

2 tablespoons sea salt

2 tablespoons freshly ground black pepper

1 tablespoon dried Greek oregano

2 red onions, quartered

3 bell peppers, any color, cut into 1-inch squares

Lemon slices, for garnishing

1. Preheat a grill to medium-high heat.

2. In a large bowl, combine the pork, lemon juice, olive oil, salt, pepper, and oregano. Let sit for 15 minutes.

3. Assemble the skewers: Alternate pork pieces with red onion and bell pepper. When adding the onion to the skewer, pull apart two layers from each quarter.

4. Grill the souvlaki for 7 minutes. Turn and cook for 7 to 8 minutes more, or until the pork is done (at least 145°F).

Cooking tip: The good news is that new food-safety guidelines state that it's safe to cook pork to 145°F. This yields a juicy souvlaki, much more so than cooking it to 160°F.

Serving tip: Serve over *Pilaffi me Fides* / Rice Pilaf with Vermicelli (page 86) or *Aginares me Patates sto Fourno* / Roasted Artichokes and Potatoes (page 111). Also consider topping with *Den Ine Y Dika Sou Yiayia's Tzatziki* / Not Your *Yiayia's* Tzatziki (page 23) or Avocado *Skordalia* / Avocado Garlic Spread (page 34).

PER SERVING: Calories: 381; Total Fat: 19g; Saturated Fat: 4g; Protein: 43g; Total Carbs: 10g; Fiber: 3g; Sodium: 2,476mg

Hirino me Damaskina kai Syka

BRAISED PORK SHOULDER WITH PLUMS AND FIGS

GLUTEN-FREE NUT-FREE	SERVES 6 TO 8	PREP TIME: 20 MINUTES	COOK TIME: 2 HOURS, 30 MINUTES

In Greece, as in California, plums and figs reach their peak in the summer. This pork braise is the result of that sensational seasonality. Half the recipe's tangy plums disintegrate and form the rich base of a sauce that cuts through the richness of a pork shoulder roast. That is teamed with even more plums and voluptuous black Mission figs in the final minutes of cooking to yield a decadent dish.

3 pounds pork shoulder, cut into 1½-inch cubes

3 tablespoons extra-virgin olive oil, divided

Kosher salt

Freshly ground black pepper

1 onion, chopped

1½ pounds plums, pitted and sliced, divided

1 cup white wine

½ cup balsamic vinegar

2 tablespoons honey

2 bay leaves

2½ cups chicken broth, plus more as needed

½ teaspoon ground nutmeg

½ pound black Mission figs

1. Preheat the oven to 325°F.

2. In a large bowl, toss the pork with 1 tablespoon of olive oil and season with salt and pepper.

3. In a 7- to 9-quart Dutch oven over medium-high heat, heat 1 tablespoon of olive oil.

4. Working in batches, add the pork and cook for 5 to 7 minutes per side to brown. Transfer the pork to a bowl and set aside. Drain the fat from the pot and return it to medium heat.

5. Add the remaining 1 tablespoon of olive oil to the pot along with the onions. Cook for 3 to 5 minutes, until translucent.

6. Add 1 pound of plums and cook for 1 or 2 minutes.

7. Stir in the wine, vinegar, and honey. Cook for about 5 minutes, until reduced by half.

8. Return the pork to the pot.

9. Add the bay leaves, the ground nutmeg, and enough chicken broth to cover the pork. Cover the pot and place it in the oven. Braise for 90 minutes.

10. Remove the pot from the oven and place it on the stove top. With a slotted spoon, remove the pork from the pot into a serving dish.

11. Add the remaining ½ pound of plums and the figs to the pot. Cook uncovered over medium heat for about 8 minutes to reduce the sauce just a bit.

12. Add the reduced sauce along with the plums and figs to the pork in the serving dish, toss together, and enjoy.

Serving tip: This braise can stand on its own, but it's also delicious paired with *Pilaffi me Fides* / Rice Pilaf with Vermicelli (page 86) or orzo pasta.

PER SERVING: Calories: 483; Total Fat: 17g; Saturated Fat: 4g; Protein: 45g; Total Carbs: 31g; Fiber: 3g; Sodium: 950mg

PORK TENDERLOIN WITH SWEET FRUIT GLAZE

GLUTEN-FREE NUT-FREE	SERVES 4	PREP TIME: 10 MINUTES	COOK TIME: 20 MINUTES

We're so lucky to have access to fresh, ranch-raised pork on the central coast of California. If you don't have local access to organic, non-antibiotic-raised meats, seek them out at your local market. They are widely available and may cost more, but the texture, flavor, and health benefits are worth it. Greeks pride themselves on *katheaftou* (real) food. Pork is the least common meat eaten by Greeks. It's a treat when served, always surrounded with lots of vegetable dishes, good Greek bread, and olive oil. Pork tenderloin is very lean, yet succulent, meat. Do not overcook it! Our trick is to cook it quickly at high heat to lock in the juices and flavor. The *glyko*, a traditional sweet-cooked fruit sauce from northern Greece, adds texture and flavor.

For the meat
1 (about 1¼-pound) pork tenderloin

2 tablespoons extra-virgin olive oil

2 teaspoons sea salt

1 teaspoon dried garlic

½ teaspoon dried Greek oregano

¼ teaspoon dried ground rosemary

2 tablespoons minced fresh basil

For the sauce
1½ cups chopped fresh fruit, such as tart cherries, strawberries, or blueberries

¼ cup honey

1 tablespoon water

To make the meat

1. Preheat the oven to 500°F.

2. Rub the tenderloin with the olive oil.

3. In a small bowl, combine the salt, garlic, oregano, and rosemary. Thoroughly rub the mixture into the meat. Place the seasoned tenderloin in a large glass or ceramic baking dish and cover tightly with aluminum foil. Roast for 20 minutes. The meat will continue to cook once it is removed from the oven.

4. Pierce the foil upon removal from the oven, allowing steam to escape so the meat does not overcook.

5. Cut the pork tenderloin into 1-inch slices and arrange evenly on 4 plates.

6. Top with the sauce and garnish with the basil.

To make the sauce

Five minutes before the meat comes out of the oven, in a small saucepan over medium-high heat, combine the fruit, honey, and water. Cook for 5 minutes (longer for harder fruits), stirring until warm and soft.

Substitution tip: Truly, most fruits will do! Use whatever is in season, from hard to soft fruits (except melons—cooked melon?!). Oranges can be wonderful in winter. Add an extra tablespoon of sugar when using them.

Cooking tip: If you're cooking for 12 to 16 servings and decide to make a whole pork loin (versus a small pork *tender*loin), multiply each ingredient here by the weight of the loin (5 to 6 pounds on average).

PER SERVING: Calories: 308; Total Fat: 10g; Saturated Fat: 2g; Protein: 31g; Total Carbs: 26g; Fiber: 2g; Sodium: 1,012mg

Cretan Kreatopita

MEAT PIE

NUT-FREE	SERVES 8	PREP TIME: 1 HOUR, 30 MINUTES	COOK TIME: 1 HOUR

You can make this meat pie ahead and not bake it, putting the entire pie in a rubber freezer container for up to two months without the finishing yolk and sesame seeds on the outside crust. It's truly worth the extra time (and bragging rights!) to make the pastry yourself. The flavor combinations are exquisite.

For the pastry

1 cup warm tap water (not steaming hot)

1 (¼-ounce) packet yeast

3 cups all-purpose flour, plus more as needed

¼ teaspoon sea salt

¼ teaspoon freshly, finely ground black pepper

¼ cup extra-virgin olive oil

For the filling

4 tablespoons extra-virgin olive oil, divided, plus more for preparing the baking dish

1 medium onion, cut into ¼-inch pieces

½ cup white wine

2 tablespoons chopped fresh mint

1½ teaspoons sea salt

½ teaspoon freshly ground black pepper

1½ pounds lean ground beef

¼ teaspoon ground nutmeg

2 hard-boiled eggs, finely diced

1 cup *mizithra* cheese, crumbled (yes, it's creamy!)

½ cup whole-grain bread crumbs

3 eggs, beaten

1 egg yolk

2 tablespoons sesame seeds

To make the pastry

1. In a small bowl, add the water and immediately sprinkle the yeast over it. Stir well to dissolve.

2. In a large bowl, add the flour and make a well in the center.

3. Add the salt, pepper, olive oil, and yeast mixture to the well. Using clean hands, blend the ingredients well, making sure the dough is not sticking to the sides of the bowl or your hands. If it is too sticky, add up to 1 cup flour, ½ cup at a time, until the consistency is smoother and peels easily off your hands. (Do not use more than 4 cups flour total.)

4. Return the dough to the bowl and let rise for 30 minutes.

To make the filling

1. Preheat the oven to 350°F.

2. Lightly grease a 9-inch round or square baking pan or ceramic dish with olive oil and set aside.

3. In large skillet over medium-high heat, cook the onion with 2 tablespoons of olive oil for 5 minutes, until brown. Transfer the onion to a large bowl.

4. Return the skillet to the heat and add the remaining 2 tablespoons of olive oil along with the wine, mint, salt, pepper, and ground beef. Cook over medium-high heat for 8 to 10 minutes, browning the meat and not stirring too frequently so it sticks to the pot a little for color, and not cooking it thoroughly. Remove from the heat and add to the onion in the bowl. Sprinkle the meat mixture with the nutmeg.

5. In a medium bowl, mix together the hard-boiled eggs, cheese, bread crumbs, and beaten eggs. Add to the meat mixture and stir well to combine.

(CONTINUED)

Meat Pie, continued

6. After the pastry has risen for 30 minutes, separate it into thirds. Use two thirds for the bottom crust; roll out the bottom and top portions flat to fit the prepared baking pan (the top crust will be thinner).

7. Pour the onion-meat-egg mixture over the bottom crust. Cover with the top crust. Brush with the egg yolk and scatter the sesame seeds over the top. Bake in the center of the oven for 45 to 50 minutes, until golden brown.

8. Cover and refrigerate leftovers for up to 3 days.

Substitution tip: If you can't find authentic *mizithra* cheese from Crete, use feta cheese or shredded kasseri cheese instead. To save an hour of prep time, you can purchase ready-made pastry (not to be confused with phyllo dough), in the freezer section of your grocery store. Thaw it before using. If you have access to a Mediterranean grocery, ready-made pastry will often come from Greece, without a lot of additives.

Cooking tip: Leave the top part of the pie without a crust, and use all the dough for the bottom crust to make a double deep-dish pie instead. If you do, top the pie with thinly sliced tomatoes seasoned with salt and pepper. Brush with 1 tablespoon olive oil before baking. If you freeze the pie to cook later, start it in a 250°F oven for 15 minutes, finishing at 350°F for 35 to 40 minutes more, until golden brown.

PER SERVING: Calories: 548; Total Fat: 26g; Saturated Fat: 7g; Protein: 31g; Total Carbs: 45g; Fiber: 2g; Sodium: 663mg

Ellinika Biftekia

GREEK BURGERS

GLUTEN-FREE NUT-FREE	SERVES 4	PREP TIME: 15 MINUTES	COOK TIME: 10 TO 20 MINUTES

Theo's mom's favorite treat on Mother's Day, or summer picnic days, was always burgers and hot dogs on the grill; yeah, we grew up in the '60s. Seldom was the holiday celebrated at home—the whole family would drive out to a beautiful lake, canasta cards smacking the picnic table, *tiropitas* wrapped in foil as nibbles while the meat cooked, joining later with *Patata Salata* / Greek Potato Salad (page 62), wine, and Greek pastries. Our charcoal grill always got some stares from passersby because the drifting smells were something better than your usual burger meat. Secret ingredients make all the difference—and now you know them, too.

1 pound 90% lean ground chuck

½ pound ground lamb

½ pound ground pork

½ cup chopped (¼-inch) onion

¼ cup minced fresh parsley

2 teaspoons sea salt

1 teaspoon freshly ground black pepper

1 teaspoon dried Greek oregano

1 teaspoon dried garlic

¼ teaspoon ground cloves

4 (1½-inch-square-by-¼-inch-thick) feta cheese slices

1. Preheat a grill to medium-high heat (about 350°F on a gas grill; if using a charcoal grill, cooking will take a bit longer).

2. In a large bowl, combine the chuck, lamb, pork, onion, parsley, salt, pepper, oregano, garlic, and cloves. With clean hands, thoroughly mix the ingredients. Divide the mixture into 6 equal portions, squeezing each to form a ball. Cut the balls in half, insert 1 feta square into each, and re-form the halves into patties. Place the burgers on the grill and cook to your desired doneness: 8 minutes for medium rare to 15 minutes for well-done on a gas grill; 10 to 20 minutes, respectively, on a charcoal grill.

(CONTINUED)

3. Alternatively, in a skillet over high heat, heat 2 tablespoons olive oil. Add the burgers and cook for 2 to 3 minutes per side, for a nice sear on the outside and a medium-rare inside.

Substitution tip: If you use only ground beef, eliminating the lamb and pork, use 85% lean ground beef, not 90% lean.

Serving tip: These make a pretty rich burger on a bun, but if you decide to go for it, use an egg bread bun with plenty of sliced onion and tomato to layer over the burgers. We like to eat these without a bun yet with all the crunchy raw ingredients that go on the bun. The richness of the meat is a decadent stand-alone with fresh garden tomatoes, sweet bell peppers, onions, and corn on the cob.

PER SERVING: Calories: 498; Total Fat: 31g; Saturated Fat: 11g; Protein: 47g; Total Carbs: 4g; Fiber: 1g; Sodium: 1,396mg

Horiatiki Stroma Piato
COUNTRY-STYLE LAYERED DISH

NUT-FREE	SERVES 8 TO 12	PREP TIME: 2 HOURS	COOK TIME: 50 MINUTES

Traditional moussaka is the best known of all Greek foods—you see it at all the Greek festivals, oozing with thick béchamel. On Theo's recent trip to Crete she witnessed a large Greek family dining seaside. A little girl, about eight years old, had eyes as big as tennis balls when a thick slab of rich moussaka was placed before her. Her mom told her that certainly she wouldn't eat the whole thing (moussaka being a decadent treat, her mom was probably hoping for a bite) . . . she did, all by herself, with no help! Theo came up with this (relatively) quicker, healthier, high-protein version. It's like making lasagna—it does take a while, but it's worth it and is good for a large party or multiple meals.

2 medium globe eggplant, cut into ½-inch slices

2 tablespoons sea salt, plus 3½ teaspoons, divided

1 egg, beaten, plus 3 eggs, beaten separately

2½ teaspoons freshly ground black pepper, divided

½ cup seasoned bread crumbs, such as Progresso brand

9 tablespoons extra-virgin olive oil, divided

1 medium onion, cut into ½-inch chunks

2 pounds lean ground chuck

¼ cup minced fresh parsley

1 large (28-ounce) can chopped tomatoes

1 cup crumbled feta cheese

½ pound raw spinach

½ teaspoon ground nutmeg

1. Place the sliced eggplant in a colander. Using 2 tablespoons of salt, salt the slices on both sides. Let the eggplant drain for 1 hour in the sink. Rinse off the salt and dry the eggplant slices with paper towels.

2. Place 1 beaten egg in a shallow dish and add ½ teaspoon of salt and ½ teaspoon of pepper. Into another shallow dish, pour the bread crumbs.

3. With a fork, dip an eggplant slice into the egg, coating it on both sides, then pat it into the bread crumbs, lightly coating both sides. Set the breaded eggplant on a plate and repeat with the remaining slices.

4. In a large skillet over medium-high heat, heat 2 tablespoons of olive oil.

(CONTINUED)

5. Add the onion and 1 teaspoon of salt. Cook for 5 minutes until brown. Transfer to a large bowl.

6. Return the skillet to the heat. Add 2 tablespoons of olive oil and the ground chuck. Season with 1 teaspoon of salt and 1 teaspoon of pepper. Cook for 8 to 10 minutes, until brown, breaking up the meat with a spoon. Transfer to the onion in the bowl, add the parsley, and stir to mix.

7. Return the skillet to the medium-high heat and add 4 tablespoons of olive oil. Heat for 30 seconds, using a spatula to scrape up any browned bits (*fond*) from the bottom of the skillet.

8. Place the breaded eggplant slices, in batches, into the hot oil. Fry for 3 to 4 minutes per side, until golden brown. Drain on a paper towel–lined plate.

9. Preheat the oven to 350°F.

10. In a small bowl, stir together the tomatoes, feta, ½ teaspoon of salt, and ½ teaspoon of pepper.

11. Coat the bottom of a 9-by-13-inch casserole dish, or something similar, with 3 tablespoons of juice from the tomato mixture and the remaining 1 tablespoon of olive oil.

12. Layer half the fried eggplant slices in the dish, not overlapping but close together.

13. Layer half of the meat.

14. Top with half of the tomato mixture.

15. Layer on the remaining eggplant slices.

16. Cover with the remaining meat.

17. In a medium bowl, mix 3 beaten eggs with the spinach and the remaining ½ teaspoon of salt and 1½ teaspoons of pepper. Pour the egg and spinach mixture over the top, pressing the spinach in between slices of eggplant, creating an even layer over the meat and eggplant.

18. Pour the remaining tomato and feta mixture over the egg and spinach mixture. Sprinkle the top with the nutmeg. Bake for 25 to 30 minutes, until the egg is set.

19. Cover and refrigerate any leftovers for up to 3 days.

Cooking tip: Theo loves using whole nutmeg, freshly grating it over the top of many of her Greek dishes. Don't mix it into other spices or it will lose its subtle qualities; it's truly a stand-alone, use-alone spice that adds another dimension to the savory qualities of Greek cooking. If you don't have whole nutmeg, get some the next time you're in a spice shop; you'll taste the difference!

PER SERVING: Calories: 519; Total Fat: 35g; Saturated Fat: 11g; Protein: 35g; Total Carbs: 15g; Fiber: 6g; Sodium: 697mg

Gemisto Olokliro Kotopoulo

STUFFED WHOLE CHICKEN

GLUTEN-FREE NUT-FREE	SERVES 4	PREP TIME: 30 MINUTES	COOK TIME: 1 HOUR, 20 MINUTES

Theo adopted her daughters from Nepal in 2001 when they were five and six years old. Chicken was a delicacy to them, their main dish having been *dal bhat* (a combination of lentils and rice), but they loved this recipe and learned to fight over the wishbone as soon as they were shown this tradition from Theo's childhood—they still like to squabble over the wishbone when they're together. This recipe is so easy they often make it for their own friends now. Here again, we're into using good organic chicken for flavor and health, never those antibiotic-infused birds.

1 (3.5- to 4-pound) whole organic chicken

2 tablespoons sea salt, plus 2 teaspoons, divided

1 medium artichoke, quartered

½ cup chopped (½-inch chunks) red or yellow bell pepper

½ cup cremini mushrooms, quartered

½ cup chopped (1-inch chunks) zucchini

8 tablespoons extra-virgin olive oil, divided

Juice of 1 lemon, including some pulp but no seeds

1 tablespoon freshly ground black pepper

1 tablespoon dried Greek oregano

4 medium Yukon Gold potatoes, quartered

4 medium, firm tomatoes, such as Early Girl variety, halved

½ cup Kalamata olives, pitted

2 (4-inch) fresh rosemary sprigs

2 teaspoons lemon zest

1. Preheat the oven to 375°F.

2. Chicken cooks from the inside out, so salt the inside of the cavity: Pour 2 tablespoons of salt into one of your hands and rub the inside thoroughly.

3. In a medium bowl, toss together the artichoke, bell pepper, mushrooms, zucchini, and 3 tablespoons of olive oil. With a large spoon, put the veggies into the chicken cavity. Place the chicken breast-side up on a rack inserted in the bottom of a deep roasting pan.

4. In the empty veggie bowl, whisk 3 tablespoons of olive oil, the lemon juice, remaining 2 teaspoons of salt, pepper, and oregano. Add the potatoes and tomatoes and stir to coat.

5. Add the olives. Arrange the veggies around the edge of the roasting pan, being careful not to tuck them under the chicken but to surround it.

6. Using your fingertips, gently get under the skin of the chicken breast, peeling the membrane from underneath the skin, yet keeping it intact on top of the breast. This allows you to rub the breast itself with the remaining 3 tablespoons of olive oil and the lemon zest.

7. Insert 2 rosemary sprigs under the skin on top of each breast. Using your oiled hand, rub the outside of the chicken to sweep off any oil, lemon zest, or rosemary from the outer skin. Roast for 1 hour, 20 minutes, until an instant-read thermometer reaches 165°F on the breast meat.

Cooking tip: Use any fresh veggies that you like for stuffing, but in the same proportion. If you love feta cheese like we do, slide 2 tablespoons of crumbled feta under the skin, alongside the rosemary sprigs and lemon zest, before roasting. Add a whole sliced onion and another tablespoon of olive oil to the potato/tomato mix if you like cooked onions.

Serving tip: If you possess great carving skills, bring the bird to the table whole to wow a small dinner party. Scoop the stuffing from inside the cavity first, before carving.

PER SERVING: Calories: 1,126; Total Fat: 78g; Saturated Fat: 18g; Protein: 64g; Total Carbs: 48g; Fiber: 11g; Sodium: 2,116mg

Stithos Kotopoulo Gemisto me Spanaki kai Feta

SPINACH AND FETA STUFFED CHICKEN BREASTS

GLUTEN-FREE NUT-FREE	SERVES 4	PREP TIME: 15 MINUTES	COOK TIME: 30 MINUTES

Christina loves taking everyday ingredients and making them interesting for her catering clients. This dish is a mainstay. It dresses up the familiar spinach, scallion, feta, and dill combination with briny capers and stuffs it into a chicken breast for an easy-to-make yet equally indulgent main course.

2 tablespoons extra-virgin olive oil, divided

3 scallions, white and green parts, minced

2 garlic cloves, minced

12 ounces fresh spinach

2 tablespoons capers, chopped

2 tablespoons sun-dried tomatoes, chopped

½ cup chopped fresh dill

½ cup feta cheese

4 boneless skinless chicken breasts, pounded ½ to ¼ inch thick

Kosher salt

Freshly ground black pepper

1. Preheat the oven to 375°F.

2. Heat a large skillet over medium heat.

3. Add 1 tablespoon of olive oil, the scallions, and the garlic. Cook for 5 minutes. Transfer to a medium bowl.

4. Return the skillet to the heat and add the spinach to wilt, 3 to 5 minutes. Drain to remove any excess liquid and add to the onions and garlic.

5. Mix in the capers, dill, sun-dried tomatoes, and feta to combine.

6. Season the chicken with salt and pepper, and drizzle with the remaining 2 tablespoons of olive oil.

7. Place ¼ of the spinach mixture in the lower-middle portion of a chicken breast. Roll it up and secure with a toothpick. Repeat with the remaining spinach and the other 3 chicken breasts. Place the finished rolls in a baking dish.

8. Bake for 20 to 30 minutes, or until the internal temperature of the chicken reaches 165°F.

PER SERVING: Calories: 265; Total Fat: 14g; Saturated Fat: 4g; Protein: 30g; Total Carbs: 9g; Fiber: 3g; Sodium: 508mg

Kotopoulo Kapama

BRAISED CHICKEN WITH TOMATO SAUCE AND SPICES

GLUTEN-FREE NUT-FREE	SERVES 6	PREP TIME: 20 MINUTES	COOK TIME: 2 HOURS, 30 MINUTES

This comforting dish is bright in flavor with tangy tomato sauce enriched with spices and Christina's addition of honey—a revered Greek ingredient. It's the dish Christina loves to make for her friends (and that keeps them asking for invitations to dinner). It's traditionally served with egg noodles but is perfect accompanied by her *Spanakorizo* / Spinach Rice (page 85).

3 pounds chicken thighs, or 1 (4- to 4.5-pound) whole chicken, cut into 8 pieces

2 tablespoons extra-virgin olive oil, divided

1 onion, chopped

5 garlic cloves, minced

3 carrots, diced

3 celery stalks, diced

1 teaspoon ground cinnamon, or 2 cinnamon sticks

1 cup white wine

½ cup red wine vinegar

¼ cup honey

2 tablespoons tomato paste

2 cups chicken broth

1 bay leaf

1. Preheat the oven to 325°F.

2. In a heated 7- to 9-quart Dutch oven over medium-high heat, cook the chicken in 1 tablespoon of olive oil for 5 to 7 minutes, until brown. Cook it in batches, if needed, so as not to crowd the pan. Drain any excess fat that accumulates. Transfer the chicken to a plate.

3. Return the pot to the heat and heat the remaining 1 tablespoon of olive oil.

4. Add the onion and stir. Cook for 5 minutes, scraping up any browned bits (*fond*) from the bottom of the pot.

5. Add the garlic and cook for 1 minute more.

6. Add the carrots, celery, and cinnamon. Cook for 5 minutes.

7. Stir in the wine, vinegar, honey, and tomato paste. Simmer for 5 to 7 minutes, until reduced by half.

8. Return the chicken to the pot. Cover it with the chicken broth, add the bay leaf, cover the pot, and place it in the oven. Braise for 2 hours.

9. Cover and refrigerate any leftovers for up to 3 days. Like the *Youvetsi* / Braised Lamb or Beef with Spiced Tomato Sauce (page 163), it's better after letting it sit overnight to let the flavors develop.

Serving tip: Traditional *kapama* is served topped with *mizithra* cheese. If that isn't available, try Romano, or even the saltiness of feta would make a nice addition.

PER SERVING: Calories: 603; Total Fat: 37g; Saturated Fat: 9g; Protein: 41g; Total Carbs: 20g; Fiber: 2g; Sodium: 732mg

GREEKIFIED COBBLER, PAGE 213;
OLIVE OIL ICE CREAM WITH FETA,
CINNAMON, AND BASIL, PAGE 194

CHAPTER NINE

Desserts

"You eat dessert every day?" Yes, most often midday with dark Greek coffee. Theo has converted family-favorite recipes from using butter to using extra-virgin olive oil; she is an organic extra-virgin olive oil producer in California, inspired to make dessert a bit healthier and lighter, with a perfect crumb never left on the plate. Theo recommends using Greek varietal olive oils because they are denser, fruitier, and more buttery—promising the purity of savory Greek flavors.

Vasilopita
GREEK HOLIDAY BREAD 191

Eleaolado Pagoto me Feta, Kanelli, kai Vasiliko
**OLIVE OIL ICE CREAM WITH
FETA, CINNAMON, AND BASIL** 194

Kourambiedes
SHORTBREAD COOKIES 197

Den Ine To Baklava Tis Miteras Sas
NOT YOUR MOTHER'S BAKLAVA 198

Kolokithakia Lemoni Keik Elaioladou
ZUCCHINI LEMON OLIVE OIL CAKE 200

Koulouria
GREEK COFFEE COOKIE 203

Karidopita
GREEK WALNUT CAKE 206

Elliniki Yiaourti Metaxa Keik
GREEK YOGURT BRANDY CAKE 208

Efkolo Halva
EASY HALVA 210

Eliniki Frouta Cobbler
GREEKIFIED COBBLER 213

Vasilopita

GREEK HOLIDAY BREAD

VEGETARIAN	MAKES 8 OR 9 LOAVES	PREP TIME: 6 HOURS	COOK TIME: 30 MINUTES

Sometimes called *tsoureki*, this sweet egg bread is a mainstay during Easter and New Year's holidays. Similar to challah, Theo's version uses olive oil instead of butter. Traditionally, it is eaten fresh on New Year's Day and Easter, as part of breaking Great Lent, but Theo loves to cut half-inch slices, spread each side with olive oil, and either toast the bread in the oven on both sides or, better yet, fry it in a skillet, fresh jam becoming its best friend. Dipping it into beaten egg like a Greek version of French toast makes for breakfast food utopia in your very own home. This bread really isn't a dessert, but we included it in this chapter because it's a mainstay, must-know-how-to-make bread that is a significant "sweet spot" on savory holiday tables. This recipe does have a large yield, so make a big batch, share it, freeze it, or give it as gifts.

4 cups whole milk

2½ cups sugar, plus ½ teaspoon, divided

Cinnamon, for dusting

3 (¼-ounce) packets yeast

17 cups organic all-purpose flour, divided, plus more as needed

2 cups extra-virgin olive oil

12 organic eggs

1 tablespoon vanilla extract

1 teaspoon sea salt

¼ cup raw sesame seeds (optional)

¼ cup raw slivered almonds (optional)

1. In a medium saucepan over medium heat, slowly heat the milk to a scald (just below boiling to 180°F; it's important that the skin forms on top). Skim off the skin and place it in a small bowl. Shake ½ teaspoon sugar and dust some cinnamon over the top and give it to any child with whom you want to create a favorite memory, or sneak it for yourself; it's one of the joys of making this recipe!

2. Transfer 1 cup of hot milk to another small bowl. Test the milk with the back of your pinky; if you can hold the middle

(CONTINUED)

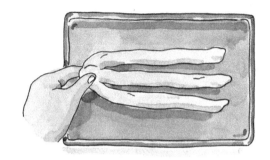

knuckle in the milk for 3 seconds without getting burned, add the yeast and dissolve it, stirring slowly to form a thin paste. (If you can't hold your pinky there, wait a little longer and test again.)

3. In a large bowl, add 8 cups of flour, make a well in the center, and pour the remaining warm milk and the yeast/milk mixture in. Mix thoroughly with your clean hands, but do not knead or overwork the dough. Cover with a clean kitchen towel and place in a warm spot to rise for 2 hours. A sunny window or a chair near a heating vent is perfect.

4. After 1 hour and 45 minutes pass, in the bowl of a stand mixer or other large bowl using a handheld electric mixer, cream together the olive oil and remaining 2½ cups of sugar.

5. In a separate bowl, beat together 10 eggs, the vanilla, and the salt with a fork. Add the eggs to the creamed olive oil and sugar, mixing on medium speed, blending the eggs in thoroughly.

6. After 2 hours, on a work surface or in very large bowl, scatter 2 cups of flour. Punch down the risen dough and gather any sticky bits from around the outside of the bowl. Transfer the dough to the floured work surface or bowl and create a well.

7. Pour the egg and sugar mixture into the well.

8. Add the remaining 7 cups of flour. With your hands, gather the dough from the outside edges, kneading the flour from underneath together with the dough, egg and sugar mixture, and the flour you just added. Continue to knead until the dough becomes elastic. If the dough is too sticky and doesn't peel away from your hands easily, add another cup of flour. Cover with a clean kitchen towel and let rise for 2 more hours.

9. Line 9 (9-inch) round cake pans or 3 large baking sheets with parchment paper and set aside.

10. After 2 hours, punch down the dough. Split it into 8 or 9 equal pieces and either place them into the prepared cake pans or divide each portion into three strips and make braid-shaped loaves (see Preparation tip), placing no more than 3 loaves horizontally on each prepared sheet.

11. In a small bowl, whisk the remaining 2 eggs. Using your clean fingertips or a pastry brush, spread the beaten egg over each loaf, getting into any braided crevices but not leaving pooled egg residue.

12. Decorate the loaves by sprinkling them with the raw sesame seeds (if using) and arranging the almond slivers (if using) in a decorative pattern. Cover with a clean kitchen towel and let rise for 45 minutes.

13. While the loaves are rising, preheat the oven to 350°F.

14. Bake the bread for 30 minutes, until a toothpick inserted in the center comes out clean. The bread will be golden brown on the top and bottom. If you don't use parchment, it may get too brown on the bottom.

15. The bread can be stored in resealable plastic bags, where it stays moist and delicious for 3 days. It also freezes beautifully.

Preparation tip: If you want to braid your loaves, roll 3 (4-inch) balls into 12-inch strands. Squeeze the tops of all 3 strands together at one end so you can braid them. When finished braiding, tuck the end of the dough under the loaf for a finished look.

PER SERVING (1 SLICE BREAD ASSUMING 8 SLICES EACH OUT OF 8 LOAVES): Calories: 227; Total Fat: 8g; Saturated Fat: 2g; Protein: 5g; Total Carbs: 34g; Fiber: 1g; Sodium: 50mg

Eleaolado Pagoto me Feta, Kanelli, kai Vasiliko

OLIVE OIL ICE CREAM WITH FETA, CINNAMON, AND BASIL

GLUTEN-FREE NUT-FREE VEGETARIAN	SERVES 12	PREP TIME: 80 MINUTES, PLUS 4 HOURS TO FREEZE	COOK TIME: 15 MINUTES

It took Theo and her daughter Anita a few batches to perfect a superior texture and flavor for olive oil ice cream. For one year, their olive oil ice cream had kids and adults alike standing in line for this creamy confection. The melting point of this recipe is a bit lower than that of other ice creams, so enjoy it creamy just out of your ice cream maker, or frozen hard.

2½ cups 2% milk, divided

1 pint heavy (whipping) cream, divided

1 cup sugar

3 eggs, beaten

¾ cup Greek Kalamata or Koroneiki varietal extra-virgin olive oil, divided

3 tablespoons ground cinnamon

½ cup crumbled feta cheese

3 tablespoons chopped fresh Greek basil

1. In 2-quart saucepan over medium heat, whisk ½ cup of milk, ½ cup of heavy cream, the sugar, eggs, and ¼ cup of olive oil. Cook for about 15 minutes, until the mixture turns a light yellow and thickens. Do not allow the mixture to simmer or boil.

2. Remove the pan from the heat, cover the pan, and refrigerate for about 40 minutes to cool enough to add the remaining ingredients without cooking them.

(CONTINUED)

Olive Oil Ice Cream with Feta, Cinnamon, and Basil, continued

3. After cooling, add the remaining milk, cream, and olive oil, and the cinnamon, feta, and basil. Mix well with a large spoon.

4. Churn the mixture in an ice cream maker for 30 to 45 minutes, until thick and creamy. Freeze in an airtight container for at least 4 hours before serving.

Serving tip: This makes a lovely accompaniment to Theo's *Karidopita* / Greek Walnut Cake (page 206) and *Eliniki Frouta Cobbler* / Greekified Cobbler (page 213) or a pretty stand-alone dessert served in black or dark blue cups, garnished with fresh basil flowers.

PER SERVING: Calories: 365; Total Fat: 30g; Saturated Fat: 13g; Protein: 5g; Total Carbs: 22g; Fiber: 1g; Sodium: 107mg

Kourambiedes
SHORTBREAD COOKIES

NUT-FREE VEGETARIAN	MAKES 40 TO 60 COOKIES, DEPENDING ON THEIR SHAPE	PREP TIME: 1 HOUR, 30 MINUTES	COOK TIME: 20 MINUTES

Oh my... so many lovely memories with our *yiayias* making these melt-in-your-mouth wonders. There are recipes using rosewater and crushed almonds in the dough, but Theo's *yiayia* made them this way—then Theo converted the recipe from using a pound of browned butter to using Greek olive oil for a lighter, healthier cookie. They still melt in your mouth, with the aromatics from fresh Kalamata olive oil leaving a little Greek dance on your willing taste buds.

4 cups all-purpose flour, sifted

2 egg yolks, beaten

¾ cup Greek Kalamata varietal extra-virgin olive oil

2 cups confectioners' sugar

1. Preheat the oven to 350°F.

2. Line 2 baking sheets with parchment paper.

3. In a large bowl, add the sifted flour and make a well in the center.

4. Add the egg yolks and olive oil into the well. Stir to combine. The dough will seem fragile. Squeeze it into 2-inch half-moon shapes, or form ¾-inch balls and squeeze 3 balls together to form a triangle shape. Place them on the prepared sheets and bake for 20 minutes, switching and

rotating the pans about halfway through cooking. The finished cookies will be just brown on the bottom and still creamy white on the top.

5. Remove from the oven. Using a small strainer and a spoon to direct the sugar only on each individual cookie. Immediately divide the confectioners' sugar among the tops of each cookie. Let cool.

6. Store the cooled cookies in a sealable plastic container between sheets of wax paper or parchment paper.

PER SERVING (1 COOKIE IF RECIPE MAKES 40): Calories: 105; Total Fat: 4g; Saturated Fat: 1g; Protein: 1g; Total Carbs: 16g; Fiber: 0g; Sodium: 1mg

NOT YOUR MOTHER'S BAKLAVA

VEGETARIAN	MAKES ABOUT 48 PIECES	PREP TIME: 2 HOURS	COOK TIME: 40 MINUTES

Please don't be intimidated by baklava! Recipes using phyllo are all over this book, and Theo's version of baklava, using olive oil instead of butter, makes this truly a healthy dessert recipe that keeps perfectly for a few days. She calls her version Not Your Mother's Baklava because her mom used browned butter, walnuts only, and 1 pound of phyllo. Theo stole her sister Kathy's idea of using 2 pounds of phyllo instead of 1, creating a thick, gooey middle texture complementary to the crunchiness of the outer phyllo and the nuts inside.

For the simple syrup

2 cups water

1 cup sugar

¼ cup freshly squeezed lemon juice

For the baklava

2½ cups Greek Kalamata or Koroneiki varietal extra-virgin olive oil

2 pounds (4 rolls) phyllo, at room temperature

2 cups organic walnuts, ground

2 cups organic pistachio kernels, ground

¼ cup sugar

¼ cup ground cinnamon

1 tablespoon ground cloves

To make the simple syrup

1. Up to 1 day ahead but at least 2 hours before baking, making certain it has time to chill, in a 1-quart saucepan over medium-high heat, combine the water, sugar, and lemon juice, stirring until the sugar dissolves.

2. Bring the syrup to a boil and boil for 2 minutes. Test for doneness by placing a ¼-inch dot of hot syrup on your thumbnail. If it doesn't roll off, remove from the heat and let it cool. Keep boiling until the nail test is solid.

3. Cover the pan with a lid or plastic wrap and refrigerate for a minimum of 2 hours and up to 24 hours.

To make the baklava

1. Spread a thin layer of olive oil on the bottom of a 9-by-13-inch baking dish.

2. One sheet at a time, layer 1 roll of phyllo into the pan, brushing each sheet with a thin layer of olive oil before adding the next (see Baking tip).

3. In a large bowl, mix together the walnuts, pistachios, sugar, cinnamon, and cloves. Spread 2 cups of the nut mixture over the phyllo.

4. One sheet at a time, layer 2 rolls phyllo on top, brushing each sheet with a thin layer of olive oil before adding the next.

5. Spread the remaining nut mixture over the phyllo.

6. Top with the remaining 1 roll of phyllo, layering one sheet at a time and brushing each sheet with a thin coat of olive oil before adding the next.

7. Preheat the oven to 375°F.

8. With a very sharp, long, nonserrated knife, cut the phyllo lengthwise into 6 equal strips about 1½ inches wide, making sure to slice through to the bottom of the pan. Use your thumb and forefinger placed on either side of your knife to hold the phyllo down as you cut. Then cut diagonal slices, 1½ inches wide, across the strips. The cut baklava pieces will be diamond shaped.

9. Bake for 10 minutes. Reduce the heat to 325°F and bake for 30 minutes more, until golden brown.

10. Remove from the oven and immediately pour the cold syrup over the hot baklava. It will sizzle and absorb the syrup perfectly this way.

Baking tip: Use a wide 3- or 4-inch paintbrush from your hardware store as a pastry brush—your baklava assembly will go much faster! Don't forget to cut any phyllo dish you make before baking. Make sure to pour the syrup evenly over the baklava, covering the edges and middle of the pastry equally. You might use a pitcher or vessel with a pour spout—even a squeeze bottle with a large tip—to control even syrup distribution.

PER SERVING (1 PIECE) : Calories: 205; Total Fat: 15g; Saturated Fat: 2g; Protein: 3g; Total Carbs: 17g; Fiber: 1g; Sodium: 61mg

Kolokithakia Lemoni Keik Elaioladou

ZUCCHINI LEMON OLIVE OIL CAKE

NUT-FREE VEGETARIAN	SERVES 16	PREP TIME: 40 MINUTES	COOK TIME: 30 MINUTES	TOTAL TIME: 2 HOURS

Modern-style cakes call for triple layers and a "naked siding" approach to the frosting. With bushels of zucchini coming out of every angle of Theo's farm stand garden, she had to develop her own zucchini cake recipe. Many of us desperately look for solutions to our zucchini bonanzas, but we promise this light summer cake will become a year-round favorite for all occasions. It tastes as pretty as it looks.

For the frosting

4 ounces cream cheese, at room temperature

2 tablespoons butter, at room temperature

2 tablespoons extra-virgin lemon olive oil

2 teaspoons vanilla extract

2 tablespoons grated lemon zest

3 cups confectioners' sugar

For the cake

2½ cups sugar

¾ cup extra-virgin lemon olive oil

4 eggs, beaten

⅔ cup unsweetened vanilla almond milk

2 teaspoons vanilla extract

4 cups cake flour

2½ teaspoons baking powder

1 teaspoon sea salt

2½ cups coarsely shredded zucchini, excess moisture removed by blotting with paper towels

1 tablespoon slivered lemon zest, for garnishing

To make the frosting

1. In a large bowl, with an electric handheld mixer, beat together the cream cheese, butter, olive oil, vanilla, and grated lemon zest until light and fluffy.

2. Add the confectioners' sugar and beat until well combined. You will have about 2 cups of frosting.

To make the cake

1. Preheat the oven to 350°F.

2. Prepare 3 (8-inch) round cake pans: Trace the bottom of the pan's shape on parchment paper. Cut out the circles and place them on the bottoms of the pans.

3. In a large bowl, whisk the sugar and olive oil.

(CONTINUED)

4. Add the eggs, almond milk, and vanilla and whisk to combine.

5. Add the flour, baking powder, and salt. Mix thoroughly to make a smooth batter.

6. Stir in the zucchini.

7. Pour 2 cups of batter into each pre-pared pan. Bake for 30 minutes until a toothpick inserted into the center comes out clean.

8. Remove from the oven and cool on wire racks for 15 minutes.

9. Invert the pans: Working over wire racks or your prep table, place your thumbs on the bottom of the pan and your fingers over the cake, slipping the cake from the pan.

10. When completely cooled, place 1 cake layer on a serving dish. Spread it lightly with frosting. Repeat with the 2 remaining cake layers.

11. Frost the top with a ½-inch-thick layer of frosting.

12. Frost the sides minimally with the remaining frosting, allowing the cake to show through.

13. Garnish the top of the cake with slivered lemon zest.

Substitution tip: Use orange olive oil, swapping out the grated zest and zest slivers for orange also. You can also use real milk instead of almond milk, but almond milk gives the cake a unique flavor. Last, you may use regular olive oil if you don't have lemon or orange olive oil, but the character of the cake's flavor will change.

PER SERVING: Calories: 431; Total Fat: 18g; Saturated Fat: 5g; Protein: 5g; Total Carbs: 65g; Fiber: 1g; Sodium: 174mg

Koulouria
GREEK COFFEE COOKIE

NUT-FREE VEGETARIAN	MAKES ABOUT 60 COOKIES, DEPENDING ON THEIR SHAPE	PREP TIME: 30 MINUTES	COOK TIME: 25 MINUTES

Theo's favorite memories, hands down, are literally her hands on the table making *koulourakia* with her mom and *yiayia*. They would sing a traditional Greek song that her own daughters have learned, which she hopes will be carried down for generations to come. Even most simple Greek words have four or five syllables each, which makes the tempo of the song one you cannot help but smile to yourself about while singing. Common shapes for these cookies are S or braided shapes. Theo's *yiayia* was an artist, as is Theo, so when *yiayia* was around, she got to play with the dough . . . with Mom, it was a strict "No!" In her later years, Theo's mom softened when she herself became a *yiayia*, allowing her grandchildren to break tradition with their own unique letters and shapes. Sure didn't change the delicious flavor you could always count on.

1 cup extra-virgin olive oil

3 eggs, beaten, plus 1 egg, beaten separately

½ cup freshly squeezed orange juice

4½ cups all-purpose flour

1½ teaspoons baking powder

2 teaspoons ground cinnamon

¼ cup raw sesame seeds (optional)

1. Preheat the oven to 350°F.

2. Line 2 baking sheets with parchment paper.

3. In a medium bowl, whisk the olive oil, 3 beaten eggs, and orange juice.

4. In a large bowl, mix together the flour, baking powder, and cinnamon. Make a well in the center.

(CONTINUED)

5. Add the liquid ingredients to the well and blend the dough thoroughly with a rubber spatula. Squeeze the dough into 1½-inch balls. With your fingertips, roll the balls into ½-inch-thick tubes. Make *S* shapes with the tubes, or gently fold them in half to form twists. Place the cookies on the prepared baking sheets 2 inches apart.

6. Using your fingertips or a pastry brush, lightly coat the tops of the cookies with 1 beaten egg and sprinkle with sesame seeds (if using).

7. Bake for 25 minutes, covering the baking sheets loosely with aluminum foil for the first 10 minutes. Remove the foil after 10 minutes, switch and rotate the pans, and finish baking. The finished cookies will be dark golden brown on the bottom and lightly browned on top. Let cool. Make these ahead to save some time. These keep well for up to 8 days in a tin or resealable bag.

Serving tip: Traditionally, these cookies are eaten like a biscotti, dipped in coffee, or as a coffee cookie. Kids young and old love them with milk.

PER SERVING (1 COOKIE): Calories: 68; Total Fat: 4g; Saturated Fat: 1g; Protein: 1g; Total Carbs: 8g; Fiber: 0g; Sodium: 4mg

Karidopita
GREEK WALNUT CAKE

VEGETARIAN	MAKES 48 PIECES	PREP TIME: 20 MINUTES	COOK TIME: 40 TO 45 MINUTES

This recipe has evolved over the 35 years Theo has been making it. She's added more spice and baking powder to the original recipe to make it lighter and more complex in flavor. Still, our favorite part of this recipe is the gooey crumbs left in the bottom of the pan, versus enjoying an entire piece of cake. Well . . . we enjoy that, too!

For the cake

1½ cups sugar

1 cup Greek Kalamata or Koroneiki varietal extra-virgin olive oil

3 eggs, beaten

1 cup 2% milk

1 teaspoon balsamic vinegar

2 cups sifted all-purpose flour

1 tablespoon baking powder

1 tablespoon ground cinnamon

1 teaspoon ground allspice

½ teaspoon ground cloves

1 cup ground walnuts

For the syrup

2 cups sugar

1 cup water

2 tablespoons freshly squeezed lemon juice

To make the cake

1. Preheat the oven to 350°F.

2. In a large bowl with an electric hand-held mixer or in the bowl of a stand mixer, cream together the sugar and olive oil on high speed until well blended.

3. Reduce the speed to medium-high and add the beaten eggs, milk, and vinegar, blending well.

4. In a medium bowl, mix together the flour, baking powder, cinnamon, allspice, and cloves. With the mixer running, slowly add the flour mixture and mix until well blended.

5. Stir in the walnuts. Pour the batter into an ungreased 9-by-13-inch baking pan.

6. Bake for 40 to 45 minutes, or until a toothpick inserted in the center comes out clean.

7. Remove from the oven and let the cake cool completely before pouring the hot syrup over the cake, and before cutting. Any leftover cake should be covered with aluminum foil. It will keep at room temperature for up to 3 days.

To make the syrup

1. In a 1-quart saucepan over medium-high heat, combine the sugar, water, and lemon juice, stirring until sugar dissolves.

2. Bring the syrup to a boil and boil for 2 minutes. Test for doneness by placing a ¼-inch dot of hot syrup on your thumbnail. If it doesn't roll off, remove from the heat. Keep boiling until the nail test is solid.

3. Pour the hot syrup over the completely cooled cake and cut for serving, or let cool to room temperature.

Serving tip: Makes a perfect pairing with *Eleaolado Pagoto me Feta, Kanelli, kai Vasiliko* / Olive Oil Ice Cream with Feta, Cinnamon, and Basil (page 194).

PER SERVING (1 PIECE) : Calories: 118; Total Fat: 6g; Saturated Fat: 1g; Protein: 1g; Total Carbs: 16g; Fiber: 0g; Sodium: 7mg

Elliniki Yiaourti Metaxa Keik

GREEK YOGURT BRANDY CAKE

NUT-FREE VEGETARIAN	SERVES 16	PREP TIME: 20 MINUTES	COOK TIME: 60 TO 70 MINUTES

The best of all worlds was discovered in Theo's kitchen on a snowy winter's night in Yellow Springs, Ohio—she wanted Greek brandy and dessert and decided to put it all together. Next to hamburgers, cake is her favorite thing in the world—yes, the organic queen has a sweet tooth. This recipe is a keeper for a lot of reasons: It tastes great for several days after making it, makes a perfect coffee cake (yes, why not brandy for breakfast?), and is really pretty, too.

2 cups sugar

½ cup Greek Kalamata or Koroneiki varietal extra-virgin olive oil, plus more for preparing the pan

3 eggs

2 cups all-purpose flour or cake flour, sifted

2 teaspoons baking powder

½ teaspoon sea salt

1 cup Greek yogurt

½ cup Metaxa Greek brandy

1 tablespoon orange zest

2 teaspoons ground cinnamon

1 teaspoon vanilla extract

¼ cup confectioners' sugar

1. Preheat the oven to 350°F.

2. Lightly grease a standard Bundt pan with olive oil.

3. In a large bowl with an electric hand-held mixer or in the bowl of a stand mixer, cream together the sugar and olive oil on high speed until well blended.

4. Add eggs one at a time, beating thoroughly after each addition.

5. In a medium bowl, combine the flour, baking powder, and salt.

6. In a small bowl, stir together the yogurt, brandy, orange zest, cinnamon, and vanilla.

7. Alternate adding the flour mixture and yogurt mixture slowly to the batter, and beat on medium speed after each addition until well blended. Pour the batter into the prepared Bundt pan.

8. Bake for 60 to 70 minutes, or until a toothpick inserted into the center comes out clean.

9. Remove from the oven and let the cake cool. Invert the pan onto a serving dish and dust with the confectioners' sugar before cutting and serving.

Substitution tip: Use any brandy or schnapps. Flavored fruit brandies work fine, too, as does Armagnac, Grand Marnier—almost whatever is in your liquor cupboard!

PER SERVING: Calories: 259; Total Fat: 8g; Saturated Fat: 1g; Protein: 5g; Total Carbs: 40g; Fiber: 1g; Sodium: 78mg

Efkolo Halva

EASY HALVA

VEGETARIAN	SERVES 16	PREP TIME: 5 MINUTES, PLUS 2 HOURS TO COOL	COOK TIME: 25 MINUTES	TOTAL TIME: 2 HOURS, 30 MINUTES

One might argue that true halva is sesame-based, a bit grainy, and rich. But our favorite halva is a brown, dense, Jell-O-like mass of tasty beauty. When Theo and her sisters were little, they would often surprise her *yiayia's* oldest friend on Sundays after church. Who wouldn't want to surprise Nouna Anna—she always wore an apron and was constantly in the middle of making some type of treat. Never too sweet, but with the perfect balance, it took a while to recreate her halva just the way Theo remembers it. Treat yourself to a pretty tin mold of some nice shape, or seek one out at a vintage store. Semolina is a power grain, and this is a satisfying, healthy dessert.

1 cup fine semolina flour
  (we like Bob's Red Mill)

1 cup coarse semolina flour

1 cup Kalamata or Koroneiki varietal
  extra-virgin olive oil

4 cups water

3 cups cane sugar

2 tablespoons ground cinnamon,
  plus 1 teaspoon, divided

½ cup raisins

½ cup toasted nuts, such as walnuts,
  almonds, or pine nuts

2 tablespoons confectioners' sugar

1. In a 2-quart saucepan over medium-high heat, combine the fine semolina, coarse semolina, and olive oil. Cook for 3 to 4 minutes, stirring constantly, until brown.

2. In another 2-quart saucepan over medium-high heat, combine the water and sugar, bring to a boil, and boil for 10 minutes, stirring until the sugar dissolves and being careful that the mixture does not boil over.

(CONTINUED)

3. While stirring, slowly pour the sugar syrup into the browned semolina paste, making sure to stir the bottom of the pot thoroughly so nothing sticks.

4. Sprinkle in 2 tablespoons of cinnamon. Reduce the heat to low and simmer for about 10 minutes, continuing to stir the mixture thoroughly. The halva is finished when it peels away easily from the sides of the pan.

5. Stir in the raisins and pour the mixture into a pretty mold (like an old-fashioned gelatin mold or decorative cake mold). Cool for about 2 hours on the countertop or in the refrigerator. Remove the halva from the mold and place on a serving dish.

6. In a small bowl, mix together the confectioners' sugar and remaining 1 teaspoon of cinnamon. Dust the halva with the cinnamon-sugar and arrange the toasted nuts decoratively over it.

7. Cut into ½-inch slabs. Keeps refrigerated in an airtight container for up to 1 week.

Serving tip: This halva makes a fine stand-alone simple dessert with coffee. Make it decadent with a couple tablespoons of fresh cream and/or a drizzle of chocolate syrup.

PER SERVING: Calories: 315; Total Fat: 14g; Saturated Fat: 2g; Protein: 2g; Total Carbs: 49g; Fiber: 1g; Sodium: 1mg

Eliniki Frouta Cobbler
GREEKIFIED COBBLER

NUT-FREE VEGETARIAN	SERVES 8	PREP TIME: 20 MINUTES	COOK TIME: 40 TO 45 MINUTES

We wanted to have a little fun with the last dessert recipe in the book. Theo is a dessert hound, and all the recipes in this chapter are hers. She's from Ohio, where summer cobbler was always a necessary staple on her dinner menus. She's also goat cheese crazed. The combination of fruit, cheese, and biscuit flavors makes her swoon. The best part about this recipe, though, is that it's healthy—not much sugar and an olive oil biscuit. Perfection! Oh, add a bottle of French champagne to share and she'll start speaking French instead of Greek. . .just sayin'! We hope you enjoy the dessert recipes in this book as much as Theo has enjoyed sharing them with you.

For the filling

2 cups sliced peaches

1 cup fresh blueberries

½ cup sugar

1 tablespoon ground cinnamon

6 ounces *mizithra* cheese, crumbled

For the biscuit

1 cup all-purpose flour

1 teaspoon baking soda

¼ teaspoon sea salt

½ cup Greek Kalamata or Koroneiki varietal extra-virgin olive oil

⅓ cup sugar

1 egg, beaten

To make the filling

1. Place a large bowl in the freezer for 15 minutes.

2. In a 1-quart saucepan over medium heat, combine the peaches, blueberries, and sugar. Cook for 5 minutes, stirring. Remove from the heat and transfer the mixture to the chilled bowl to cool. When the fruit is cool enough that it won't melt the cheese, arrange it in a deep 9-inch square or oval baking dish.

3. Sprinkle with the cinnamon.

4. Spoon the cheese in ½-teaspoon amounts randomly over the fruit.

(CONTINUED)

Greekified Cobbler, continued

To make the biscuit

1. Preheat the oven to 350°F.

2. In a medium bowl, whisk the flour, baking soda, and salt.

3. Add the olive oil, sugar, and egg and whisk until smooth, scraping the sides of the bowl to mix the ingredients thoroughly. Pour the biscuit batter into the center of the baking dish over the fruit and cheese. The batter will not go all the way to the sides, allowing some fruit to show through.

4. Bake for 40 to 45 minutes, until golden brown. The finished cobbler will be smooth and cakelike on top.

Substitution tip: Strawberries, apricots, apples, or pears can be substituted for the peaches. Raspberries, blackberries, or strawberries can be substituted for the blueberries. Chèvre cheese may be substituted for *mizithra* cheese if you can't find it.

PER SERVING: Calories: 323; Total Fat: 15g; Saturated Fat: 3g; Protein: 5g; Total Carbs: 45g; Fiber: 2g; Sodium: 252mg

Holiday Menus

The Greek Wedding Menu

Forget squeezing into a svelte dress when going to a Greek wedding, knowing you'll be treated to the food and festivities of a lifetime. Weddings begin at sundown—eating, dancing, drinking ouzo with plenty of "OPAs!"—repeat until dawn. Your cheeks may hurt from smiling, but you won't feel like you've eaten the colossal amount of food you have, because you'll have danced those calories away, whether you know anyone at the party or not!

MEZZE
- *Phyllo Krotides* / Phyllo Crackers (page 24)
- *Strangisto Yiaourti Tiri* / Greek Yogurt Cheese (page 26)
- *Kalamata Elia Mezze* / Kalamata Olive Spread (page 29)
- *Den Ine Y Dika Sou Yiayia's Tzatziki* / Not Your *Yiayia's* Tzatziki (page 23)
- *Horiatiki Salata* / Greek Country Salad (page 55)

MAINS
- *Pastitsio* / Baked Pasta with Meat Sauce (page 80)
- *Gemisto Olokliro Kotopoulo* / Stuffed Whole Chicken (page 182)

DESSERTS
- *Kourambiedes* / Shortbread Cookies (page 197)
- *Koulouria* / Greek Coffee Cookie (page 203)
- *Den Ine To Baklava Tis Miteras Sas* / Not Your Mother's Baklava (page 198)

New Year's Day Menu

Epiphany (Day of the Enlightenment, January 6), is a major Greek Orthodox holiday, when special *Kalandas* (carols) are sung honoring the creation of the world and her waters, ending with the celebration of the baptism of Jesus. To *Neo Hrono* (the New Year) often is the largest family gathering of the year, the biggest gift being time together with *yiayia*, *papou*, and extended family, relishing loving conversation and the comfort foods of winter.

Vasilopita / Greek Holiday Bread (page 191) is a must—bury a silver coin wrapped in foil in the dough before baking. Cut the entire loaf, offering a piece for each person in the family, as well as a designated piece for God and the homestead. The person who receives the coin will have special good luck for the entire year.

MEZZE
- *Throumpi Baklava* / Savory Baklava Rolls (page 36)
- *Feta-Kalamata Apogymnomena Avga* / Feta-Kalamata Deviled Eggs (page 35)

SOUP
- *Avgolemono* / Egg-Lemon Chicken Soup (page 46)

MAINS
- *Stifado* / Beef Stew (page 165)
- *Hirino Kreas me Glyko* / Pork Tenderloin with Sweet Fruit Glaze (page 172)
- *Makaronada* / Pasta with Meat Sauce (page 79)

SIDES
- *Spanakorizo* / Spinach Rice (page 85)
- *Gigandes Plaki* / Braised Giant Beans in Tomato Sauce (page 71)

DESSERT
- *Efkolo Halva* / Easy Halva (page 210)
- *Karidopita* / Greek Walnut Cake (page 206)
- *Den Ine To Baklava Tis Miteras Sas* / Not Your Mother's Baklava (page 198)

Christmas Menu

Christmas in a Greek household has evolved throughout the generations to take on similar traditions as the rest of the West. People sing carols, indulge in sweets, and feast on Christmas Day because they were supposed to be fasting for the 40 days leading up to it. *Christopsomo* or "Christ Bread" is similar to a *vasilopita* and is a traditional fixture for the Greek table. Slaughtering hogs is typically done in the winter in Greece, so a warm and comforting braise is the perfect centerpiece for the Greek Christmas table.

MEZZE

- *Strangisto Yiaourti Tiri* / Greek Yogurt Cheese (page 26)
- *Htipiti* / Roasted Red Pepper and Feta Cheese Dip (page 32)
- *Phyllo Krotides* / Phyllo Crackers (page 24)

SOUP

- *Avgolemono* / Egg-Lemon Chicken Soup (page 46)

SALAD

- *Salata me Roka, Portokali, Maratho, kai Rodi* / Arugula Salad with Oranges, Fennel, and Pomegranate (page 53)

MAIN

- *Hirino me Damaskina kai Syka* / Braised Pork Shoulder with Plums and Figs (page 170)

SIDES

- *Pilaffi me Fides* / Rice Pilaf with Vermicelli (page 86)
- *Gigandes Plaki* / Braised Giant Beans in Tomato Sauce (page 71)
- *Spanakopita* / Spinach Pie (page 103)

DESSERTS

- *Karidopita* / Greek Walnut Cake (page 206)
- *Vasilopita* / Greek Holiday Bread (page 191)
- *Kourambiedes* / Shortbread Cookies (page 197)
- *Den Ine To Baklava Tis Miteras Sas* / Not Your Mother's Baklava (page 198)

Easter Menu

The most important of all the Greek holidays usually conjures the biggest feast as well. Greek Easter is preceded by Great Lent, a period of 40 days of fasting and prayers. On midnight of Easter Sunday, Greeks proclaim Christ's resurrection, and that is followed by a bowl of *magiritsa* and the cracking of red eggs—Greeks dye eggs red to signify the blood of Jesus Christ.

Easter Sunday proper is a day of feasting, and lamb, signifying Christ's sacrifice for His people, is the centerpiece of the feast. Larger affairs will roast a whole lamb or two, while more intimate parties will roast a leg. The rest of the feast is filled in with spreads of mezze, spring vegetables, and countless desserts.

MEZZE

- *Kalamata Elia Mezze* / Kalamata Olive Spread (page 29)
- Avocado *Skordalia* / Avocado Garlic Spread (page 34)
- *Phyllo Krotides* / Phyllo Crackers (page 24)
- Tomato *Diples* / Tomato Foldover (page 38)

SOUP

- *Mock Magiritsa* / Easter Lamb Soup (page 48)

SALAD

- *Salata me Sparangi, Arakas, kai Avgo Pose* / Asparagus Salad with Peas and Poached Egg (page 58)

MAIN

- *Gemisto Podi Arniou* / Stuffed Leg of Lamb (page 158)

SIDES

- *Spanakorizo* / Spinach Rice (page 85)
- *Aginares me Patates sto Fourno* / Roasted Artichokes and Potatoes (page 111)

DESSERT

- *Eliniki Frouta Cobbler* / Greekified Cobbler (page 213)
- *Kourambiedes* / Shortbread Cookies (page 197)
- *Vasilopita* / Greek Holiday Bread (page 191)
- *Koulouria* / Greek Coffee Cookie (page 203)

Glossary

AVGOLEMONO: A sauce of beaten eggs and lemon used in soup—especially avgolemono soup—or to dress meats and vegetables.

BASIL: The Greek "globe" varietal basil is a natural accompaniment to tomatoes in sauces and salads. As with Greek oregano, use the authentic globe varietal.

CINNAMON: In Greek cooking, this warming spice is used not only in desserts but also in meat sauces.

DILL: An essential Greek herb with an earthy quality, used in everything from sauces to dips and pies.

EXTRA-VIRGIN OLIVE OIL: Less than 1 percent acidic, certified by the International Olive Council.

FDA: Food and Drug Administration, operated by the U.S. federal government.

FETA: A soft Greek sheep's- or goat's-milk cheese preserved in brine.

FOND: Those delicious browned bits left in the bottom of the pan when roasting or sautéing; often deglazed by adding liquid to the hot pan, and scraping and stirring them into the dish or a sauce for flavor.

GRAVIERA: A semihard sheep's-milk (cow's-milk on Naxos) cheese made in different variations throughout Greece with a taste and texture similar to Gruyère.

GREEK COFFEE: Traditionally brewed in a long-handled open kettle and often served mid- to late morning and, again, after the midday nap.

GREEK YOGURT: Made from sheep's, goat's, or cow's milk; thick and rich. Authentic Greek yogurt is naturally thick and does not use thickening additives.

HALLOUMI: Semihard cheese from Cyprus with an elastic texture that is either grilled or served fresh, and can be eaten along with or incorporated into salads and other dishes.

HONEY: One of the original sweeteners used in Greek cuisine; evidence of its use dates back to Minoan times.

IOC: The International Olive Council is an intergovernmental organization bringing together olive oil and table olive producers as an informational gateway for consumers.

KASSERI: Hard cow's-milk cheese similar to Asiago or Parmesan.

KEFALOTIRI: A hard, salty white cheese made from sheep's and goat's milk.

KEFALOGRAVIERA: A hard, salty cheese made predominantly from sheep's milk, but can also contain a small percentage of goat's milk; a cross between *kefalotiri* and Graviera.

KORONEIKI: Tiny olive varietal, high in oil content, indigenous to Crete.

METAXA: Greek brandy made from dry white and Muscat wines, aged in oak casks.

MEZZETHES (MEZZE): appetizers; small bites of food served as a snack or before a meal. Common mezzethes are cheese, olives, and dips.

MINT: An essential aromatic herb in Greek cooking, commonly used to flavor a variety of pies, meatballs, and stuffing.

MIZITHRA: A sheep's- or goat's-milk cheese made from milk and whey in a similar process to making ricotta, except the outcome is a harder cheese.

OREGANO: Greek oregano is the most common herb used in Greek cuisine. Using Italian or Mexican oregano will not impart the same flavors; use the Greek varietal for the most genuine flavor.

PARSLEY: A common Greek herb with a mild flavor used to enhance and garnish a variety of dishes.

PHYLLO: Thin layers of pastry dough used for pitas and desserts by brushing with olive oil or butter.

PLAKI: A dish cooked in the oven with onions, tomatoes, and olive oil.

PSAROSOUPA/KAKAVIA: A traditional fish soup that has been made by fishermen in Greece since ancient times.

RAKI: A clear, distilled spirit made from the mash of the grapes after wine production. It is called *tsipouro* in other parts of Greece and *raki* or *tsikoudia* on Crete. It should not be confused with Turkish *raki*, which has an aniseed flavor similar to ouzo. The people of Crete drink *raki* with mezze in the early evening and after dinner, to calm the stomach and mind.

SAGANAKI: Commonly known as fried cheese, *saganaki* is also the term for the shallow dish in which any *saganaki* is served.

SCORE: To precut; score your phyllo pies before you bake them so you can easily divide it into pieces without damaging the cooked flaky crust.

STAKA: A cheeselike product from Crete created from making a roux from the milk solids derived from clarifying butter.

TEMPERING: Bringing your ingredients up to a desired temperature. This is commonly used in Greek cooking with an *avgolemono* sauce.

XINOMIZITHRA: A tangy, soft, creamy sheep's- or goat's-milk cheese with a similar texture to ricotta but more sour.

YOUVETSI/GIOUVETSID: Typically, a braise of meat in a tomato-based sauce served over pasta or rice. The name is derived from the historical clay vessel used to make it.

The Dirty Dozen & the Clean Fifteen

The Environmental Working Group (EWG) is a nonprofit, nonpartisan organization dedicated to protecting human health and the environment. Its mission is to empower people to live healthier lives in a healthier environment. This organization publishes an annual list of the twelve kinds of produce, in sequence, that have the highest amount of pesticide residue—the Dirty Dozen—as well as a list of the fifteen kinds of produce that have the least amount of pesticide residue—the Clean Fifteen).

THE DIRTY DOZEN

The Dirty Dozen includes the following produce. These are considered among this year's most important produce to buy organically:

1. Strawberries
2. Apples
3. Nectarines
4. Peaches
5. Celery
6. Grapes
7. Cherries
8. Spinach
9. Tomatoes
10. Bell peppers
11. Cherry tomatoes
12. Cucumbers
    + Kale/collard greens*
    + Hot peppers*

*The Dirty Dozen list contains two additional items—kale/collard greens and hot peppers—because they tend to contain trace levels of highly hazardous pesticides.

THE CLEAN FIFTEEN

The least critical to buy organically are the Clean Fifteen list. The following are on the list:

1. Avocados
2. Corn
3. Pineapples
4. Cabbage
5. Sweet peas
6. Onions
7. Asparagus
8. Mangos
9. Papayas
10. Kiwi
11. Eggplant
12. Honeydew
13. Grapefruit
14. Cantaloupe
15. Cauliflower

Appendix B
Conversion Tables

VOLUME EQUIVALENTS (LIQUID)

US Standard	US Standard (ounces)	Metric (approximate)
2 tablespoons	1 fl. oz.	30 mL
¼ cup	2 fl. oz.	60 mL
½ cup	4 fl. oz.	120 mL
1 cup	8 fl. oz.	240 mL
1½ cups	12 fl. oz.	355 mL
2 cups or 1 pint	16 fl. oz.	475 mL
4 cups or 1 quart	32 fl. oz.	1 L
1 gallon	128 fl. oz.	4 L

OVEN TEMPERATURES

Fahrenheit (F)	Celsius (C) (approximate)
250°F	120°C
300°F	150°C
325°F	165°C
350°F	180°C
375°F	190°C
400°F	200°C
425°F	220°C
450°F	230°C

VOLUME EQUIVALENTS (DRY)

US Standard	Metric (approximate)
⅛ teaspoon	0.5 mL
¼ teaspoon	1 mL
½ teaspoon	2 mL
¾ teaspoon	4 mL
1 teaspoon	5 mL
1 tablespoon	15 mL
¼ cup	59 mL
⅓ cup	79 mL
½ cup	118 mL
⅔ cup	156 mL
¾ cup	177 mL
1 cup	235 mL
2 cups or 1 pint	475 mL
3 cups	700 mL
4 cups or 1 quart	1 L

WEIGHT EQUIVALENTS

US Standard	Metric (approximate)
½ ounce	15 g
1 ounce	30 g
2 ounces	60 g
4 ounces	115 g
8 ounces	225 g
12 ounces	340 g
16 ounces or 1 pound	455 g

Recipe Index

A

Agapimeni Salata Tis
     Oikogeneias, 64–65
Aginares me Patates sto
     Fourno, 111
Arni Psito, 161–162
Arugula Salad with
     Oranges, Fennel, and
     Pomegranate, 53
Asparagus Salad with Peas and
     Poached Egg, 58–59
Atmismena Mydia me
     Aspri Crassi kai
     Maratho, 148–150
Avgolemono, 46–47
Avocado Garlic Spread, 34
Avocado Skordalia, 34

B

Baked Pasta with Meat
     Sauce, 80–81
Baked Zucchini Patties, 96
Beef Stew, 165–166
Braised Chicken with Tomato
     Sauce and Spices, 186–187
Braised Giant Beans in Tomato
     Sauce, 71–72
Braised Lamb or Beef with Spiced
     Tomato Sauce, 163–164
Braised Pork Shoulder with
     Plums and Figs, 170–171
Butternut Squash and Hazelnut
     Pasta, 77–78

C

Cabbage Rolls Greek
     Style, 118–119
Chortofagos Moussaka, 92–94
Country-Style Layered
     Dish, 179–180
Cretan Kreatopita, 174–176
Crispy Greek Fried Eggplant and
     Zucchini, 112–113

D

Den Ine To Baklava Tis Miteras
     Sas, 198–199
Den Ine Y Dika Sou Yiayia's
     Tzatziki, 23
Dolmathes me Frankostafyla kai
     Koukounari, 108–110
Drosistikos Karpouzi Soupa, 43

E

Easter Lamb Soup, 48–49
Easy Halva, 210–212
The Easy Greek, 117
I Efkoli Elliniki, 117
Efkolo Halva, 210–212
Egg-Lemon Chicken Soup, 46–47
Eggplant Dip, 30–31
Eggplant Slippers, 100–101
Eleaolado Pagoto me
     Feta, Kanelli, kai
     Vasiliko, 194–196
Eliniki Frouta Cobbler, 213–215
Ellinika Biftekia, 177–178
Elliniki Yiaourti Metaxa
     Keik, 208–209
Elliniko Kokteil Garides, 136

F

Fakes, 52
Family Favorite Salad, 64–65
Fasolakia me Patates, 91
Feta Crab Cakes, 146–147
Feta-Kalamata Apogymnomena
     Avga, 35
Feta-Kalamata Deviled Eggs, 35
Feta Keik Kavourion, 146–147
Fish Soup, 50–51
Fish Steamed in Parchment
     with Tomato, Fennel, and
     Olives, 128–129
Fried Calamari, 137–138

G

Garides Santorini, 133–134
Gemisto Monacho Psari, 131–132
Gemisto Olokliro
     Kotopoulo, 182–183
Gemisto Podi Arniou, 158–160
Gigandes Plaki, 71–72
Grape Leaves Stuffed with
     Currants and Pine
     Nuts, 108–110
Greek Burgers, 177–178
Greek Coffee Cookie, 203–205
Greek Country Salad, 55
Greek Gazpacho, 44
Greek Holiday Bread, 191–193
Greekified Cobbler, 213–215
Greek Potato Salad, 62–63
Greek-Style Shrimp Cocktail, 136
Greek Walnut Cake, 206–207
Greek-y Creamed Spinach, 27
Greek Yogurt Brandy
     Cake, 208–209

Greek Yogurt Cheese, 26
Green Beans with Potatoes, 91
Grilled Rack of Lamb, 157
Grilled Whole Sea Bass, 125

H

Halloumi and Peach Summer
    Salad, 56–57
Halloumi me Rodakino Kalokeri
    Salata, 56–57
Hifias Souvlaki, 130
Hirino Kreas me Glyko, 172–173
Hirino me Damaskina kai
    Syka, 170–171
Horiatiki Frittata, 120–121
Horiatiki Gazpacho, 44
Horiatiki Stroma Piato, 179–180
Horiatiki Salata, 55
Htapodi me Patates, 143–145
Htapodi me Syka kai
    Rodákina, 141–142
Htipiti, 32

K

Kalamari Gemeista, 139–140
Kalamari Tiganites, 137–138
Kalamata Elia Mezze, 29
Kalamata Olive Spread, 29
Karidopita, 206–207
Keftedes, 167
Kolokithakia Lemoni Keik
    Elaioladou, 200–202
Kolokithokeftedes, 96
Kolokythiaki kai
    Fountoukia, 77–78
Kotopoulo Kapama, 186–187
Koulouria, 203–205
Kourambiedes, 197
Krema Spanaki, 27

L

Lahanodolmades, 118–119
Lavraki Skara, 125
Lemoni Krimidi Pita, 115–116

Lemony Onion Pie, 115–116
Lentil Soup, 52

M

Makaronada, 79
Makaronia me Domates, Garida,
    kai Vasilikos, 75
Manestra, 84
Meatballs, 167
Meat Pie, 174–176
Meikta Thalassina me Krasi kai
    Kapari, 153
Melitzana Papoutsakia, 100–101
Melitzanosalata, 30–31
Melizantes kai Kolokithakia
    Tiganites, 112–113
Mixed Seafood with Wine and
    Capers, 153
Mock Magiritsa, 48–49

N

Not Your Mother's
    Baklava, 198–199
Not Your Yiayia's Tzatziki, 23

O

Octopus with Figs and
    Peaches, 141–142
Octopus with Potatoes, 143–145
Olive Oil Ice Cream with
    Feta, Cinnamon, and
    Basil, 194–196
Orzo Pasta with Tomato, 84

P

Paidakia Skara, 157
Pan-Cooked Fish with
    Tomatoes, 126–127
Pasta Salad with Orzo, Tomato,
    Olives, and Feta, 83
Pasta with Meat Sauce, 79
Pastitsio, 80–81
Patata Salata, 62–63
Phyllo Crackers, 24

Phyllo Krotides, 24
Pilaffi me Fides, 86
Pork Souvlaki, 169
Pork Tenderloin with Sweet Fruit
    Glaze, 172–173
Psarakia Spetsiota, 126–127
Psari ston Atmo me Domata,
    Maratho, kai Eiles, 128–129
Psarosoupa, 50–51
Psiti Melitzana kai Kolokythia me
    Revithia, Xinomizithra, kai
    Vasilikos, 106–107

R

Refreshing Watermelon Soup, 43
Rice Pilaf with Vermicelli, 86
Rizi me Thalassina, 151–152
Roasted Artichokes and
    Potatoes, 111
Roasted Eggplant and Zucchini
    with Crunchy Spiced
    Chickpeas, Xinomizithra,
    and Basil, 106–107
Roasted Leg of Lamb, 101–102
Roasted Red Pepper and Feta
    Cheese Dip, 32

S

Salata me Kritharaki, Domates,
    Elies, kai Feta, 83
Salata me Roka, Portokali,
    Maratho, kai Rodi, 53
Salata me Sparangi, Arakas, kai
    Avgo Pose, 58–59
Savory Baklava Rolls, 36–37
Seafood Rice, 151–152
Shortbread Cookies, 197
Shrimp Santorini, 133–134
Skioufikta me Manitaria kai
    Kotopoulo, 74
Skioufikta with Wild Mushrooms
    and Chicken, 74
Souvlaki, 169

Spaghetti with Tomato, Shrimp, and Basil, 75
Spanakopita, 103–105
Spanakorizo, 85
Spinach and Feta Stuffed Chicken Breasts, 185
Spinach Pie, 103–105
Spinach Rice, 85
Steamed Mussels with White Wine and Fennel, 148–150
Stifado, 165–166
Stithos Kotopoulo Gemisto me Spanaki kai Feta, 185
Strangisto Yiaourti Tiri, 26
Stuffed Leg of Lamb, 158–160
Stuffed Monkfish, 131–132
Stuffed Squid, 139–140

Stuffed Tomatoes with Quinoa, 95
Stuffed Whole Chicken, 182–183
Swordfish Souvlaki, 130

T

Theo's Eliniki Salata Kipou, 60–61
Theo's Garden Greek Salad, 60–61
Throumpi Baklava, 36–37
Tomato Diples, 38–39
Tomato Foldover, 38–39
Tourlou, 98–99

V

Vasilopita, 191–193
Vegetable Medley, 98–99
Vegetable Moussaka, 92–94
Village Frittata, 120–121

W

Warm Harvest Salad, 66

Y

Yemista me Kinoa Pligouri, 95
Youvetsi, 163–164

Z

Zesti Salata Synkomidís, 66
Zucchini Lemon Olive Oil Cake, 200–202

Index

A

Almond milk
 Zucchini Lemon Olive Oil
  Cake (Kolokithakia Lemoni
  Keik Elaioladou), 200–202
Almonds
 Avocado Garlic Spread
  (Avocado Skordalia), 34
 Greek Holiday Bread
  (Vasilopita), 191–193
 Kalamata Olive Spread
  (Kalamata Elia Mezze), 29
 Rice Pilaf with Vermicelli
  (Pilaffi me Fides), 86
Apostolis Restaurant
 (Chania, Crete), 56
Artichokes
 The Easy Greek (I Efkoli
  Elliniki), 117
 Roasted Artichokes and
  Potatoes (Aginares me
  Patates sto Fourno), 111
 Stuffed Whole Chicken
  (Gemisto Olokliro
  Kotopoulo), 182–183
Arugula
 Arugula Salad with Oranges,
  Fennel, and Pomegranate
  (Salata me Roka, Portokali,
  Maratho,
  kai Rodi), 53
Asparagus
 Asparagus Salad with Peas
  and Poached Egg (Salata
  me Sparangi, Arakas, kai
  Avgo Pose), 58–59
Avocados
 Avocado Garlic Spread
  (Avocado Skordalia), 34

Theo's Garden Greek Salad
  (Theo's Eliniki Salata
  Kipou), 60–61
 Village Frittata (Horiatiki
  Frittata), 120–121

B

Baking, 16, 39
Basil
 about, 12, 14
 Beef Stew (Stifado), 165–166
 Crispy Greek Fried Eggplant
  and Zucchini (Melizantes
  kai Kolokithakia
  Tiganites), 112–113
 Kalamata Olive Spread
  (Kalamata Elia Mezze), 29
 Not Your Yiayia's Tzatziki
  (Den Ine Y Dika Sou
  Yiayia's Tzatziki), 23
 Olive Oil Ice Cream with
  Feta, Cinnamon, and
  Basil (Eleaolado Pagoto
  me Feta, Kanelli, kai
  Vasiliko), 194–196
 Pork Tenderloin with Sweet
  Fruit Glaze (Hirino Kreas
  me Glyko), 172–173
 Roasted Eggplant and
  Zucchini with Crunchy
  Spiced Chickpeas,
  Xinomizithra, and Basil
  (Psiti Melitzana kai
  Kolokythia me Revithia,
  Xinomizithra, kai
  Vasilikos), 106–107

Spaghetti with Tomato,
  Shrimp, and Basil
  (Makaronia me Domates,
  Garida, kai Vasilikos), 75
 Stuffed Monkfish (Gemisto
  Monacho Psari), 131–132
 Stuffed Squid (Kalamari
  Gemeista), 139–140
 Theo's Garden Greek Salad
  (Theo's Eliniki Salata
  Kipou), 60–61
Beans and legumes. See specific
Beef
 Baked Pasta with Meat Sauce
  (Pastitsio), 80–81
 Beef Stew (Stifado), 165–166
 Braised Lamb or Beef with
  Spiced Tomato Sauce
  (Youvetsi), 163–164
 Country-Style Layered
  Dish (Horiatiki Stroma
  Piato), 179–180
 Greek Burgers (Ellinika
  Biftekia), 177–178
 Meatballs (Keftedes), 167
 Meat Pie (Cretan
  Kreatopita), 174–176
 Pasta with Meat Sauce
  (Makaronada), 79
Beets
 Theo's Garden Greek Salad
  (Theo's Eliniki Salata
  Kipou), 60–61
Bell peppers
 Beef Stew (Stifado), 165–166
 Feta Crab Cakes (Feta Keik
  Kavourion), 146–147
 Greek Gazpacho (Horiatiki
  Gazpacho), 44

Bell peppers, *continued*
Greek Potato Salad
(Patata Salata), 62–63
Kalamata Olive Spread
(Kalamata Elia Mezze), 29
Pasta Salad with Orzo, Tomato,
Olives, and Feta (Salata me
Kritharaki, Domates, Elies,
kai Feta), 83
Pork Souvlaki (Souvlaki), 169
Roasted Red Pepper and Feta
Cheese Dip (Htipiti), 32
Savory Baklava Rolls
(Throumpi Baklava), 36–37
Stuffed Leg of Lamb (Gemisto
Podi Arniou), 158–160
Stuffed Whole Chicken
(Gemisto Olokliro
Kotopoulo), 182–183
Vegetable Medley
(Tourlou), 98–99
Blenders, 14
Blueberries
Greekified Cobbler (Eliniki
Frouta Cobbler), 213–215
Braising, 16
Breakfast, 19

C

Cabbage
Cabbage Rolls Greek Style
(Lahanodolmades), 118–119
Cantaloupe
Family Favorite Salad
(Agapimeni Salata Tis
Oikogeneias), 64–65
Capers
Fish Steamed in Parchment
with Tomato, Fennel, and
Olives (Psari ston Atmo
me Domata, Maratho, kai
Eiles), 128–129

Mixed Seafood with Wine and
Capers (Meikta Thalassina
me Krasi kai
Kapari), 153
Pasta Salad with Orzo, Tomato,
Olives, and Feta (Salata me
Kritharaki, Domates, Elies,
kai Feta), 83
Spinach and Feta Stuffed
Chicken Breasts (Stithos
Kotopoulo Gemisto me
Spanaki kai Feta), 185
Carrots
Baked Pasta with Meat Sauce
(Pastitsio), 80–81
Braised Chicken with
Tomato Sauce and
Spices (Kotopoulo
Kapama), 186–187
Braised Giant Beans in
Tomato Sauce (Gigandes
Plaki), 71–72
Braised Lamb or Beef with
Spiced Tomato Sauce
(Youvetsi), 163–164
Lentil Soup (Fakes), 52
Spinach Rice (Spanakorizo), 85
Cauliflower
Vegetable Moussaka
(Chortofagos
Moussaka), 92–94
Celery
Baked Pasta with Meat Sauce
(Pastitsio), 80–81
Beef Stew (Stifado), 165–166
Braised Chicken with
Tomato Sauce and
Spices (Kotopoulo
Kapama), 186–187
Braised Giant Beans in
Tomato Sauce
(Gigandes Plaki), 71–72

Braised Lamb or Beef with
Spiced Tomato Sauce
(Youvetsi), 163–164
Easter Lamb Soup (Mock
Magiritsa), 48–49
Fish Soup (Psarosoupa), 50–51
Greek Potato Salad
(Patata Salata), 62–63
Lentil Soup (Fakes), 52
Seafood Rice (Rizi me
Thalassina), 151–152
Spinach Rice (Spanakorizo), 85
Central Greece, 4
Cheese. *See specific*
Chicken
Braised Chicken with
Tomato Sauce and
Spices (Kotopoulo
Kapama), 186–187
Egg-Lemon Chicken Soup
(Avgolemono), 46–47
Skioufikta with Wild
Mushrooms and Chicken
(Skioufikta me Manitaria
kai Kotopoulo), 74
Spinach and Feta Stuffed
Chicken Breasts (Stithos
Kotopoulo Gemisto me
Spanaki kai Feta), 185
Stuffed Whole Chicken
(Gemisto Olokliro
Kotopoulo), 182–183
Chickpeas
Roasted Eggplant and
Zucchini with Crunchy
Spiced Chickpeas,
Xinomizithra, and Basil
(Psiti Melitzana kai
Kolokythia me Revithia,
Xinomizithra, kai
Vasilikos), 106–107
Vegetable Moussaka
(Chortofagos
Moussaka), 92–94

Chiffonading, 14

Chiles
  Feta Crab Cakes (Feta Keik
    Kavourion), 146–147

Christianity, 3, 7

Christmas, 7, 219

Cilantro
  Lentil Soup (Fakes), 52

Cinnamon, 14

Crab
  Feta Crab Cakes (Feta Keik
    Kavourion), 146–147

Cream. See also Half-and-half
  Olive Oil Ice Cream with
    Feta, Cinnamon, and
    Basil (Eleaolado Pagoto
    me Feta, Kanelli, kai
    Vasiliko), 194–196
  Skioufikta with Wild
    Mushrooms and Chicken
    (Skioufikta me Manitaria
    kai Kotopoulo), 74

Cream cheese
  Spinach Pie
    (Spanakopita), 103–105
  Zucchini Lemon Olive Oil
    Cake (Kolokithakia Lemoni
    Keik Elaioladou), 200–202

Crete, 2, 5–6, 56

Cucumbers
  Greek Country Salad
    (Horiatiki Salata), 55
  Greek Gazpacho (Horiatiki
    Gazpacho), 44
  Pasta Salad with Orzo,
    Tomato, Olives, and Feta
    (Salata me Kritharaki,
    Domates, Elies, kai
    Feta), 83
  Refreshing Watermelon Soup
    (Drosistikos Karpouzi
    Soupa), 43
  Village Frittata (Horiatiki
    Frittata), 120–121

Culture, and food, 3, 7

Currants
  Grape Leaves Stuffed
    with Currants and
    Pine Nuts (Dolmathes
    me Frankostafyla kai
    Koukounari), 108–110

Cyprus, 5

D

Demeter, 2

Dill
  about, 14
  Asparagus Salad with Peas
    and Poached Egg (Salata
    me Sparangi, Arakas, kai
    Avgo Pose), 58–59
  Baked Zucchini Patties
    (Kolokithokeftedes), 96
  Crispy Greek Fried Eggplant
    and Zucchini (Melizantes
    kai Kolokithakia
    Tiganites), 112–113
  Easter Lamb Soup
    (Mock Magiritsa), 48–49
  Feta Crab Cakes (Feta Keik
    Kavourion), 146–147
  Fish Soup (Psarosoupa), 50–51
  Fried Calamari (Kalamari
    Tiganites), 137–138
  Grape Leaves Stuffed
    with Currants and
    Pine Nuts (Dolmathes
    me Frankostafyla kai
    Koukounari), 108–110
  Greek-Style Shrimp
    Cocktail (Elliniko Kokteil
    Garides), 136
  Green Beans with Potatoes
    (Fasolakia me Patates), 91
  Not Your Yiayia's Tzatziki
    (Den Ine Y Dika Sou
    Yiayia's Tzatziki), 23

Seafood Rice (Rizi me
  Thalassina), 151–152

Spinach and Feta Stuffed
  Chicken Breasts (Stithos
  Kotopoulo Gemisto me
  Spanaki kai Feta), 185

Spinach Pie
  (Spanakopita), 103–105

Spinach Rice
  (Spanakorizo), 85

Stuffed Monkfish (Gemisto
  Monacho Psari), 131–132

Dionysus, 2

Dittany, 6

Dutch ovens, 15

E

Easter, 3, 7, 48–49, 161, 191, 220

Eggplants
  Country-Style Layered
    Dish (Horiatiki Stroma
    Piato), 179–180
  Crispy Greek Fried Eggplant
    and Zucchini (Melizantes
    kai Kolokithakia
    Tiganites), 112–113
  Eggplant Dip
    (Melitzanosalata), 30–31
  Eggplant Slippers (Melitzana
    Papoutsakia), 100–101
  Roasted Eggplant and
    Zucchini with Crunchy
    Spiced Chickpeas,
    Xinomizithra, and Basil
    (Psiti Melitzana kai
    Kolokythia me Revithia,
    Xinomizithra, kai
    Vasilikos), 106–107
  Vegetable Medley
    (Tourlou), 98–99
  Vegetable Moussaka
    (Chortofagos
    Moussaka), 92–94

Eggs
  Asparagus Salad with Peas and
    Poached Egg (Salata me
    Sparangi, Arakas, kai Avgo
    Pose), 58–59
  Baked Pasta with Meat Sauce
    (Pastitsio), 80–81
  Easter Lamb Soup (Mock
    Magiritsa), 48–49
  The Easy Greek
    (I Efkoli Elliniki), 117
  Egg-Lemon Chicken Soup
    (Avgolemono), 46–47
  Feta-Kalamata Deviled
    Eggs (Feta-Kalamata
    Apogymnomena Avga), 35
  Greek Holiday Bread
    (Vasilopita), 191–193
  Lemony Onion Pie (Lemoni
    Krimidi Pita), 115–116
  Meat Pie (Cretan
    Kreatopita), 174–176
  Spinach Pie
    (Spanakopita), 103–105
  Theo's Garden Greek Salad
    (Theo's Eliniki Salata
    Kipou), 60–61
  Village Frittata (Horiatiki
    Frittata), 120–121
Equipment, 14–15

F
Farmer, Fannie, 35
Fasting, 3
Fats, 7–9
Fava beans
  The Easy Greek
    (I Efkoli Elliniki), 117
Feasting, 3, 7, 217–220
Fennel
  Arugula Salad with Oranges,
    Fennel, and Pomegranate
    (Salata me Roka, Portokali,
    Maratho, kai Rodi), 53

Easter Lamb Soup (Mock
    Magiritsa), 48–49
Feta Crab Cakes (Feta Keik
    Kavourion), 146–147
Fish Steamed in Parchment
    with Tomato, Fennel, and
    Olives (Psari ston Atmo me
    Domata, Maratho,
    kai Eiles), 128–129
Octopus with Potatoes
    (Htapodi me
    Patates), 143–145
Steamed Mussels with
    White Wine and Fennel
    (Atmismena Mydia
    me Aspri Crassi kai
    Maratho), 148–150
Feta cheese
  Baked Zucchini Patties
    (Kolokithokeftedes), 96
  Country-Style Layered
    Dish (Horiatiki Stroma
    Piato), 179–180
  The Easy Greek
    (I Efkoli Elliniki), 117
  Feta Crab Cakes (Feta Keik
    Kavourion), 146–147
  Feta-Kalamata Deviled
    Eggs (Feta-Kalamata
    Apogymnomena Avga), 35
  Greek Burgers (Ellinika
    Biftekia), 177–178
  Greek Country Salad (Horiatiki
    Salata), 55
  Greek Gazpacho
    (Horiatiki Gazpacho), 44
  Olive Oil Ice Cream with
    Feta, Cinnamon, and
    Basil (Eleaolado Pagoto
    me Feta, Kanelli, kai
    Vasiliko), 194–196

Pasta Salad with Orzo, Tomato,
    Olives, and Feta (Salata me
    Kritharaki, Domates, Elies,
    kai Feta), 83
Roasted Red Pepper and Feta
    Cheese Dip (Htipiti), 32
Savory Baklava Rolls
    (Throumpi Baklava), 36–37
Shrimp Santorini (Garides
    Santorini), 133–134
Spinach and Feta Stuffed
    Chicken Breasts (Stithos
    Kotopoulo Gemisto me
    Spanaki kai Feta), 185
Spinach Pie
    (Spanakopita), 103–105
Stuffed Monkfish (Gemisto
    Monacho Psari), 131–132
Theo's Garden Greek Salad
    (Theo's Eliniki Salata
    Kipou), 60–61
Tomato Foldover
    (Tomato Diples), 38–39
Village Frittata (Horiatiki
    Frittata), 120–121
Figs
  Braised Pork Shoulder with
    Plums and Figs (Hirino
    me Damaskina kai
    Syka), 170–171
  Octopus with Figs and Peaches
    (Htapodi me Syka kai
    Rodákina), 141–142
  Theo's Garden Greek Salad
    (Theo's Eliniki Salata
    Kipou), 60–61
Fish
  Fish Soup (Psarosoupa), 50–51
  Fish Steamed in Parchment
    with Tomato, Fennel, and
    Olives (Psari ston Atmo
    me Domata, Maratho, kai
    Eiles), 128–129

Grilled Whole Sea Bass (Lavraki Skara), 125
Pan-Cooked Fish with Tomatoes (Psarakia Spetsiota), 126–127
Stuffed Monkfish (Gemisto Monacho Psari), 131–132
sustainable, 51
Swordfish Souvlaki (Hifias Souvlaki), 130
Flaounes, 5
Flavor combinations, 13
Food processors, 14
Food storage, 17
Fruits. See also specific
Pork Tenderloin with Sweet Fruit Glaze (Hirino Kreas me Glyko), 172–173
Frying, 113
Funerals, 7

G
Garlic
Asparagus Salad with Peas and Poached Egg (Salata me Sparangi, Arakas, kai Avgo Pose), 58–59
Avocado Garlic Spread (Avocado Skordalia), 34
Baked Pasta with Meat Sauce (Pastitsio), 80–81
Baked Zucchini Patties (Kolokithokeftedes), 96
Beef Stew (Stifado), 165–166
Braised Chicken with Tomato Sauce and Spices (Kotopoulo Kapama), 186–187
Braised Giant Beans in Tomato Sauce (Gigandes Plaki), 71–72
Braised Lamb or Beef with Spiced Tomato Sauce (Youvetsi), 163–164

Butternut Squash and Hazelnut Pasta (Kolokythiaki kai Fountoukia), 77–78
Cabbage Rolls Greek Style (Lahanodolmades), 118–119
Eggplant Dip (Melitzanosalata), 30–31
Eggplant Slippers (Melitzana Papoutsakia), 100–101
Fish Steamed in Parchment with Tomato, Fennel, and Olives (Psari ston Atmo me Domata, Maratho, kai Eiles), 128–129
Greek Gazpacho (Horiatiki Gazpacho), 44
Greek Potato Salad (Patata Salata), 62–63
Greek-Style Shrimp Cocktail (Elliniko Kokteil Garides), 136
Greek-y Creamed Spinach (Krema Spanaki), 27
Green Beans with Potatoes (Fasolakia me Patates), 91
Grilled Rack of Lamb (Paidakia Skara), 157
Grilled Whole Sea Bass (Lavraki Skara), 125
Kalamata Olive Spread (Kalamata Elia Mezze), 29
Lentil Soup (Fakes), 52
Meatballs (Keftedes), 167
Not Your Yiayia's Tzatziki (Den Ine Y Dika Sou Yiayia's Tzatziki), 23
Octopus with Potatoes (Htapodi me Patates), 143–145
Orzo Pasta with Tomato (Manestra), 84
Pan-Cooked Fish with Tomatoes (Psarakia Spetsiota), 126–127

Pasta with Meat Sauce (Makaronada), 79
Roasted Leg of Lamb (Arni Psito), 161–162
Roasted Red Pepper and Feta Cheese Dip (Htipiti), 32
roasting, 34
Seafood Rice (Rizi me Thalassina), 151–152
Shrimp Santorini (Garides Santorini), 133–134
Skioufikta with Wild Mushrooms and Chicken (Skioufikta me Manitaria kai Kotopoulo), 74
Spaghetti with Tomato, Shrimp, and Basil (Makaronia me Domates, Garida, kai Vasilikos), 75
Spinach and Feta Stuffed Chicken Breasts (Stithos Kotopoulo Gemisto me Spanaki kai Feta), 185
Spinach Rice (Spanakorizo), 85
Steamed Mussels with White Wine and Fennel (Atmismena Mydia me Aspri Crassi kai Maratho), 148–150
Stuffed Leg of Lamb (Gemisto Podi Arniou), 158–160
Stuffed Squid (Kalamari Gemeista), 139–140
Stuffed Tomatoes with Quinoa (Yemista me Kinoa Pligouri), 95
Tomato Foldover (Tomato Diples), 38–39
Vegetable Medley (Tourlou), 98–99
Vegetable Moussaka (Chortofagos Moussaka), 92–94

Gluten-free recipes
  Arugula Salad with Oranges,
      Fennel, and Pomegranate
      (Salata me Roka, Portokali,
      Maratho,
      kai Rodi), 53
  Asparagus Salad with Peas
      and Poached Egg (Salata
      me Sparangi, Arakas, kai
      Avgo Pose), 58–59
  Avocado Garlic Spread
      (Avocado Skordalia), 34
  Beef Stew (Stifado), 165–166
  Braised Chicken with
      Tomato Sauce and
      Spices (Kotopoulo
      Kapama), 186–187
  Braised Giant Beans in
      Tomato Sauce
      (Gigandes Plaki), 71–72
  Braised Lamb or Beef with
      Spiced Tomato Sauce
      (Youvetsi), 163–164
  Braised Pork Shoulder with
      Plums and Figs (Hirino
      me Damaskina kai
      Syka), 170–171
  Cabbage Rolls Greek Style
      (Lahanodolmades), 118–119
  Easter Lamb Soup (Mock
      Magiritsa), 48–49
  The Easy Greek
      (I Efkoli Elliniki), 117
  Eggplant Dip
      (Melitzanosalata), 30–31
  Family Favorite Salad
      (Agapimeni Salata Tis
      Oikogeneias), 64–65
  Feta-Kalamata Deviled
      Eggs (Feta-Kalamata
      Apogymnomena Avga), 35
  Fish Soup (Psarosoupa), 50–51

Fish Steamed in Parchment
      with Tomato, Fennel, and
      Olives (Psari ston Atmo me
      Domata, Maratho,
      kai Eiles), 128–129
  Fried Calamari (Kalamari
      Tiganites), 137–138
  Grape Leaves Stuffed
      with Currants and
      Pine Nuts (Dolmathes
      me Frankostafyla kai
      Koukounari), 108–110
  Greek Burgers (Ellinika
      Biftekia), 177–178
  Greek Country Salad
      (Horiatiki Salata), 55
  Greek Gazpacho
      (Horiatiki Gazpacho), 44
  Greek Potato Salad
      (Patata Salata), 62–63
  Greek-Style Shrimp Cocktail
      (Elliniko Kokteil
      Garides), 136
  Greek-y Creamed Spinach
      (Krema Spanaki), 27
  Greek Yogurt Cheese
      (Strangisto
      Yiaourti Tiri), 26
  Green Beans with Potatoes
      (Fasolakia me Patates), 91
  Grilled Rack of Lamb
      (Paidakia Skara), 157
  Grilled Whole Sea Bass
      (Lavraki Skara), 125
  Halloumi and Peach Summer
      Salad (Halloumi me
      Rodakino Kalokeri
      Salata), 56–57
  Kalamata Olive Spread
      (Kalamata Elia Mezze), 29
  Lentil Soup (Fakes), 52

Mixed Seafood with Wine and
      Capers (Meikta Thalassina
      me Krasi kai
      Kapari), 153
  Not Your Yiayia's Tzatziki
      (Den Ine Y Dika Sou
      Yiayia's Tzatziki), 23
  Octopus with Figs and
      Peaches (Htapodi me Syka
      kai Rodákina), 141–142
  Octopus with Potatoes
      (Htapodi me
      Patates), 143–145
  Olive Oil Ice Cream with
      Feta, Cinnamon, and
      Basil (Eleaolado Pagoto
      me Feta, Kanelli, kai
      Vasiliko), 194–196
  Orzo Pasta with Tomato
      (Manestra), 84
  Pork Souvlaki (Souvlaki), 169
  Pork Tenderloin with Sweet
      Fruit Glaze (Hirino Kreas
      me Glyko), 172–173
  Refreshing Watermelon Soup
      (Drosistikos Karpouzi
      Soupa), 43
  Roasted Leg of Lamb
      (Arni Psito), 161–162
  Roasted Red Pepper and Feta
      Cheese Dip (Htipiti), 32
  Seafood Rice (Rizi me
      Thalassina), 151–152
  Shrimp Santorini (Garides
      Santorini), 133–134
  Spinach and Feta Stuffed
      Chicken Breasts (Stithos
      Kotopoulo Gemisto me
      Spanaki kai Feta), 185
  Spinach Rice
      (Spanakorizo), 85

Steamed Mussels with
White Wine and Fennel
(Atmismena Mydia
me Aspri Crassi kai
Maratho), 148–150
Stuffed Leg of Lamb (Gemisto
Podi Arniou), 158–160
Stuffed Monkfish (Gemisto
Monacho Psari), 131–132
Stuffed Squid (Kalamari
Gemeista), 139–140
Stuffed Whole Chicken
(Gemisto Olokliro
Kotopoulo), 182–183
Swordfish Souvlaki
(Hifias Souvlaki), 130
Theo's Garden Greek Salad
(Theo's Eliniki Salata
Kipou), 60–61
Vegetable Medley
(Tourlou), 98–99
Vegetable Moussaka
(Chortofagos
Moussaka), 92–94
Village Frittata (Horiatiki
Frittata), 120–121
Warm Harvest Salad (Zesti
Salata Synkomidís), 66
Grape leaves
Grape Leaves Stuffed
with Currants and
Pine Nuts (Dolmathes
me Frankostafyla kai
Koukounari), 108–110
Greece
food regions of, 4–5
map, 5
Greek cuisine
cooking techniques, 14,
16–17, 113
Creten eating habits, 6
equipment used, 14–15
essential flavors, 7

flavor combinations, 13
food culture, 3, 7
history of, 2–3, 5
and the Mediterranean diet, 9
pantry staples, 12, 14
recipes, 18
Greek "diet," 8–9
Greek oregano (rigani)
about, 12
Beef Stew (Stifado), 165–166
Braised Giant Beans in
Tomato Sauce
(Gigandes Plaki), 71–72
Cabbage Rolls Greek Style
(Lahanodolmades), 118–119
Eggplant Slippers (Melitzana
Papoutsakia), 100–101
Family Favorite Salad
(Agapimeni Salata Tis
Oikogeneias), 64–65
Feta Crab Cakes (Feta Keik
Kavourion), 146–147
Feta-Kalamata Deviled
Eggs (Feta-Kalamata
Apogymnomena Avga), 35
Greek Burgers (Ellinika
Biftekia), 177–178
Greek Country Salad
(Horiatiki Salata), 55
Greek Potato Salad
(Patata Salata), 62–63
Greek-Style Shrimp Cocktail
(Elliniko Kokteil
Garides), 136
Kalamata Olive Spread
(Kalamata Elia Mezze), 29
Lemony Onion Pie (Lemoni
Krimidi Pita), 115–116
Lentil Soup (Fakes), 52
Meatballs (Keftedes), 167
Not Your Yiayia's Tzatziki
(Den Ine Y Dika Sou Yiayia's
Tzatziki), 23

Octopus with Figs and
Peaches (Htapodi me Syka
kai Rodákina), 141–142
Orzo Pasta with Tomato
(Manestra), 84
Pan-Cooked Fish with
Tomatoes (Psarakia
Spetsiota), 126–127
Pasta Salad with Orzo,
Tomato, Olives, and Feta
(Salata me Kritharaki,
Domates, Elies, kai
Feta), 83
Phyllo Crackers
(Phyllo Krotides), 24
Pork Souvlaki (Souvlaki), 169
Pork Tenderloin with Sweet
Fruit Glaze (Hirino Kreas
me Glyko), 172–173
Roasted Red Pepper and Feta
Cheese Dip (Htipiti), 32
Savory Baklava Rolls
(Throumpi Baklava), 36–37
Shrimp Santorini (Garides
Santorini), 133–134
Stuffed Leg of Lamb (Gemisto
Podi Arniou), 158–160
Stuffed Whole Chicken
(Gemisto Olokliro
Kotopoulo), 182–183
Swordfish Souvlaki
(Hifias Souvlaki), 130
Tomato Foldover
(Tomato Diples), 38–39
Village Frittata (Horiatiki
Frittata), 120–121
Greek yogurt
about, 19
Butternut Squash and
Hazelnut Pasta
(Kolokythiaki kai
Fountoukia), 77–78

Greek yogurt, *continued*
    Greek Yogurt Brandy Cake
        (Elliniki Yiaourti Metaxa
        Keik), 208–209
    Greek Yogurt Cheese
        (Strangisto
        Yiaourti Tiri), 26
    Refreshing Watermelon Soup
        (Drosistikos Karpouzi
        Soupa), 43
    Vegetable Moussaka
        (Chortofagos
        Moussaka), 92–94
    Village Frittata (Horiatiki
        Frittata), 120–121
Green beans
    Green Beans with Potatoes
        (Fasolakia me Patates), 91
Green olives
    Stuffed Monkfish (Gemisto
        Monacho Psari), 131–132
Grilling, 16
Grills, 15

H
Half-and-half
    Tomato Foldover
        (Tomato Diples), 38–39
Halloumi cheese, 5
    Halloumi and Peach Summer
        Salad (Halloumi me
        Rodakino Kalokeri
        Salata), 56–57
Hazelnuts
    Butternut Squash and
        Hazelnut Pasta
        (Kolokythiaki kai
        Fountoukia), 77–78
Holiday menus, 217–220
Honey
    about, 3
    Braised Chicken with
        Tomato Sauce and
        Spices (Kotopoulo
        Kapama), 186–187

Braised Pork Shoulder with
    Plums and Figs (Hirino
    me Damaskina kai
    Syka), 170–171
Halloumi and Peach Summer
    Salad (Halloumi me
    Rodakino Kalokeri
    Salata), 56–57
Pork Tenderloin with Sweet
    Fruit Glaze (Hirino Kreas
    me Glyko), 172–173
Hospitality, 3

I
Islands, 4

K
Kalamata olives
    The Easy Greek
        (I Efkoli Elliniki), 117
    Feta-Kalamata Deviled
        Eggs (Feta-Kalamata
        Apogymnomena Avga), 35
    Fish Steamed in Parchment
        with Tomato, Fennel, and
        Olives (Psari ston Atmo me
        Domata, Maratho,
        kai Eiles), 128–129
    Fried Calamari (Kalamari
        Tiganites), 137–138
    Greek Country Salad (Horiatiki
        Salata), 55
    Greek Potato Salad
        (Patata Salata), 62–63
    Greek-Style Shrimp Cocktail
        (Elliniko Kokteil
        Garides), 136
    Kalamata Olive Spread
        (Kalamata Elia Mezze), 29
    Not Your Yiayia's Tzatziki
        (Den Ine Y Dika Sou Yiayia's
        Tzatziki), 23

Pasta Salad with Orzo, Tomato,
    Olives, and Feta (Salata me
    Kritharaki, Domates, Elies,
    kai Feta), 83
Savory Baklava Rolls
    (Throumpi Baklava), 36–37
Shrimp Santorini (Garides
    Santorini), 133–134
Stuffed Whole Chicken
    (Gemisto Olokliro
    Kotopoulo), 182–183
Theo's Garden Greek Salad
    (Theo's Eliniki Salata
    Kipou), 60–61
Village Frittata (Horiatiki
    Frittata), 120–121
Kale
    Fish Soup (Psarosoupa), 50–51
    Warm Harvest Salad (Zesti
        Salata Synkomidís), 66
Karvouna, 15
Kasseri cheese
    Eggplant Slippers (Melitzana
        Papoutsakia), 100–101
    Family Favorite Salad
        (Agapimeni Salata Tis
        Oikogeneias), 64–65
    Phyllo Crackers
        (Phyllo Krotides), 24
    Village Frittata (Horiatiki
        Frittata), 120–121
Kefalotiri cheese
    Baked Pasta with Meat Sauce
        (Pastitsio), 80–81
    Baked Zucchini Patties
        (Kolokithokeftedes), 96
    Lemony Onion Pie (Lemoni
        Krimidi Pita), 115–116
    Pasta with Meat Sauce
        (Makaronada), 79
    Skioufikta with Wild
        Mushrooms and Chicken
        (Skioufikta me Manitaria kai
        Kotopoulo), 74

Spinach Pie
(Spanakopita), 103–105
Vegetable Moussaka
(Chortofagos
Moussaka), 92–94
Koliva, 7

L
Lamb
Braised Lamb or Beef with
Spiced Tomato Sauce
(Youvetsi), 163–164
Easter Lamb Soup (Mock
Magiritsa), 48–49
Greek Burgers (Ellinika
Biftekia), 177–178
Grilled Rack of Lamb
(Paidakia Skara), 157
Meatballs (Keftedes), 167
Roasted Leg of Lamb (Arni
Psito), 161–162
Stuffed Leg of Lamb (Gemisto
Podi Arniou), 158–160
Leeks
Lemony Onion Pie (Lemoni
Krimidi Pita), 115–116
Leftovers, 17
Lemons, lemon juice, and zest
about, 12
Asparagus Salad with Peas
and Poached Egg (Salata
me Sparangi, Arakas, kai
Avgo Pose), 58–59
Avocado Garlic Spread
(Avocado Skordalia), 34
Crispy Greek Fried Eggplant
and Zucchini (Melizantes
kai Kolokithakia
Tiganites), 112–113
Easter Lamb Soup
(Mock Magiritsa), 48–49
The Easy Greek
(I Efkoli Elliniki), 117
Egg-Lemon Chicken Soup
(Avgolemono), 46–47

Eggplant Dip
(Melitzanosalata), 30–31
Eggplant Slippers (Melitzana
Papoutsakia), 100–101
Fish Soup (Psarosoupa), 50–51
Fish Steamed in Parchment
with Tomato, Fennel, and
Olives (Psari ston Atmo me
Domata, Maratho,
kai Eiles), 128–129
Fried Calamari (Kalamari
Tiganites), 137–138
Grape Leaves Stuffed
with Currants and
Pine Nuts (Dolmathes
me Frankostafyla kai
Koukounari), 108–110
Greek Potato Salad
(Patata Salata), 62–63
Greek Walnut Cake
(Karidopita), 206–207
Green Beans with Potatoes
(Fasolakia me Patates), 91
Grilled Whole Sea Bass
(Lavraki Skara), 125
Halloumi and Peach Summer
Salad (Halloumi me
Rodakino Kalokeri
Salata), 56–57
Kalamata Olive Spread
(Kalamata Elia Mezze), 29
Lemony Onion Pie (Lemoni
Krimidi Pita), 115–116
Not Your Mother's Baklava
(Den Ine To Baklava Tis
Miteras Sas), 198–199
Octopus with Potatoes
(Htapodi me
Patates), 143–145
Pork Souvlaki (Souvlaki), 169
Refreshing Watermelon Soup
(Drosistikos Karpouzi
Soupa), 43

Roasted Artichokes and
Potatoes (Aginares me
Patates sto Fourno), 111
Roasted Leg of Lamb
(Arni Psito), 161–162
Roasted Red Pepper and Feta
Cheese Dip (Htipiti), 32
Seafood Rice (Rizi me
Thalassina), 151–152
Spaghetti with Tomato,
Shrimp, and Basil
(Makaronia me Domates,
Garida, kai Vasilikos), 75
Steamed Mussels with
White Wine and Fennel
(Atmismena Mydia
me Aspri Crassi kai
Maratho), 148–150
Stuffed Squid (Kalamari
Gemeista), 139–140
Stuffed Whole Chicken
(Gemisto Olokliro
Kotopoulo), 182–183
Swordfish Souvlaki
(Hifias Souvlaki), 130
Theo's Garden Greek Salad
(Theo's Eliniki Salata
Kipou), 60–61
Zucchini Lemon Olive Oil Cake
(Kolokithakia Lemoni Keik
Elaioladou), 200–202
Lentils
Lentil Soup (Fakes), 52
Lettuce
Family Favorite Salad
(Agapimeni Salata Tis
Oikogeneias), 64–65
Lima beans
Braised Giant Beans in
Tomato Sauce
(Gigandes Plaki), 71–72
Loukoumades, 5

M

Mahlepi, 5

Makaria, 7

Mayo clinic, 9, 17

Meat thermometers, 15

Mediterranean diet, 9

Menus, 217–220

Mezze, 21

Milk. *See also* Cream;
  Half-and-half
  Baked Pasta with Meat Sauce
    (Pastitsio), 80–81
  Butternut Squash and
    Hazelnut Pasta
    (Kolokythiaki kai
    Fountoukia), 77–78
  Crispy Greek Fried Eggplant
    and Zucchini (Melizantes
    kai Kolokithakia
    Tiganites), 112–113
  Greek Holiday Bread
    (Vasilopita), 191–193
  Greek Walnut Cake
    (Karidopita), 206–207
  Olive Oil Ice Cream with
    Feta, Cinnamon, and
    Basil (Eleaolado Pagoto
    me Feta, Kanelli, kai
    Vasiliko), 194–196

Mint
  about, 14
  Grape Leaves Stuffed
    with Currants and
    Pine Nuts (Dolmathes
    me Frankostafyla kai
    Koukounari), 108–110
  Meatballs (Keftedes), 167
  Meat Pie (Cretan
    Kreatopita), 174–176
  Refreshing Watermelon Soup
    (Drosistikos Karpouzi
    Soupa), 43
  Roasted Leg of Lamb
    (Arni Psito), 161–162
  Spinach Pie
    (Spanakopita), 103–105

Stuffed Tomatoes with
  Quinoa (Yemista me Kinoa
  Pligouri), 95

Mizithra cheese
  Greekified Cobbler (Eliniki
    Frouta Cobbler), 213–215
  Greek-y Creamed Spinach
    (Krema Spanaki), 27
  Meat Pie (Cretan
    Kreatopita), 174–176
  Warm Harvest Salad
    (Zesti Salata
    Synkomidís), 66

Mortars and pestles, 15

Mushrooms
  Beef Stew (Stifado), 165–166
  Skioufikta with Wild
    Mushrooms and Chicken
    (Skioufikta me Manitaria
    kai Kotopoulo), 74
  Stuffed Whole Chicken
    (Gemisto Olokliro
    Kotopoulo), 182–183
  Vegetable Moussaka
    (Chortofagos
    Moussaka), 92–94
  Warm Harvest Salad (Zesti
    Salata Synkomidís), 66

Mussels
  Steamed Mussels with
    White Wine and Fennel
    (Atmismena Mydia
    me Aspri Crassi kai
    Maratho), 148–150

N

New Year's Day, 7, 191, 219

Northern Greece, 4

Nut-free recipes
  Arugula Salad with Oranges,
    Fennel, and Pomegranate
    (Salata me Roka, Portokali,
    Maratho, kai Rodi), 53

Asparagus Salad with Peas
  and Poached Egg (Salata
  me Sparangi, Arakas, kai
  Avgo Pose), 58–59

Baked Pasta with Meat Sauce
  (Pastitsio), 80–81

Baked Zucchini Patties
  (Kolokithokeftedes), 96

Beef Stew (Stifado), 165–166

Braised Chicken with
  Tomato Sauce and
  Spices (Kotopoulo
  Kapama), 186–187

Braised Giant Beans in
  Tomato Sauce
  (Gigandes Plaki), 71–72

Braised Lamb or Beef with
  Spiced Tomato Sauce
  (Youvetsi), 163–164

Braised Pork Shoulder with
  Plums and Figs (Hirino
  me Damaskina kai
  Syka), 170–171

Country-Style Layered
  Dish (Horiatiki Stroma
  Piato), 179–180

Crispy Greek Fried Eggplant
  and Zucchini (Melizantes
  kai Kolokithakia
  Tiganites), 112–113

Easter Lamb Soup
  (Mock Magiritsa), 48–49

Egg-Lemon Chicken Soup
  (Avgolemono), 46–47

Eggplant Dip
  (Melitzanosalata), 30–31

Eggplant Slippers (Melitzana
  Papoutsakia), 100–101

Family Favorite Salad
  (Agapimeni Salata Tis
  Oikogeneias), 64–65

Feta Crab Cakes (Feta Keik
  Kavourion), 146–147

Feta-Kalamata Deviled
  Eggs (Feta-Kalamata
  Apogymnomena Avga), 35

Fish Soup (Psarosoupa), 50–51

Fish Steamed in Parchment with Tomato, Fennel, and Olives (Psari ston Atmo me Domata, Maratho, kai Eiles), 128–129

Fried Calamari (Kalamari Tiganites), 137–138

Greek Burgers (Ellinika Biftekia), 177–178

Greek Coffee Cookie (Koulouria), 203–205

Greek Country Salad (Horiatiki Salata), 55

Greek Gazpacho (Horiatiki Gazpacho), 44

Greekified Cobbler (Eliniki Frouta Cobbler), 213–215

Greek Potato Salad (Patata Salata), 62–63

Greek-y Creamed Spinach (Krema Spanaki), 27

Greek Yogurt Brandy Cake (Elliniki Yiaourti Metaya Keik), 208–209

Greek Yogurt Cheese (Strangisto Yiaourti Tiri), 26

Green Beans with Potatoes (Fasolakia me Patates), 91

Grilled Rack of Lamb (Paidakia Skara), 157

Grilled Whole Sea Bass (Lavraki Skara), 125

Halloumi and Peach Summer Salad (Halloumi me Rodakino Kalokeri Salata), 56–57

Lemony Onion Pie (Lemoni Krimidi Pita), 115–116

Lentil Soup (Fakes), 52

Meatballs (Keftedes), 167

Meat Pie (Cretan Kreatopita), 174–176

Mixed Seafood with Wine and Capers (Meikta Thalassina me Krasi kai Kapari), 153

Not Your Yiayia's Tzatziki (Den Ine Y Dika Sou Yiayia's Tzatziki), 23

Octopus with Figs and Peaches (Htapodi me Syka kai Rodákina), 141–142

Octopus with Potatoes (Htapodi me Patates), 143–145

Olive Oil Ice Cream with Feta, Cinnamon, and Basil (Eleaolado Pagoto me Feta, Kanelli, kai Vasiliko), 194–196

Orzo Pasta with Tomato (Manestra), 84

Pan-Cooked Fish with Tomatoes (Psarakia Spetsiota), 126–127

Pasta Salad with Orzo Tomato, Olives, and Feta (Salata me Kritharaki, Domates, Elies, kai Feta), 83

Pasta with Meat Sauce (Makaronada), 79

Phyllo Crackers (Phyllo Krotides), 24

Pork Souvlaki (Souvlaki), 169

Pork Tenderloin with Sweet Fruit Glaze (Hirino Kreas me Glyko), 172–173

Refreshing Watermelon Soup (Drosistikos Karpouzi Soupa), 43

Roasted Artichokes and Potatoes (Aginares me Patates sto Fourno), 111

Roasted Eggplant and Zucchini with Crunchy Spiced Chickpeas, Xinomizithra, and Basil (Psiti Melitzana kai Kolokythia me Revithia, Xinomizithra, kai Vasilikos), 106–107

Roasted Leg of Lamb (Arni Psito), 161–162

Roasted Red Pepper and Feta Cheese Dip (Htipiti), 32

Seafood Rice (Rizi me Thalassina), 151–152

Shortbread Cookies (Kourambiedes), 197

Shrimp Santorini (Garides Santorini), 133–134

Skioufikta with Wild Mushrooms and Chicken (Skioufikta me Manitaria kai Kotopoulo), 74

Spaghetti with Tomato, Shrimp, and Basil (Makaronia me Domates, Garida, kai Vasilikos), 75

Spinach and Feta Stuffed Chicken Breasts (Stithos Kotopoulo Gemisto me Spanaki kai Feta), 185

Spinach Pie (Spanakopita), 103–105

Spinach Rice (Spanakorizo), 85

Steamed Mussels with White Wine and Fennel (Atmismena Mydia me Aspri Crassi kai Maratho), 148–150

Stuffed Leg of Lamb (Gemisto Podi Arniou), 158–160

Stuffed Monkfish (Gemisto Monacho Psari), 131–132

Stuffed Tomatoes with Quinoa (Yemista me Kinoa Pligouri), 95

Nut-free recipes, *continued*
Stuffed Whole Chicken
(Gemisto Olokliro
Kotopoulo), 182–183
Swordfish Souvlaki
(Hifias Souvlaki), 130
Theo's Garden Greek Salad
(Theo's Eliniki Salata
Kipou), 60–61
Tomato Foldover
(Tomato Diples), 38–39
Vegetable Medley
(Tourlou), 98–99
Vegetable Moussaka
(Chortofagos
Moussaka), 92–94
Zucchini Lemon Olive Oil
Cake (Kolokithakia Lemoni
Keik Elaioladou), 200–202
Nutmeg, 180
Nuts. *See also specific*
Easy Halva (Efkolo
Halva), 210–212

O

Octopus
Octopus with Figs and
Peaches (Htapodi me Syka
kai Rodákina), 141–142
Octopus with Potatoes
(Htapodi me
Patates), 143–145
Olive oil, 6–7, 12, 17
Olives. *See* Green olives;
Kalamata olives
Onions. *See also* Scallions
Baked Pasta with Meat Sauce
(Pastitsio), 80–81
Beef Stew (Stifado), 165–166
Braised Chicken with
Tomato Sauce and
Spices (Kotopoulo
Kapama), 186–187

Braised Giant Beans in
Tomato Sauce
(Gigandes Plaki), 71–72
Braised Lamb or Beef with
Spiced Tomato Sauce
(Youvetsi), 163–164
Braised Pork Shoulder with
Plums and Figs (Hirino
me Damaskina kai
Syka), 170–171
Butternut Squash and
Hazelnut Pasta
(Kolokythiaki kai
Fountoukia), 77–78
Country-Style Layered
Dish (Horiatiki Stroma
Piato), 179–180
Eggplant Dip
(Melitzanosalata), 30–31
Greek Burgers (Ellinika
Biftekia), 177–178
Greek Country Salad
(Horiatiki Salata), 55
Greek-y Creamed Spinach
(Krema Spanaki), 27
Lemony Onion Pie (Lemoni
Krimidi Pita), 115–116
Lentil Soup (Fakes), 52
Meatballs (Keftedes), 167
Meat Pie (Cretan
Kreatopita), 174–176
Orzo Pasta with Tomato
(Manestra), 84
Pan-Cooked Fish with
Tomatoes (Psarakia
Spetsiota), 126–127
Pasta Salad with Orzo,
Tomato, Olives, and Feta
(Salata me Kritharaki,
Domates, Elies,
kai Feta), 83
Pasta with Meat Sauce
(Makaronada), 79

Pork Souvlaki (Souvlaki), 169
Roasted Red Pepper and Feta
Cheese Dip (Htipiti), 32
Seafood Rice (Rizi me
Thalassina), 151–152
Shrimp Santorini (Garides
Santorini), 133–134
Skioufikta with Wild
Mushrooms and Chicken
(Skioufikta me Manitaria
kai Kotopoulo), 74
Spinach Rice
(Spanakorizo), 85
Stuffed Squid (Kalamari
Gemeista), 139–140
Stuffed Tomatoes with
Quinoa (Yemista me Kinoa
Pligouri), 95
Swordfish Souvlaki
(Hifias Souvlaki), 130
Vegetable Medley
(Tourlou), 98–99
Vegetable Moussaka
(Chortofagos
Moussaka), 92–94
Village Frittata (Horiatiki
Frittata), 120–121
Warm Harvest Salad (Zesti
Salata Synkomidís), 66
Oranges, orange juice, and zest
Arugula Salad with Oranges,
Fennel, and Pomegranate
(Salata me Roka, Portokali,
Maratho, kai Rodi), 53
Greek Coffee Cookie
(Koulouria), 203–205
Greek Yogurt Brandy Cake
(Elliniki Yiaourti Metaxa
Keik), 208–209
Stuffed Monkfish (Gemisto
Monacho Psari), 131–132

P

Pantry staples, 12, 14
Parsley
  about, 14
  Braised Giant Beans in
    Tomato Sauce
    (Gigandes Plaki), 71–72
  Country-Style Layered
    Dish (Horiatiki Stroma
    Piato), 179–180
  Eggplant Dip
    (Melitzanosalata), 30–31
  Eggplant Slippers (Melitzana
    Papoutsakia), 100–101
  Feta Crab Cakes (Feta Keik
    Kavourion), 146–147
  Fish Soup (Psarosoupa), 50–51
  Greek Burgers (Ellinika
    Biftekia), 177–178
  Grilled Whole Sea Bass
    (Lavraki Skara), 125
  Halloumi and Peach Summer
    Salad (Halloumi me
    Rodakino Kalokeri
    Salata), 56–57
  Mixed Seafood with Wine and
    Capers (Meikta Thalassina
    me Krasi kai
    Kapari), 153
  Octopus with Figs and
    Peaches (Htapodi me Syka
    kai Rodákina), 141–142
  Octopus with Potatoes
    (Htapodi me
    Patates), 143–145
  Pan-Cooked Fish with
    Tomatoes (Psarakia
    Spetsiota), 126–127
  Seafood Rice (Rizi me
    Thalassina), 151–152
  Shrimp Santorini (Garides
    Santorini), 133–134
  Spinach Pie
    (Spanakopita), 103–105

  Stuffed Tomatoes with
    Quinoa (Yemista me Kinoa
    Pligouri), 95
  Warm Harvest Salad (Zesti
    Salata Synkomidís), 66
Pasta
  Baked Pasta with Meat Sauce
    (Pastitsio), 80–81
  Butternut Squash and
    Hazelnut Pasta
    (Kolokythiaki kai
    Fountoukia), 77–78
  Orzo Pasta with Tomato
    (Manestra), 84
  Pasta Salad with Orzo,
    Tomato, Olives, and Feta
    (Salata me Kritharaki,
    Domates, Elies,
    kai Feta), 83
  Pasta with Meat Sauce
    (Makaronada), 79
  Rice Pilaf with Vermicelli
    (Pilaffi me Fides), 86
  Skioufikta with Wild
    Mushrooms and Chicken
    (Skioufikta me Manitaria
    kai Kotopoulo), 74
  Spaghetti with Tomato,
    Shrimp, and Basil
    (Makaronia me Domates,
    Garida, kai Vasilikos), 75
Pastries, 17
Pastry brushes, 15, 199
Peaches
  Greekified Cobbler (Eliniki
    Frouta Cobbler), 213–215
  Halloumi and Peach Summer
    Salad (Halloumi me
    Rodakino Kalokeri
    Salata), 56–57
  Octopus with Figs and
    Peaches (Htapodi me Syka
    kai Rodákina), 141–142

Peas
  Asparagus Salad with Peas
    and Poached Egg (Salata
    me Sparangi, Arakas, kai
    Avgo Pose), 58–59
Peloponnese, 4
Persephone, 2
Philoxenia, 3
Phyllo dough
  about, 16
  Lemony Onion Pie (Lemoni
    Krimidi Pita), 115–116
  Not Your Mother's Baklava
    (Den Ine To Baklava Tis
    Miteras Sas), 198–199
  Phyllo Crackers
    (Phyllo Krotides), 24
  Savory Baklava Rolls
    (Throumpi Baklava), 36–37
  Spinach Pie
    (Spanakopita), 103–105
Pine nuts
  Grape Leaves Stuffed
    with Currants and
    Pine Nuts (Dolmathes
    me Frankostafyla kai
    Koukounari), 108–110
  Rice Pilaf with Vermicelli
    (Pilaffi me Fides), 86
  Stuffed Squid (Kalamari
    Gemeista), 139–140
Pistachios
  Not Your Mother's Baklava
    (Den Ine To Baklava Tis
    Miteras Sas), 198–199
  Savory Baklava Rolls
    (Throumpi Baklava), 36–37
  Warm Harvest Salad (Zesti
    Salata Synkomidís), 66
Plums
  Braised Pork Shoulder with
    Plums and Figs (Hirino
    me Damaskina kai
    Syka), 170–171

Pomegranate seeds
    Arugula Salad with Oranges,
        Fennel, and Pomegranate
        (Salata me Roka, Portokali,
        Maratho, kai Rodi), 53
Pork
    Braised Pork Shoulder with
        Plums and Figs (Hirino
        me Damaskina kai
        Syka), 170–171
    Greek Burgers (Ellinika
        Biftekia), 177–178
    Pork Souvlaki (Souvlaki), 169
    Pork Tenderloin with Sweet
        Fruit Glaze (Hirino Kreas
        me Glyko), 172–173
Potatoes. *See also* Sweet potatoes
    Beef Stew (Stifado), 165–166
    Cabbage Rolls Greek Style
        (Lahanodolmades), 118–119
    Fish Soup (Psarosoupa), 50–51
    Greek Potato Salad
        (Patata Salata), 62–63
    Green Beans with Potatoes
        (Fasolakia me Patates), 91
    Octopus with Potatoes
        (Htapodi me
        Patates), 143–145
    Roasted Artichokes and
        Potatoes (Aginares me
        Patates sto Fourno), 111
    Stuffed Whole Chicken
        (Gemisto Olokliro
        Kotopoulo), 182–183

Q
Quinoa
    Stuffed Tomatoes with Quinoa
        (Yemista me
        Kinoa Pligouri), 95

R
Raisins
    Easy Halva (Efkolo
        Halva), 210–212
Rice
    basmati, 86
    Easter Lamb Soup (Mock
        Magiritsa), 48–49
    Egg-Lemon Chicken Soup
        (Avgolemono), 46–47
    Rice Pilaf with Vermicelli
        (Pilaffi me Fides), 86
    Seafood Rice (Rizi me
        Thalassina), 151–152
    Spinach Rice (Spanakorizo), 85
    Stuffed Squid (Kalamari
        Gemeista), 139–140
Roasting, 16
Rosemary
    Grilled Rack of Lamb (Paidakia
        Skara), 157
    Pork Tenderloin with Sweet
        Fruit Glaze (Hirino Kreas
        me Glyko), 172–173
    Roasted Leg of Lamb
        (Arni Psito), 161–162
    Stuffed Whole Chicken
        (Gemisto Olokliro
        Kotopoulo), 182–183
Rusk, 6

S
Scallions
    Baked Zucchini Patties
        (Kolokithokeftedes), 96
    Easter Lamb Soup
        (Mock Magiritsa), 48–49
    Feta Crab Cakes (Feta Keik
        Kavourion), 146–147
    Fish Soup (Psarosoupa), 50–51

Fish Steamed in Parchment
        with Tomato, Fennel, and
        Olives (Psari ston Atmo
        me Domata, Maratho, kai
        Eiles), 128–129
    Grape Leaves Stuffed
        with Currants and
        Pine Nuts (Dolmathes
        me Frankostafyla kai
        Koukounari), 108–110
    Greek Potato Salad
        (Patata Salata), 62–63
    Octopus with Potatoes
        (Htapodi me
        Patates), 143–145
    Rice Pilaf with Vermicelli
        (Pilaffi me Fides), 86
    Spinach and Feta Stuffed
        Chicken Breasts (Stithos
        Kotopoulo Gemisto me
        Spanaki kai Feta), 185
    Spinach Pie
        (Spanakopita), 103–105
Seafood. *See also specific*
    Mixed Seafood with Wine and
        Capers (Meikta Thalassina
        me Krasi kai
        Kapari), 153
    Seafood Rice (Rizi me
        Thalassina), 151–152
Searing, 16
Seasoning, 17
Semolina
    Easy Halva (Efkolo
        Halva), 210–212
Sesame seeds
    Greek Coffee Cookie
        (Koulouria), 203–205
    Greek Holiday Bread
        (Vasilopita), 191–193
    Meat Pie (Cretan
        Kreatopita), 174–176
    Tomato Foldover
        (Tomato Diples), 38–39

Shallots
  Arugula Salad with Oranges, Fennel, and Pomegranate (Salata me Roka, Portokali, Maratho, kai Rodi), 53
  Green Beans with Potatoes (Fasolakia me Patates), 91
Shrimp
  farm-raised, 136
  Greek-Style Shrimp Cocktail (Elliniko Kokteil Garides), 136
  Shrimp Santorini (Garides Santorini), 133–134
  Spaghetti with Tomato, Shrimp, and Basil (Makaronia me Domates, Garida, kai Vasilikos), 75
Spinach
  Cabbage Rolls Greek Style (Lahanodolmades), 118–119
  Country-Style Layered Dish (Horiatiki Stroma Piato), 179–180
  Eggplant Slippers (Melitzana Papoutsakia), 100–101
  Greek-y Creamed Spinach (Krema Spanaki), 27
  Halloumi and Peach Summer Salad (Halloumi me Rodakino Kalokeri Salata), 56–57
  Spinach and Feta Stuffed Chicken Breasts (Stithos Kotopoulo Gemisto me Spanaki kai Feta), 185
  Spinach Pie (Spanakopita), 103–105
  Spinach Rice (Spanakorizo), 85
  Stuffed Leg of Lamb (Gemisto Podi Arniou), 158–160
  Warm Harvest Salad (Zesti Salata Synkomidís), 66

Squash. See also Zucchini
  Butternut Squash and Hazelnut Pasta (Kolokythiaki kai Fountoukia), 77–78
  Vegetable Medley (Tourlou), 98–99
Squid
  Fried Calamari (Kalamari Tiganites), 137–138
  Stuffed Squid (Kalamari Gemeista), 139–140
Staka cheese, 111
Steamer baskets, 15
Strawberries
  Family Favorite Salad (Agapimeni Salata Tis Oikogeneias), 64–65
Sweet potatoes
  Warm Harvest Salad (Zesti Salata Synkomidís), 66
Syrups, 17

T
Tahini
  Eggplant Dip (Melitzanosalata), 30–31
Techniques, 14, 16–17, 113
Tempering, 16
Terroir, 158
Thyme
  Grilled Whole Sea Bass (Lavraki Skara), 125
  Skioufikta with Wild Mushrooms and Chicken (Skioufikta me Manitaria kai Kotopoulo), 74
Tomatoes
  about, 14
  Baked Pasta with Meat Sauce (Pastitsio), 80–81
  Beef Stew (Stifado), 165–166
  Braised Giant Beans in Tomato Sauce (Gigandes Plaki), 71–72

  Braised Lamb or Beef with Spiced Tomato Sauce (Youvetsi), 163–164
  Cabbage Rolls Greek Style (Lahanodolmades), 118–119
  Country-Style Layered Dish (Horiatiki Stroma Piato), 179–180
  Feta Crab Cakes (Feta Keik Kavourion), 146–147
  Fish Soup (Psarosoupa), 50–51
  Fish Steamed in Parchment with Tomato, Fennel, and Olives (Psari ston Atmo me Domata, Maratho, kai Eiles), 128–129
  Greek Country Salad (Horiatiki Salata), 55
  Greek Gazpacho (Horiatiki Gazpacho), 44
  Green Beans with Potatoes (Fasolakia me Patates), 91
  Lentil Soup (Fakes), 52
  Orzo Pasta with Tomato (Manestra), 84
  Pan-Cooked Fish with Tomatoes (Psarakia Spetsiota), 126–127
  Pasta Salad with Orzo, Tomato, Olives, and Feta (Salata me Kritharaki, Domates, Elies, kai Feta), 83
  Pasta with Meat Sauce (Makaronada), 79
  Seafood Rice (Rizi me Thalassina), 151–152
  Shrimp Santorini (Garides Santorini), 133–134
  Spaghetti with Tomato, Shrimp, and Basil (Makaronia me Domates, Garida, kai Vasilikos), 75
  Spinach Rice (Spanakorizo), 85

Tomatoes, *continued*
    Stuffed Squid (Kalamari
        Gemeista), 139–140
    Stuffed Tomatoes with Quinoa
        (Yemista me
        Kinoa Pligouri), 95
    Stuffed Whole Chicken
        (Gemisto Olokliro
        Kotopoulo), 182–183
    Swordfish Souvlaki
        (Hifias Souvlaki), 130
    Tomato Foldover
        (Tomato Diples), 38–39
    Vegetable Medley
        (Tourlou), 98–99
    Vegetable Moussaka
        (Chortofagos
        Moussaka), 92–94
    Village Frittata (Horiatiki
        Frittata), 120–121

V
Vegan recipes
    Arugula Salad with Oranges,
        Fennel, and Pomegranate
        (Salata me Roka, Portokali,
        Maratho,
        kai Rodi), 53
    Avocado Garlic Spread
        (Avocado Skordalia), 34
    Braised Giant Beans in
        Tomato Sauce
        (Gigandes Plaki), 71–72
    Eggplant Dip
        (Melitzanosalata), 30–31
    Grape Leaves Stuffed
        with Currants and
        Pine Nuts (Dolmathes
        me Frankostafyla kai
        Koukounari), 108–110
    Greek Potato Salad
        (Patata Salata), 62–63
    Green Beans with Potatoes
        (Fasolakia me Patates), 91

Kalamata Olive Spread
    (Kalamata Elia Mezze), 29
Orzo Pasta with Tomato
    (Manestra), 84
Spinach Rice
    (Spanakorizo), 85
Stuffed Tomatoes with
    Quinoa (Yemista me Kinoa
    Pligouri), 95
Vegetable Medley
    (Tourlou), 98–99
Vegetables. *See specific*
Vegetarian recipes
    Asparagus Salad with Peas
        and Poached Egg (Salata
        me Sparangi, Arakas, kai
        Avgo Pose), 58–59
    Baked Zucchini Patties
        (Kolokithokeftedes), 96
    Butternut Squash and
        Hazelnut Pasta
        (Kolokythiaki kai
        Fountoukia), 77–78
    Cabbage Rolls Greek Style
        (Lahanodolmades), 118–119
    Crispy Greek Fried Eggplant
        and Zucchini (Melizantes
        kai Kolokithakia
        Tiganites), 112–113
    The Easy Greek
        (I Efkoli Elliniki), 117
    Easy Halva (Efkolo
        Halva), 210–212
    Eggplant Slippers (Melitzana
        Papoutsakia), 100–101
    Family Favorite Salad
        (Agapimeni Salata Tis
        Oikogeneias), 64–65
    Feta-Kalamata Deviled
        Eggs (Feta-Kalamata
        Apogymnomena Avga), 35
    Greek Coffee Cookie
        (Koulouria), 203–205

Greek Country Salad
    (Horiatiki Salata), 55
Greek Gazpacho
    (Horiatiki Gazpacho), 44
Greek Holiday Bread
    (Vasilopita), 191–193
Greekified Cobbler (Eliniki
    Frouta Cobbler), 213–215
Greek Walnut Cake
    (Karidopita), 206–207
Greek-y Creamed Spinach
    (Krema Spanaki), 27
Greek Yogurt Brandy Cake
    (Elliniki Yiaourti Metaxa
    Keik), 208–209
Greek Yogurt Cheese
    (Strangisto Yiaourti
    Tiri), 26
Halloumi and Peach Summer
    Salad (Halloumi me
    Rodakino Kalokeri
    Salata), 56–57
Lemony Onion Pie (Lemoni
    Krimidi Pita), 115–116
Not Your Mother's Baklava
    (Den Ine To Baklava Tis
    Miteras Sas), 198–199
Not Your Yiayia's Tzatziki
    (Den Ine Y Dika Sou
    Yiayia's Tzatziki), 23
Olive Oil Ice Cream with
    Feta, Cinnamon, and
    Basil (Eleaolado Pagoto
    me Feta, Kanelli, kai
    Vasiliko), 194–196
Pasta Salad with Orzo,
    Tomato, Olives, and Feta
    (Salata me Kritharaki,
    Domates, Elies,
    kai Feta), 83
Phyllo Crackers
    (Phyllo Krotides), 24

Refreshing Watermelon Soup (Drosistikos Karpouzi Soupa), 43

Roasted Artichokes and Potatoes (Aginares me Patates sto Fourno), 111

Roasted Eggplant and Zucchini with Crunchy Spiced Chickpeas, Xinomizithra, and Basil (Psiti Melitzana kai Kolokythia me Revithia, Xinomizithra, kai Vasilikos), 106–107

Roasted Red Pepper and Feta Cheese Dip (Htipiti), 32

Savory Baklava Rolls (Throumpi Baklava), 36–37

Shortbread Cookies (Kourambiedes), 197

Spinach Pie (Spanakopita), 103–105

Theo's Garden Greek Salad (Theo's Eliniki Salata Kipou), 60–61

Tomato Foldover (Tomato Diples), 38–39

Vegetable Moussaka (Chortofagos Moussaka), 92–94

Village Frittata (Horiatiki Frittata), 120–121

Warm Harvest Salad (Zesti Salata Synkomidís), 66

Zucchini Lemon Olive Oil Cake (Kolokithakia Lemoni Keik Elaioladou), 200–202

Vinegar, 12

W

Walnuts

Greek Walnut Cake (Karidopita), 206–207

Not Your Mother's Baklava (Den Ine To Baklava Tis Miteras Sas), 198–199

Watermelon

Refreshing Watermelon Soup (Drosistikos Karpouzi Soupa), 43

Weddings, 217

X

Xinomizithra cheese

Roasted Artichokes and Potatoes (Aginares me Patates sto Fourno), 111

Roasted Eggplant and Zucchini with Crunchy Spiced Chickpeas, Xinomizithra, and Basil (Psiti Melitzana kai Kolokythia me Revithia, Xinomizithra, kai Vasilikos), 106–107

Z

Zucchini

Baked Zucchini Patties (Kolokithokeftedes), 96

Crispy Greek Fried Eggplant and Zucchini (Melizantes kai Kolokithakia Tiganites), 112–113

Roasted Eggplant and Zucchini with Crunchy Spiced Chickpeas, Xinomizithra, and Basil (Psiti Melitzana kai Kolokythia me Revithia, Xinomizithra, kai Vasilikos), 106–107

Stuffed Tomatoes with Quinoa (Yemista me Kinoa Pligouri), 95

Stuffed Whole Chicken (Gemisto Olokliro Kotopoulo), 182–183

Vegetable Medley (Tourlou), 98–99

Zucchini Lemon Olive Oil Cake (Kolokithakia Lemoni Keik Elaioladou), 200–202

Acknowledgments

Theo Biggest thanks to Meg Mateo Ilasco for asking me to write this book. I so appreciate being a first-generation Greek, particularly as it relates to my personal food culture—how I love to eat, garden, and create happiness surrounding my table from fork to conversation. Meg's immediate acceptance of my suggestion to bring on Christina Xenos as my coauthor established a perfect pairing for recipe content, personality, and meeting our deadline. Christina and I have a lot of personal history, and we promise to make flavorful fun whenever promoting this book together. Brian Hurley, our senior editor, was so patient as we brainstormed an agreeable title for this book, fielding our needs most efficiently; thanks, Brian!

The recipes would not be as wonderful as they are without the detailed eye and articulate nature our developmental editor Mary Cassells brought to the pages here—truly encapsulating the vision of each dish. I wish my parents were alive to celebrate this book with me. Without them, these recipes could never have been developed, nor would my love for entertaining and living the good life exist.

Christina My most sincere thanks to Theo Stephan, for having faith in me and giving me the opportunity to work with her on this project. I am forever grateful for that. She truly is a phenomenal friend, writing partner, and collaborator.

A special thanks to my husband, Alex Lyras, for his love, support, and encouragement that extends far beyond this book. I would like to express my gratitude to my mother-in-law, Georgia Lyras, who forged a culinary path that I can only hope to follow, and who is always there to answer any cooking questions I might have. Thanks to the Haggis and Doyle families for connecting me to my ancestral home in Crete; thanks especially to Kalli Doyle for all her enthusiasm and love, Donald Haggis for filling in the gaps on historical Greek cooking, and my *yiayia*, Polly Haggis who introduced me to the tastes, people, and culture of Crete.

Many thanks to Lia Bozonelis for her loyal friendship and support and who, along with John Fuleras, were the best Greek culinary barometers anyone could ask for. Thanks to my super-tasters Matt Stewart and Steven Robins, who offered such thoughtful recipe feedback throughout the process of this book, and to everyone—Randy, Josh, Anu, Jessica, Gilbert, Danielle, Lucy, Lanee, and Brian—who let me test out my creations on them.

Special thanks to the Callisto Media team: Meg Ilasco, Brian Hurley, and the keen eye of our developmental editor Mary Cassells.

My sincere gratitude to the Annunciation Greek Orthodox Church in Dayton, Ohio, which has a beautiful culinary tradition of cooking and baking for their annual Greek festival, where I was able to learn so much at such a young age. Thanks to May Hennemann and the New School of Cooking, without whose formal training I would not be where I am today. Thanks to Dawn Kiko Cheng for all her encouragement, support, and sharp listening skills.

And finally, thanks to my family—Nicholas, Theodora, Tony, and Courtney Xenos, for their love and support; Mr. Peepers, who spent every day meticulously critiquing my cooking techniques and swiping bites of feta; and my aunt Marge Xenos, who still makes the world's best spanakopita.

About the Authors

 *Theodora (Theo) Stephan* is from Dayton, Ohio. She founded Global Gardens in 1998, the first olive oil producer in Santa Barbara, California, and first in the United States to plant a commercial grove of *Koroneiki* varietal olive trees imported from Greece.

Global Gardens has been featured on CNBC, *Home & Family*, Korean Broadcasting System, and a myriad of media. Feature stories have been included in *Better Homes and Gardens, Living the Country Life, AAA Westways, Sunset,* and the *Los Angeles Times*. Editors' picks have appeared in *Food and Wine, Fine Cooking, Bon Appétit, Vegetarian Times, Mother Earth Magazine,* and *Cooking Light*.

A great love for gardening and entertaining with easy-to-use-products has grown into the Global Gardens Farm Stand in Los Olivos, California—an agrotourism, "taste education" experience unique to wine country. More than 40 products comprise her brand. Theo's globalgardensonline.com website features her olive oil clubs, recipes, and useful information.

Theo's first cookbook, *Olive Oil & Vinegar for Life: Delicious Recipes for Caliterranean Living,* features her trademarked "Caliterranean" lifestyle. She will celebrate her seventeenth Certified Organic olive harvest this year. Theo is a seasoned public speaker, educator, foodie, world traveler, and olive oil expert.

Christina Xenos is a professional chef and journalist based in Los Angeles, California. Her company, Sweet Greek Personal Chef Services, tantalizes palates throughout the city with full culinary services.

Christina regularly hosts Greek-themed pop-up dining experiences through EatWith and Feastly, and also teaches cooking classes for private clients. She has been featured on TV in several cooking segments, was a judge on an international cooking show, and was a contestant on *Recipe Hunters: Appetizer Battle*, where her signature spanakopita won.

Her culinary career began at an early age, when she baked Greek delicacies for Annunciation Greek Orthodox Church in Dayton, Ohio, for its annual festival. She honed her chef skills in professional cooking and baking at the New School of Cooking in Los Angeles and often returns to her family's home on the south coast of Crete to indulge in the local flavors.

She has served as a travel correspondent for *Forbes Travel Guide* and as the online editor for *Where* Magazine/SoCalPulse.com in Southern California for more than a decade, documenting the thriving restaurant scene in and around Los Angeles. She continues to write for their suite of publications and also pens freelance food and travel pieces for a number of other publications.

CPSIA information can be obtained
at www.ICGtesting.com
Printed in the USA
BVHW051803091020
590614BV00002B/7